BTEC
FINANCE

PHILIP HOLDEN

Heinemann Educational Books

Other titles for BTEC

Business Organisations and Environments
   Book 1
   Book 2
by Matthew Glew, Michael Watts and Ronald Wells

*To my mother and father, and to John and
Alison, without whose love this book would
not have been possible*

Heinemann Educational
A division of Heinemann Educational Books Ltd
Halley Court, Jordan Hill, Oxford OX2 8EJ

OXFORD LONDON EDINBURGH
MELBOURNE SYDNEY AUCKLAND
IBADAN NAIROBI GABARONE HARARE
KINGSTON PORTSMOUTH NH (USA)
SINGAPORE MADRID

© Philip Holden 1987

First published 1987
Reprinted 1990

British Library Cataloguing in Publication Data
Holden, Philip
  BTEC finance.
  1. Finance
  I. Title
  332   HG173

ISBN 0–435–45520–6

Printed in Great Britain by
Thomson Litho Ltd, East Kilbride, Scotland

Contents

Preface *v*
Acknowledgements *v*
Introduction *1*

PART ONE: PERSONAL FINANCE

1. Personal Income and Expenditure *3*

Personal expenditure *3*
The economist's concept of opportunity cost *4*
Buying an asset *5*
Personal income *6*
Conclusion *8*

2. Saving *10*

How can you save? *10*
Personal budget *10*
General points about saving *11*
Future savings requirements *12*
Where you can invest your savings *13*
Conclusion *18*

3. Borrowing *20*

Some terms you should know *20*
Borrowing: how it's done *22*
Tips about borrowing *24*
Borrowing and the law *24*
Conclusion *25*

4. Personal Accounts *26*

Budget *26*
Receipts and payments statement *26*
Income and expenditure statement *26*
Sources and application of funds statement *26*
Balance sheet *26*
Conclusion *30*

PART TWO: ACCOUNTANCY

5. The Role of Accountants *31*

Introducing accountants *31*
Accountants in private practice *32*
Accountants in industry and commerce *33*
Conclusion *34*

PART THREE: FINANCIAL ACCOUNTING

6. Recording Financial Information I *36*

Double-entry book-keeping *36*
Accounting concepts and conventions *37*
How double entries are made *38*
Preparation of final accounts *42*
Computers and double-entry book-keeping *43*

7. Recording Financial Information II *45*

Preparation of final accounts *45*
Depreciation *48*
Other documents used to record financial information *49*
Conclusion *53*

8. Accounts in a Partnership *54*

Introducing partnerships *54*
Partnership Agreement *54*
A partnership's final accounts *55*
Conclusion *59*

9. Accounts in a Limited Company *61*

Introducing limited companies *61*
A limited company's final accounts *61*
Fruit and Veg Ltd's accounts for the year ended 31 May 1989 *63*
Case study: H. P. Bulmer Holdings plc *70*
Conclusion *73*

10. Accounts in Other Organisations *74*

Clubs *74*
Nationalised industries *75*
Local authorities *78*
Your college *80*
Conclusion *81*

PART FOUR: RAISING FINANCE

11. Raising Finance *82*

Factors to consider *82*
Sources of finance *84*
Case study: Virgin Group plc *88*
Conclusion *89*

PART FIVE: MANAGEMENT
ACCOUNTING

12. Valuation and Purchase of Assets *90*

Valuation of assets and the effects of inflation *90*
Purchase of fixed assets: investment appraisal
    techniques *93*
Conclusion *97*

13. Interpretation of Accounts *98*

Liquidity and profitability – an introduction *98*
Profitability *103*
Capital structure *106*
Limitations of financial ratios *107*
Who wants to interpret accounts? *108*
Interpreting accounts: summary *108*
Case study: Laker Airways *109*

14. Financial Planning and Control *111*

Functions of planning and control *111*
Financial planning – budgeting *112*
Financial control *115*
Costing *116*
Costs and pricing *119*
Conclusion *120*

15. Finance and Organisational Decision-Making *122*

Objectives and decision-making *122*
Organisational objectives *124*
Where financial factors are secondary in decision-
    making *125*
Case studies: Marks & Spencer and BL *129*
Conclusion *132*

PART SIX: THE FUTURE ROLE OF
COMPUTERS

16. Computers and Accounting *133*

Introducing computers *133*
Computer applications in accounting *135*
The accountant and computers: the evidence *137*
Conclusion *137*

Appendix: Present Value of 1 *139*
Appendix for Lecturers: an Integrated Teaching
    Strategy *140*
Index *151*

Preface

This book would not have been possible without the help and encouragement of so many different people. However, any errors and omissions are, of course, the sole responsibility of the author. Consequently I would be grateful for any suggested improvements from you, the reader.

I am also most grateful to the following people:

- The editorial staff at Heinemann Educational Books, particularly Janice Brown, and the anonymous reviewers. Their help has been much appreciated.
- The ladies who so skilfully typed the manuscript: M. Sawkins, M. Mundye, S. Bowes, A. Waterson and E. Woolley. Many thanks for their efficient and prompt service.
- My former colleagues at Brooklands Technical College – a great bunch of people. In particular, I would like to thank Paul Barnes, who helped me during my first years of teaching, and Terry McPherson and Neil Stamper, who helped me to formulate my ideas on the BTEC Finance module.
- My former tutors at Nottingham University and the City University Business School. I would particularly like to mention Professors Brian Chiplin and Sid Kessler.
- Most of all, my parents, my brother, and his wife, to whom this book is dedicated.

  I would also like to thank dearest Ann, who has put the value of this book into perspective.

Acknowledgements

The author and publishers would like to thank all those who gave permission to reproduce copyright material as acknowledged in the sources. Crown copyright material is reproduced with permission of the Controller of Her Majesty's Stationery Office.

Introduction

Hello, readers, and welcome to your first-year BTEC National Finance course. This module may seem incredibly dull and boring to you. However, if you think about it for one moment, the world of finance is extremely important to all of us.

The Oxford Dictionary defines finance as *'money as support for an undertaking'*, and we all need money. All the groups on *Top of the Pops* last week needed money to get started. You need money to get to college and to go out at weekends. The list could go on and on.

So how does this book attempt to explain the world of money and finance? As you might have noticed from the contents pages, the book is divided up into six parts. Each of them will now be outlined to form an overall picture of what the book is trying to achieve.

Part One: Personal Finance (Chapters 1–4)

This section should enable you to manage your own personal finances better, and so spend your money more wisely. In other words, you should waste less money and be able to spend more on the things you really like or need.

Part Two: Accountancy (Chapter 5)

The rest of the book looks at how organisations cope with financial problems. As you have probably already guessed, this is the subject of **accounting**, which tries to solve these problems with the help of professional practitioners called **accountants**. Chapter 5 looks at what accountants do.

Part Three: Financial Accounting (Chapters 6–10)

The main purpose of this area of accounting is to accurately describe an organisation's financial position. To do this, accountants prepare certain accounting documents. For example, an organisation's **profit and loss account** shows how much profit (or loss) it is making. Its **balance sheet** shows the things it owns (e.g. machinery) and the money it owes to other people on a particular day.

Various examples are used to illustrate these financial accounting chapters. An imaginary business is set up – starring two little-known fictional characters called Colin Smith and Helen Baptiste. H. P. Bulmer's (the cider-makers), West Sussex County Council and British Rail are also used as examples.

Part Four: Raising Finance (Chapter 11)

This chapter looks at how different organisations raise money to finance their activities. A real-life company, Richard Branson's Virgin Group plc, is used as the main example here. This will tell you how it provides the money to finance its recording artists like Phil Collins and Culture Club.

Part Five: Management Accounting (Chapters 12–15)

This area of accounting attempts to answer the following questions:

- *Where should an organisation invest its money?* Accountants have developed techniques to help an organisation choose between different ideas for investment. For example, they can help it choose between two different types of equipment. Such techniques are looked at in Chapter 12.
- *How is an organisation doing financially? Is it making enough profits? Has it enough cash to pay its bills?* These questions can be answered by analysing and interpreting the accounting documents which were prepared in Chapters 6–10. We look at how this is done in Chapter 13, where Laker Airways is used as the main example.
- *What are an organisation's costs and how can it reduce them?* This question is answered in Chapter 14.
- *How much are an organisation's decisions influenced by financial considerations?* This question is answered in Chapter 15, using BL and Marks & Spencer as examples.

Part Six: The Future Role of Computers (Chapter 16)

This chapter looks at how computers are used by accountants today. It also tries to predict what impact computers will have in the future.

Appendix for Lecturers

This comprises:

- An introduction to BTEC philosophy with respect to the new BTEC National courses.
- An integrated teaching strategy – a suggested teaching programme for the first year of the BTEC National course in Business and Finance. This includes: (a) suggestions as to how the three core units – Organisation in its Environment I; Finance; and People in Organisations I – can be integrated; and (b) intramodular assignments which fit into the overall teaching strategy.

That's all there is! I hope you enjoy reading the book and carrying out the activities which are included in each chapter. These will, I hope, make it more interesting for you and get you more involved in the learning process. I hope you will enjoy at least some, if not all, of the assignments.

PART ONE
Personal Finance

1
Personal Income and Expenditure

The Beatles and Abba sang about it. Some people have died for it. Others have married for it. It is meant to be the root of all evil.

Got it? Yes, it's **money**, which is one of this book's major considerations. Unfortunately I cannot give you any, but I can help you to understand it a bit better. The aim of the book is to take you on a journey through the world of money and finance and to make sense of it.

Activity

Find out the functions of money from an economics or banking textbook in your college library. Decide which of them is the most important.

You should have decided upon money's **medium of exchange** function as the most important. In other words, you need money to buy things – either **goods** (e.g. food, clothes and records) or **services** (e.g. a night out at the cinema). These are **items of expenditure**.

First of all, though, you must get the money from somewhere to pay for the things that you want. You do this either by being given the money (e.g. through a grant) or by earning it (through a job of some sort). These are your **sources of income**.

Both your expenditure and your income are obviously important to your personal finances. So the first chapter of this part of the book, on personal finance, is about how people spend their money and where they get it from. We shall look at expenditure first.

Personal Expenditure

Activity

Make a list of the goods and services you have bought in the past year.

Looking at this list, you should be able to pick out different items of expenditure. Some will remain the same in the next month or so, whilst others will vary quite a lot. Your money will also be spent on things which either are used up very quickly (e.g. food and drink) or last much longer (e.g. a radio).

Two sets of terms are used to distinguish between these different types of expenditure:

- **fixed** and **variable** expenditure; and
- **revenue** and **capital** expenditure (see Fig. 1.1).

Fig. 1.1: Types of expenditure

FIXED	VARIABLE
Does not change in the short term	Changes with how much you use something
REVENUE	CAPITAL
Spending on things used in one go or gradually over a short period of time	Spending on fixed assets

Fixed and variable expenditure

Fixed expenditure refers to items of expenditure which are unlikely to change in the next year or so.

3

Activity

Make a list of your main items of fixed expenditure.

Your list could have included:

(a) Rail fares to college.
(b) Any insurance payments (e.g. for a motor bike or car).
(c) Road tax on a car.
(d) Loan or hire-purchase repayments (e.g. on a stereo, or motor bike).

Your parents are also likely to have the following items of fixed expenditure:

(a) Mortgage repayments or rent on a house or flat.
(b) Rental charge on a telephone.
(c) Insurance payments on their home and its contents.
(d) Rates on their home.
(e) Water rates.
(f) Payments for life assurance.

Variable expenditure refers to items of expenditure which can be changed according to how much you plan to use them. The more you use them, the higher the variable expenditure. The less you use them, the lower the variable expenditure.

Activity

Make a list of your main items of variable expenditure.

This might have included:

(a) Meals out and other forms of entertainment.
(b) Christmas and birthday presents.
(c) Running and maintenance costs of a car, motor bike or stereo.
(d) Food, drink and clothing.

Your parents are also likely to have the following items of variable expenditure:

(a) Maintenance costs of their home.
(b) Telephone calls.
(c) Electricity and gas.

Revenue and capital expenditure

Revenue expenditure refers to items of expenditure which are used up either completely in one go, or gradually over a short period of time. They are paid for out of someone's current income. Therefore, revenue expenditure is sometimes referred to as **current expenditure**.

Activity

Make a list of your main items of revenue expenditure.

These might have included:

(a) Bus and train fares.
(b) Visits to discos.
(c) Snacks in the refectory.
(d) Shoes and clothing.

Your parents are also likely to have the following items of revenue expenditure:

(a) Rent and rates on their home.
(b) Food and other household expenses.
(c) Running costs of a car.

Capital expenditure refers to items of expenditure which are used over a long period of time. As we shall see later in the book, accountants call such things **fixed assets**. Therefore, to use their language, another way of defining capital expenditure would be 'spending on fixed assets'.

Activity

Make a list of your main items of capital expenditure.

This might have included:

(a) Stereo.
(b) Car or motor bike.
(c) Camera.

Your parents are also likely to have the following items of capital expenditure:

(a) Television.
(b) Video recorder.
(c) Washing-machine.
(d) Home.
(e) Refrigerator.

As we shall see in Chapter 6, this distinction between revenue and capital expenditure is an extremely important one in an organisation's accounts. Revenue expenditures are entered as costs in its profit and loss account, and capital expenditures appear as fixed assets in its balance sheet.

The economist's concept of opportunity cost

So far in this chapter we have assumed, as accountants do, that the cost of something is based upon its purchase price (or, as it is sometimes called, its **historical cost**). The problem with this is that, when you buy something, you lose not only the money you paid for it but also other benefits as well. Therefore, the true cost of something is more than just its purchase price. Consider the following example.

Example – buying a Dire Straits LP

In addition to the money you paid, the other costs (or benefits lost) of buying a Dire Straits LP would include:

1. The interest you could have earned by putting the money into the building society.
2. Not being able to afford that ZZ Top album you always wanted.
3. Not getting a cuddle from your girl- or boy-friend because (s)he hates Dire Straits!

To overcome this problem, economists define costs in a different way to accountants. They use a term, which you will also come across in Organisation in its Environment I: **opportunity cost**. An economist defines the cost of something in terms of its opportunity cost, i.e. in terms of the benefits lost to obtain it.

Two further examples should help to make clearer this difference between an accountant's and an economist's definition of cost.

Example – going to a party

Imagine that you have been invited to a party this weekend. What benefits will you lose by going? Or, to put it another way, what is the opportunity cost of going to the party?

You should have thought of the following:

1. Money – your expenditure resulting from the party, e.g. travelling expenses and the bottle of wine brought to the party. (Only these expenditures would be viewed as costs by accountants.)
2. Interest – the interest that could have been earned on this money by investing it in, for example, a building society or bank.
3. Other things you could have enjoyed doing – e.g. going to the cinema, watching television, or the wages from an evening job.

Example – a one-person greengrocer's business

An economist would view the following as costs of this business:

1. Money – expenditures resulting from the purchase of goods and services to run the business, e.g. fruit, vegetables and electricity. (Again, only these expenditures would be viewed as costs by accountants.)
2. Salary – the salary the man or woman could have earned in another job.
3. Interest – the interest they could have earned elsewhere (e.g. in a building-society account) on the money invested in the business.

Activity

Identify the opportunity cost of:

1. Buying a television set.
2. Doing a BTEC National course.

Buying an asset

An asset is something which someone owns. Accountants identify two main types of asset:

- **Fixed assets**, which are items of capital expenditure and are used for a long period of time (see p. 4).
- **Current assets**, which are either cash or things that can be easily converted into cash. A person's current assets will include any money owed to him or her by other people. These people are called a person's **debtors**.

Activity

List the fixed assets and current assets which you own.

You could have come up with the following:

- Fixed assets – car or motor bike, camera, stereo.
- Current assets – bank balance, building-society deposits, cash in wallet or handbag, money owed to you by friends (debtors).

However, where do we get the money to buy these assets? Let us look at one example to help to answer this question.

Activity: buying a stereo

Imagine that you have decided to blast your friends' eardrums with a 'stack' stereo system, worth £250. Make a list of possible ways of financing this expenditure.

Saving and borrowing

You should have come up with the answer that there are two broad possibilities:

- **Saving**, i.e. save up to buy one.
- **Borrowing**, i.e. borrow the money through, for example, a bank loan, a hire-purchase agreement or a credit sales agreement.

We shall examine the main types of saving and borrowing in the next two chapters, but first we must look at what determines how much someone will save or borrow.

The answer is, of course, their income in relation to their expenditure:

(a) They will save when their income is greater than their expenditure.
(b) They will have to borrow when their expenditure is greater than their income.

Therefore, we must look at a person's main sources of income, and at the main items in an employee's pay slip.

Personal income

People receive income from at least one of the following sources (see Fig. 1.2):

1. **Wages and salaries** – i.e. income paid to people who work for somebody else.
2. **Income from self-employment** – i.e. income received by self-employed people, such as sole traders and partners, from their business.
3. **Rent, dividends and interest received** – this includes (a) rent from property owned; (b) dividends from shares owned (see Chapter 2); (c) interest on investments (building-society accounts, etc.).
4. **Private pensions and annuities**. Retired people often receive pensions in addition to the state pension. Normally they are received from their former employers. Annuities are regular payments paid out by life-assurance companies (see Chapter 2).
5. **Social security benefits** – these are benefits, such as unemployment benefit, given out by the government to those who need them.
6. **Other sources of income** – these are mostly grants given out by the government, such as student grants.

Activity

Using books from your library, make a list of benefits available in the UK today.

The figures involved are enormous. People's incomes totalled £256,300 million in 1984 (see Fig. 1.2).

Activity

1. Calculate, using Fig. 1.2, how much each source of income was in *money terms* in 1984.
2. List your main sources of income.

As wages and salaries are by far the most important source of personal income, we shall have to examine these in further detail by looking at a pay slip.

Reading your pay slip

If you have a part-time job, look at your last pay slip (if not, have a look at your mother's or father's, or a friend's). You will notice that it includes the following main items:

- Gross pay.
- Net pay.
- Compulsory deductions.
- Voluntary deductions.

We shall now explain each of these in turn (see Fig. 1.3).

GROSS PAY

This refers to the total wages or salary earned by somebody. Wages are paid to manual employees, often on an hourly basis (i.e. a certain amount per hour). Salaries are paid annually to non-manual employees in weekly or monthly amounts.

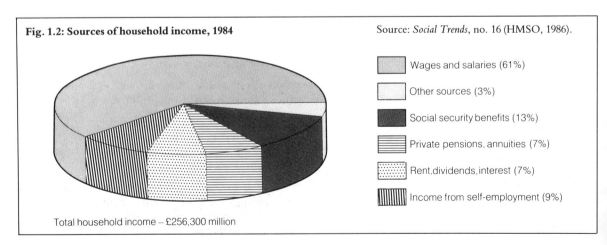

Fig. 1.2: Sources of household income, 1984

Source: *Social Trends*, no. 16 (HMSO, 1986).

Wages and salaries (61%)
Other sources (3%)
Social security benefits (13%)
Private pensions, annuities (7%)
Rent, dividends, interest (7%)
Income from self-employment (9%)

Total household income – £256,300 million

Personal Income and Expenditure

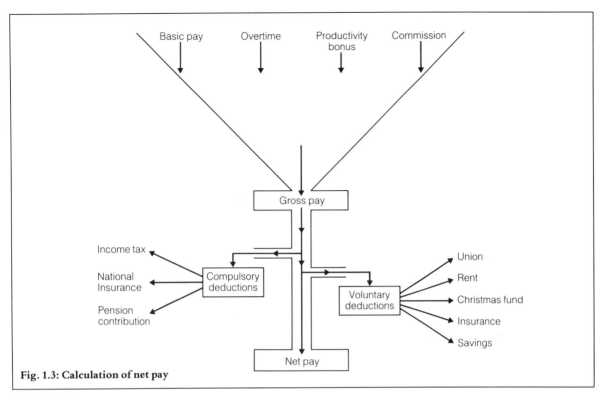

Fig. 1.3: Calculation of net pay

Someone's gross pay is calculated as follows:

(a) **basic pay** (i.e. the wages or salary paid for a normal working week); *plus*
(b) **any additional payments**, which may include:
- **overtime**;
- **productivity bonus** (paid if an employee produces more goods);
- **commission** (paid to sales personnel as a percentage of the goods or services they sell).

NET PAY

Someone's net pay is the amount they can actually spend, i.e. their gross pay *less* their total deductions (compulsory and voluntary deductions).

COMPULSORY DEDUCTIONS

These are the amounts which *have to be* deducted from gross pay. They are income tax, National Insurance and pension contribution (see Fig. 1.4).

Income tax is paid automatically to the Inland Revenue via the Pay-As-You-Earn Scheme (PAYE). The amount of tax paid is calculated as a percentage (for most people, the standard rate of tax, presently 27 per cent) of someone's **taxable income** (their gross pay less their total tax allowances). The tax rates and allowances for 1987–8 are:

Income tax rates

Rate (%)	Taxable income
27 (standard rate)	Up to £17,900
40	£17,901–£20,400
45	£20,401–£25,400
50	£25,401–£33,300
55	£33,301–£41,200
60	Over £41,200

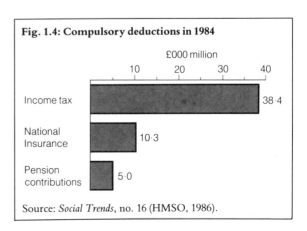

Fig. 1.4: Compulsory deductions in 1984

Income tax: 38.4
National Insurance: 10.3
Pension contributions: 5.0

Source: *Social Trends*, no. 16 (HMSO, 1986).

Tax allowances

Single person, or working wife	£2,425
Married man	£3,795

Example – single person, gross pay £8,425 p.a.:

	£
Gross pay	8,425
Less Tax allowances	2,425
Taxable income	6,000
Income tax paid (@ 27%)	1,620

A person's **tax code** on their pay slip indicates how much tax they will pay. In our example the person's code would have been 242L. The three numbers represent the person's total tax allowances divided by 10 (to the nearest whole number). The letter indicates the type of tax allowance:

L (lower) – for single people and earning wives;
H (higher) – married men and people bringing up children on their own.

When you start working, you may also be asked to complete a **tax return** by the Inland Revenue. This has two purposes: to get a statement of your income and to check the tax allowances you are claiming.

Activity

Ali is single and earns £200 per week. Calculate how much income tax (to the nearest pound) he will pay every year. What will his tax code be?

National Insurance is paid by all employees who earn above a certain weekly wage or salary. It is paid as a percentage of the employee's gross pay, and employers as well as employees pay it. National Insurance contributions are used to help pay for sickness and unemployment benefits, for state pensions, for the National Health Service and for other welfare benefits.

The National Insurance rates for 1986–7 are:

Gross pay (per week)	Employee	Employer
Under £38	Nil	Nil
£38–£59.99	5%	5%
£60–£94.99	7%	7%
£95–£139.99	9%	9%
£140–£285	9%	10.45%
Over £285	Nil	10.45%

Pension contribution (sometimes called **superannuation**). Many employers operate a private pension scheme which gives the employee a pension on top of the state old-age pension. An employee's contributions to such a scheme are usually based on a percentage of their gross pay.

VOLUNTARY DEDUCTIONS

These are amounts which *may be* deducted from gross pay. They may include:

- **Trade-union subscriptions**.
- **Rent** (where the employer provides housing, e.g. farmers).
- **Christmas fund**.
- **Insurance premiums** (e.g. for private medical care).
- **Savings** (e.g. contributions to a government savings scheme).

Activity

Joyce's basic working week is 40 hours, and she regularly works 10 hours a week overtime. Her basic rate of pay is £2 per hour, and any overtime is paid double this. She pays into a private pension scheme, and each contribution is 5 per cent of her gross pay. Her only voluntary deduction is £2 per week trade-union subscription.

On the basis of this information, calculate Joyce's gross and net pay per week (assume 1986–7 income tax, National Insurance rates and income tax allowances).

Conclusion

In this chapter we have shown how we can earn money and spend it. Now we must find out how we can save it. This is the subject of Chapter 2.

Assignment

You are required to carry out the following tasks:

1. Make a detailed list of your main items of expenditure and sources of income each week for the rest of this term.
2. Identify what types of expenditure they are, i.e. fixed or variable, revenue or capital.
3. Complete your income and expenditure statement for the term and your balance sheet for the last day of term (see Chapter 4).

Skills tested:
- Numeracy.
- Identifying and tackling problems.
- Learning and studying.
- Information gathering.
- Communicating.

Personal Income and Expenditure

Assignment (intramodular assignment with Organisation in its Environment I and People in Organisation I)

You have just been given some figures from *Social Trends* about household expenditure on luxury items (see Fig. 1.5). You are required to:

1. Illustrate expenditure by all households by means of a pie chart and a bar chart.
2. Prepare a report on the significance of these figures for:
   (a) your local football club;
   (b) W. H. Smith, the stationery chain;
   (c) McDonalds, the hamburger chain;
   (d) Intasun, the holiday operators;
   (e) H. P. Bulmer's, the cider-makers.

Fig. 1.5: Household expenditure on selected leisure items: by household income, UK 1984

	Gross normal weekly income of household						All households
	Up to £100	Over £100, up to £150	Over £150, up to £200	Over £200, up to £250	Over £250, up to £300	Over £300	
Average weekly household expenditure on (£s):							
Alcoholic drink consumed away from home	1.71	3.70	5.42	6.64	7.76	10.90	5.30
Meals consumed out*	0.97	2.18	2.52	3.73	4.30	7.66	3.18
Books, newspapers, magazines, etc.	1.41	2.02	2.29	2.84	3.05	4.06	2.42
Television, radio and musical instruments	2.06	2.85	3.93	6.10	6.48	7.85	4.36
Purchase of materials for home repairs, etc.	0.60	1.45	2.06	2.40	3.85	7.53	2.66
Holidays	0.94	3.05	4.42	3.35	6.45	10.88	4.28
Hobbies	0.03	0.02	0.08	0.05	0.08	0.23	0.08
Cinema admissions	0.02	0.07	0.06	0.10	0.14	0.21	0.09
Dance admissions	0.04	0.08	0.09	0.22	0.18	0.30	0.13
Theatre, concert, etc. admissions	0.04	0.10	0.18	0.22	0.29	0.53	0.20
Subscriptions and admission charges to participant sports	0.07	0.20	0.47	0.61	0.78	1.48	0.53
Football match admissions	—	0.03	0.07	0.07	0.06	0.10	0.05
Admissions to other spectator sports	—	0.02	0.03	0.02	0.04	0.08	0.03
Sports goods (excluding clothes)	0.04	0.11	0.26	0.39	0.58	1.72	0.47
Other entertainment	0.10	0.21	0.22	0.37	0.46	0.64	0.30
Total weekly expenditure on above	8.05	16.09	22.10	27.09	34.50	54.18	24.08
Expenditure on above items as a percentage of total household expenditure	*11.8*	*13.5*	*15.1*	*15.5*	*16.8*	*18.5*	*15.8*

*Eaten on the premises, excluding state school meals and workplace meals.

Source: *Social Trends*, no. 16 (HMSO, 1986).

2
Saving

How can you save?

To put it simply, saving is income you do not spend, i.e. your total income less your total expenditure. So there are two ways of increasing your savings:

- earn more (increase your income); and/or
- spend less (decrease your expenditure).

Because your ability to earn more may be limited (e.g. because you cannot get a better-paid job, or are unable to get overtime), often the only way of increasing your savings is by keeping a tight control over your expenditure. Making up a **personal budget** can help you do this.

Personal budget

This is an estimate of all income to be received (receipts), and all money spent (payments or expenditures) during a certain period of time (e.g. a week, month or year). A lot of people find a monthly budget to be useful, because they receive their income and pay their bills on a monthly basis. This has become particularly true since rates, electricity and gas bills can now be paid monthly instead of in a lump sum every three or six months.

How much you plan to save every month is the excess of your planned (or budgeted) income over your planned spending.

Example – Alex Brown, budget for February

Money paid out	£	Money received	£
Gas	50	Net income	1,000
Electricity	25	Interest from	
Telephone	50	building-society	
Mortgage	250	account	200
Rates	50		
Food	170		
Entertainment	150		
Transport	80		
Monthly hire-purchase payment on motor-bike	100		
Budgeted excess of income over spending (planned saving)	275		
	£1,200		£1,200

Alex would draw up the budget at the end of January and try to make sure that his actual payments in February do not exceed those stated in the budget.

So it is sometimes also useful to draw up a list of actual receipts and payments (called a **receipts and payments statement**) to compare them with those in the budget. There are two most likely explanations for actual payments being greater than budgeted payments:

- some unexpected expense which could not have been budgeted for; and
- overspending, caused by poor money management.

In our example, because of the unexpected arrival of a friend from abroad, Alex spent more on food and entertainment than he had budgeted for:

Alex Brown – receipts and payments statement for February

Payments	£	Receipts	£
Gas	50	Net income	1,000
Electricity	25	Interest from	
Telephone	50	building-society	
Mortgage	250	account	200
Rates	50		
Food	200		
Entertainment	200		
Transport	80		
Monthly hire-purchase payment on motor-bike	100		
Excess of receipts over payments	195		
	£1,200		£1,200

Alex's **income and expenditure statement** for this month would look slightly different. Only items of revenue expenditure are included in this account (see Chapter 4), unlike in the receipts and payments statement above, where items of both capital expenditure and revenue expenditure are included.

Activity

Identify the items of revenue and capital expenditure in Alex's receipts and payments statement.

Activity

Complete your own budget for next month.

General points about saving

There are three general points that people should be concerned about when saving their money: **return**, **liquidity** and **security** (see Fig. 2.1).

Fig. 2.1: Factors to consider when saving

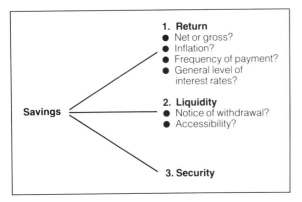

Return

Return means the rate of interest per year. When comparing the rates of interest of different savings institutions, make sure you take note of the following four points.

1. **Payment of income tax** – the word **'net'** after the rate of interest means that income tax has already been deducted. The word **'gross'** means that income tax has not yet been deducted. In other words:

gross rate − tax = net rate.

Therefore non-taxpayers (including all students) receive the gross rate and have nothing deducted from this. However, as we shall soon see, building societies and banks pay their rates of interest 'net', i.e. income tax has already been deducted at the standard rate (presently 27p in £1 or 27 per cent). Non-taxpayers, though, still receive only this net rate, because they cannot claim back from the government the tax that has already been paid.

Taxpayers, however, must convert 'net' rates into 'gross' rates when comparing the rates of different institutions (some of which will be quoted 'net' and others 'gross'). You do this as follows:

$$\text{gross rate (\%)} = \frac{\text{net rate (\%)}}{1 - \text{income tax rate (\%)}}$$

EXAMPLE

Net rate paid by building society = 10.5 per cent. For a standard-rate taxpayer this would be equivalent to a gross rate of:

$$\frac{10.5}{1 - 27\%} = \frac{10.5}{1 - (27 \div 100)} = 14.38\%.$$

Activity

Buy a *Daily Telegraph*, *Times*, *Independent* or *Guardian* on a Saturday and, using the financial pages, compare the net and gross rates of different savings institutions.

2. **Rate of inflation** – obviously you hope that the rate of interest on your savings is greater than the rate of inflation (i.e. how quickly prices are rising). This will normally be the case in times of relatively low inflation, when the rate of inflation is less than about 10 per cent.

However, if inflation rises above 10 per cent, it could well be that the rate of interest on your savings is less than inflation rate, i.e. your savings (including interest) will not be able to buy as many goods or services as before. In such circumstances it is worth getting an **index-linked** investment, where the net rate of interest given is equal to the rate of inflation.

Activity

From your newspaper, make a note of which investments are index-linked.

Activity

Using publications like the *Annual Abstract of Statistics* and *Social Trends*, find out from your library:

1. How the government measures changes in prices.
2. How much prices have risen since 1961.
3. **Frequency of payment** – it is important to note how frequently interest is paid. The more frequently it is paid, the sooner you can either

spend the interest or reinvest it to earn still more interest.

4. **General level of interest rates** – interest rates on savings vary with the general level of interest rates in the country. This is determined by factors which you will look at in the second year of your Organisation in its Environment course.

Liquidity

This refers to how easily your savings can be turned into cash and is dependent upon how much notice is required to withdraw money (often called the **notice of withdrawal**). We would expect to receive a higher rate of interest on a less liquid investment (i.e. savings which require a longer notice of withdrawal). The disadvantage is that you would have to wait longer before you could withdraw any cash.

Another factor affecting an investment's liquidity is its **accessibility**, which is dependent upon the number of outlets available to withdraw cash. In this respect, money in the account of a bank or a big building society is highly accessible because of the large number of branches and cash-dispensing machines they have.

Activity

From your newspaper, list the savings in order of liquidity (most liquid at the top, least liquid at the bottom).

Activity

Your group should make a list of all the different building societies, post offices and banks in your local area.

Divide yourselves up into groups of two. Each group should visit one of these organisations and find out:

1. How frequently they pay interest on their accounts.
2. How many branches each of them has.

Then compare your findings and prepare a 'league table' of those organisations, based upon how many branches they have (most at the top, least at the bottom).

Security

Some people want to be absolutely sure that the money value of their savings will not fall and so are prepared to accept a lower rate of return to guarantee this. Savings accounts from building societies, banks and the government (e.g. National Savings) all give this guarantee of total security.

Other investments (e.g. shares and unit trusts – see later in the chapter) are more risky in the sense that, although a high rate of return can be made from them, it is also possible to lose some or all of the money you have invested.

Activity

From your newspaper, pick out the investments which are likely to be most secure.

Future savings requirements

In the future, your saving will probably have to take account of

(a) **home-buying**,
(b) **family requirements**,
(c) **emergencies** and
(d) **retirement** (see Fig. 2.2).

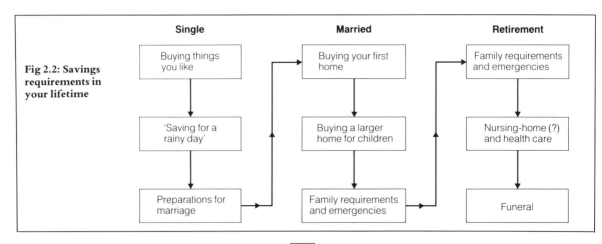

Fig 2.2: Savings requirements in your lifetime

Buying your own home

When buying a house or flat for the first time, you will have to pay for the following from your savings:

- **Deposit** (normally 5 per cent of purchase price).
- **Solicitor's fees** (normally 1 per cent of purchase price + VAT).
- **Stamp duty** (1½ per cent of purchase price, if above £30,000).
- **Removal expenses**.
- **Structural survey** – an examination by a surveyor to find out how well the property is built. This is in addition to the survey carried out by the building society or bank and usually costs about £200.
- **Building-society or bank survey** – usually costs about £50, depending upon the purchase price; the higher the price, the higher the fee.
- **Other household expenses** – furnishings, carpets, household goods, etc.

A regular savings account with a building society is an attractive way of saving to pay such expenses (see p. 15).

Activity

Calculate the total cost of buying a house for £45,000 (allow £1,500 for removal expenses, structural survey, building-society survey and other household expenses).

Family requirements

Married people must always consider what financial effect their death would have upon their family. For this reason, life assurance is considered to be an essential form of saving (see p. 18).

Emergencies

People must also save to cope with unexpected expenditures like major car repairs, or damage to your home.

Retirement

It is important that people have a private pension scheme (provided by their employer or a life-assurance company). When they retire, this will give them an income in addition to the state pension.

Where you can invest your savings (see Figs. 2.3 and 2.4)

Fig. 2.3: Where you can save

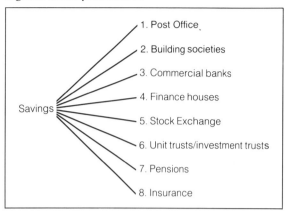

The Post Office

You can invest in the following through your local post office:

NATIONAL SAVINGS BANK ORDINARY ACCOUNT

Investment: minimum £1, maximum £10,000. Amounts of up to £100 can be withdrawn immediately.
   Verdict: both non-taxpayers and taxpayers would get a higher rate with a building-society ordinary share account.

NATIONAL SAVINGS BANK INVESTMENT ACCOUNT

Minimum £1, maximum £50,000. Notice of withdrawal: one month.
   Verdict: excellent investment for non-taxpayers.

NATIONAL GIROBANK'S CURRENT AND DEPOSIT ACCOUNTS

The National Girobank is a government-owned bank which offers similar services to the big privately owned banks like Barclays and Lloyds (see p. 16).
   Verdict: no particular advantages over other banks, except that you can use the thousands of post offices for withdrawing cash.

NATIONAL SAVINGS CERTIFICATES (PRESENT ISSUE: 31ST ISSUE)

Minimum £25, maximum £50,000. Money must be invested for five years to gain the highest possible interest.

Fig. 2.4: Percentage of adults holding different savings accounts, 1981 and 1984

Source: Inter-Bank Research Organisation, *Research Brief*, October 1985 (Association for Payment Clearing Services).

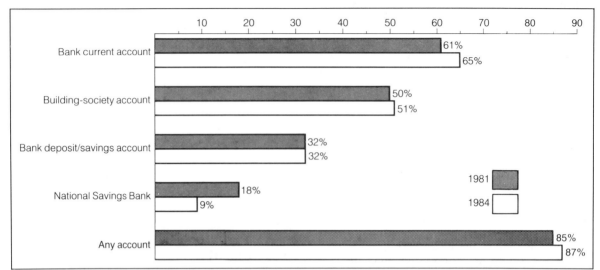

Verdict: most advantageous for top-rate taxpayers (those who pay above 27 per cent); not so good for non-taxpayers and standard-rate taxpayers.

PREMIUM BONDS

Minimum £10, maximum £10,000. You obtain a number for each £1 invested. If the government's computer, 'Ernie', chooses your number, you win a cash prize.

Verdict: strictly for the gambler. A recent *Which?* magazine survey (November 1985) stated that, if you have £10 worth of premium bonds, you have only a 1-in-14,500,000 chance of winning £250,000 or more in any one year.

YEARLY PLAN

Regular savings account (minimum £20 per month, maximum £200). You save for one year and then you can invest your savings for another four years to obtain the highest possible interest.

Verdict: good rate of interest, particularly for top-rate taxpayers, but other people could do better in a building-society account, which also ties up your money for five years.

INCOME BONDS

Minimum £2,000, maximum £50,000. Interest is paid directly into your bank account every month. Three months' notice of withdrawal needed.

Verdict: excellent for non-taxpayers; not so good for taxpayers.

DEPOSIT BONDS

Minimum £100, maximum £50,000. You must invest the money for at least one year to obtain the highest possible interest. Three months' notice of withdrawal.

Verdict: excellent for non-taxpayers; not so good for taxpayers.

NEWLY ISSUED GILT-EDGED SECURITIES

These are long-term loans to the government, issued by the government in £100 units. In other words, you can buy a newly issued unit for £100 which the government will agree to repay after a certain period of time (e.g. twenty years). You can then sell this security on the Stock Exchange (see below) to someone else, who then has the right to be repaid and to receive the interest.

Verdict: particularly good for non-taxpayers, because interest is paid gross. Some gilt-edged securities are index-linked (the interest rate is linked to the rate of inflation), and these are particularly attractive in times of high inflation.

NEWLY ISSUED LOCAL-AUTHORITY AND NATIONALISED-INDUSTRY SECURITIES

Both local authorities and nationalised industries raise money by borrowing from the public in this way. Interest is paid on the loans, and they are repaid after a certain period of time.

Verdict: good rate of interest, particularly attractive for non-taxpayers.

Activity

Visit your nearest post office and collect the leaflets available on its investment accounts. Then read them. Which are the best accounts for students and for standard-rate taxpayers?

Building societies

Building societies receive money from investors which they then lend out to home-buyers in the form of mortgages. (See Chapter 3 for a discussion of the different types of mortgage.) Building societies are extremely popular with savers. A half of all adults have an account with one (see Fig. 2.4), and at the end of 1985 £103,430 million was invested with them.

The new Building Societies Act (1986) gives societies a wide range of other powers, including the ability to lend for purposes other than house purchase and to offer insurance, legal and estate-agency services.

The five largest UK building societies are, in order of size, the Halifax, Abbey National, Nationwide, Leeds Permanent and Woolwich. Contrary to popular belief, building societies are mutual (non-profit-making) bodies. In other words, they make just enough money from interest payments on mortgages to cover their expenses and provide them with adequate reserves to meet unexpected demands for cash from their investors.

Although there are variations between societies, most building societies have the following investment accounts:

SHARE ACCOUNTS

You can pay money into these at any time. Some (often called ordinary share accounts) allow immediate withdrawal, while others require from seven days' up to three months' notice of withdrawal. Some also provide cheque-book services.

Verdict: easy withdrawal and good return, particularly for taxpayers.

REGULAR SAVINGS ACCOUNT

With these you save a regular amount every month (usually minimum £1 per month, maximum £100 per person). You receive a higher interest rate than with the ordinary share account, unless you withdraw money from the account whilst you are saving.

Verdict: an ideal account for saving up to buy a house or flat, with a good return for taxpayers.

SAVE-AS-YOU-EARN (2ND ISSUE)

You save regularly for five years (minimum £1, maximum £20 per month), at the end of which you receive a cash bonus if you have not withdrawn any of your savings. You also receive another bonus of the same size if you keep your money invested for another two years.

Verdict: particularly attractive for top-rate taxpayers.

TERM SHARE ACCOUNTS

These receive a higher rate of interest than share accounts because you cannot withdraw your money for a certain period of time (usually 1, 2, 3, 4 or 5 years). The usual minimum investment for them is £500.

Verdict: good return for taxpayers.

Activity

Choose one building society and obtain information about its investment accounts (including its rates of interest).

General points about investment in building societies

- Generally you will get a higher rate of interest if you are prepared to wait longer before you can withdraw your money.
- Always make sure that the society is a member of the **Building Societies' Association**. This guarantees that your money is absolutely safe, because if a member gets into financial difficulties, other member societies will help it out.
- The interest paid has income tax already deducted at the standard rate, i.e. it is paid net of tax. Therefore, if you pay tax at the standard rate (which most people do), you do not have to pay tax on the interest you receive. This is because the building societies have already paid the income tax to the Inland Revenue at a specially favourable rate called the **composite rate** (presently 24.75 per cent). On the other hand, non-taxpayers (e.g. students) cannot reclaim the tax that has been paid. Therefore, for them the building-society rate is effectively equivalent to a *gross* rate. Consequently building-society investment is not so attractive for non-taxpayers.
- You normally get a higher rate with smaller societies because they have lower management costs per £1 invested than the larger societies.

Activity

Buy a *Financial Times* next Saturday. On the middle right-hand page you will find a list of building-society rates. Make a note of the societies offering the highest rates for each of the different types of account. Compare these rates with those of (a) Abbey National, (b) Halifax, (c) Nationwide, (d) Woolwich, (e) Leeds Permanent.

Commercial banks

The main privately owned UK commercial banks (sometimes called **clearing banks**) are, in order of size, Barclays, National Westminster, Midland, Lloyds and Royal Bank of Scotland (which now owns William & Glyn's). Other major banks are Trustee Savings Bank (TSB), Co-operative Bank and National Girobank.

Banks provide a wide range of services to their customers, including deposit taking and lending (see Chapter 3). So they provide a variety of accounts for their depositors to invest in:

Account	Notice of withdrawal
Current account	None (the most popular type of savings account – see Fig. 2.4)
Deposit account	Seven days
High-interest accounts	One day

As with building societies, bank interest is now paid net of tax.

Verdict: high-interest accounts provide the best return and are particularly attractive for standard-rate taxpayers. However, current accounts normally give no interest, so that the money you have in them should be kept to a minimum (but make sure you do not overdraw, or you will pay bank charges).

Activity

Choose a bank and obtain information about its investment accounts.

Finance houses

You can deposit money with these institutions and in return you receive a rate of interest. They use their money to finance hire-purchase and other transactions (see Chapter 3).

Verdict: generally better than a building society if you do not pay tax, but worse if you do.

The Stock Exchange

You can buy various types of security on the Stock Exchange, including shares and debentures in public limited companies, gilt-edged securities and local-authority securities. You have to buy them through a **stockbroker**, who buys them for you from **jobbers**. Since the recent changes in the Stock Exchange (called the **Big Bang**), the same firm can act as both the stockbroker and jobber. Moreover, in the new system most shares will be bought and sold via computer, rather than by jobbers on the floor of the Stock Exchange, as happened previously.

This is only the procedure for buying **second-hand securities** (i.e. securities which have already been issued). Newly issued shares in a public limited company can be bought by completing an application form in a newspaper. This is accompanied by the company's **prospectus**, which advertises the shares and contains details about the company's financial position. This is how many people bought shares in British Telecom and the TSB.

Verdict: buying shares is a good long-term investment, but doing so through a stockbroker is not so attractive for small investors like most of us are. This is because brokers charge a small commission. So a popular way of investing on the Stock Exchange is through unit trusts (see below), which charge a smaller commission.

Activity

In the shares page of your *Financial Times*, mark the names of all the companies you recognise. Choose five of these companies and invest an imaginary £1,000 in each. Every Friday for the next ten weeks, record how much the value of your investment has risen or fallen.

Unit trusts and investment trusts

These institutions are similar to each other in that they accept money from the public and invest it for them in different securities, particularly shares. Some trusts specialise in different types of security. For example, there are unit trusts which invest only in Japanese or United States shares.

However, there are two main differences between unit and investment trusts:

SOURCE OF FUNDS

Because investment trusts are public limited companies, they raise money largely through the issue of shares and debentures. Unit trusts, on the other hand, receive money from the sale of units. They are bought direct from the unit trust.

Activity

Look up the list of unit trusts in your *Financial Times*. You will see two prices quoted for each unit. The higher price (called the **offer price**) is what you pay to buy the unit. The lower price (the **bid price**) is what you would get if you sold a unit.

RETURN TO THE INVESTOR

If an investment trust's investments are successful, it will give out a higher dividend to its shareholders, and its share price will also rise. If a unit trust's investments rise in value, the price of the units in that trust also rises, and sometimes a unit holder will receive a regular income. Therefore, there are two main types of unit trust:

- **Capital growth** – profits from the trust's investments are automatically reinvested to buy new securities.
- **Income** – some profits are given to unit holders in the form of a regular income.

Verdict: unit trusts are probably best for the small investor like you and me. They offer the choice of a high return, but there is always the chance that your units may *fall* in value, if share prices generally are falling.

If you decide to invest in a unit trust, make sure you choose one that has a record of making good investments (see *Which?* for May 1985, pp. 216–20). For those with little money (most of us!), some unit trusts operate a regular savings scheme, whereby money can be invested into them every month.

Pensions

The government provides you with a pension on reaching the age of 60 (for women) and 65 (for men). This is partly financed by National Insurance contributions (see Chapter 1). However, most employers also operate a pension scheme which gives employees an additional income when they retire. It is the job of **pension funds** to invest the employees' pension contributions wisely in various types of security, including shares. Life-assurance companies also operate similar pension schemes for self-employed people.

Verdict: an employer's pension scheme is an excellent way to provide for your retirement, particularly since income tax is not paid on any contributions to the scheme.

Insurance

The general principle of insurance is that you pay money to the insurance company (in the form of **premiums**) and in return, you or your dependants receive money from it, when the thing you have insured against takes place. To be precise, **insurance** refers to insuring for an event which *might* happen (e.g. fire and theft); **assurance** insures for something which will happen (e.g. death). So we talk about property **ins**urance and life **ass**urance, for example.

During your lifetime you should concern yourself with five broad areas of insurance: insurance for house purchase; motor insurance; travel insurance; health insurance; and life assurance.

INSURANCE FOR HOUSE PURCHASE

There are three types of insurance you should take out when buying your own home:

Household buildings insurance does not cover the contents of your home but does cover damage to your home caused by fire, lightning, explosion, earthquake, theft, flood, escape of water from pipes, and subsidence. As costs of replacing property are continually rising, it is essential that household buildings policies are linked to increases in such costs. These are called **index-linked** policies.

Household contents insurance – wherever you live you must make sure that your belongings (furniture, clothes, stereo, etc.) are insured against fire, damage and theft. At the moment, your parents' contents policy probably covers your belongings, but when you start living away from home make sure that you have your own policy. This kind of insurance is not too expensive (e.g. about £10 for covering £4,000 worth of possessions) and well worth it.

There are two types of contents policy: **indemnity**, where only the second-hand value of the damaged possessions can be claimed; and **'new for old'**, where the value of a *new* replacement can be claimed. Despite being slightly more expensive, it is better to get a 'new for old' policy.

Activity

Check whether your belongings are covered by your parents' policy.

Mortgage protection policy – this gives you life cover for repayment mortgages (see Chapter 3). In other words, if you die, the policy matures and immediately repays the mortgage.

MOTOR INSURANCE

The two most common policies for motor vehicles are the following:

Third party, fire and theft – when you have an accident, this insures you against injuries to other people involved (including your passengers) and any damage to their property (usually the other car(s) involved). You are also covered against fire and theft of your own vehicle.

Fully comprehensive – in addition to the cover given in a third party, fire and theft policy, this gives you cover against all damage to your car in an accident.

If you have a car, third party, fire and theft should be considered the minimum cover and, if you have an 'old banger', is probably sufficient. However, if you have a newer car, a fully comprehensive policy is essential.

The size of the premium depends upon a number of factors including your age, driving experience and type of car. If you do not claim on a policy, you pay a lower premium because you receive a **no-claims bonus**.

Activity

If you own a car or a motor-bike, read through your insurance policy. Make a note of its main points.

TRAVEL INSURANCE

When on holiday, this covers you for loss or theft of belongings, medical treatment and personal accidents.

MEDICAL INSURANCE

This gives you treatment in a private hospital when you are ill. Although expensive, it is worthwhile where waiting-lists at National Health Service hospitals are very long, e.g. for hip operations.

LIFE ASSURANCE

This is essential for everyone, particularly if you have a family. If something happens to you, it is reassuring to know that your loved ones will be financially secure.

The main types of life-assurance policy you should consider in your lifetime are:

- **Whole-life policies** – which give a lump-sum payment or regular income to your dependants on your death.
- **Endowment policies** – which offer a lump-sum payment when you die or reach a certain age, whichever comes sooner.
  Endowment-with-profits policies – which are particularly attractive; you get a bigger lump sum, because the insurance company invests

your premiums in shares and other securities. The bigger the profits, the bigger the payment.

- **Annuities** – where you pay a lump sum or annual premiums, and then the life-assurance company pays you a regular yearly income after you reach a certain age.

Verdict: everyone should aim to have an endowment-with-profits policy, but shop around – some insurance companies give much better deals than others (see *Which?*, September 1985).

Activity

Choose a leading insurance company from your local Yellow Pages. Write a suitable letter to it, asking for information about:

1. Its household buildings and contents policies.
2. Its motor-insurance policies.
3. Its health and medical insurance policies.
4. Its mortgage-protection and life assurance policies.

Then write brief notes on each of them.

Conclusion

These, then, are the main ways you can save, when your income is greater than your expenditure. However, unfortunately, we are not always in this position. Remember Mr Micawber in Charles Dickens's *David Copperfield*? He said: 'Annual income twenty pounds, annual expenditure nineteen, nineteen (and) six (£19–97½p!), result happiness. Annual income twenty pounds, annual expenditure twenty pounds nought and six (£20 and 2½p!), result misery.'

Fortunately, today there are also ways of borrowing to ease our difficulties when we overspend. This is the subject we turn to in Chapter 3.

Assignment

You have been asked by your Students' Union to make a survey of the services offered to students by the major banks (Barclays, Lloyds, Midland, National Westminster and the Trustee Savings Bank). As a guideline, you have been asked to compare them in terms of:

1. Bank charges.
2. Overdraft facilities.
3. Interest rates on overdrafts.
4. Cheque guarantee card.
5. Cash card.

6. Special student advisers.
7. Free gifts or discounts on certain goods.

Your findings and recommendations should be in report form.

Skills tested:
- Learning and studying.
- Information gathering.
- Communicating.

Assignment

You are working in a bank, and your superiors want some information about the bank's competitors in the savings and mortgage markets. They have asked you to choose **one** of the following articles from *Which?* magazine and make a **brief** summary of the main points. (*Note*: Students should, wherever possible, choose different ones.)

1. 'Unit Trusts', May 1985, pp. 216–20.
2. 'General Investment Tips', January 1986, pp. 26–31.
3. 'Best Buys – Investments', July 1983, pp. 302–5.
4. 'Survey on Current Accounts', September 1984, pp. 394–401 (*for two people*).
5. 'Building Society Best Buys', July 1984, pp. 294–5.

'Buying and Selling a House' (update), February 1985, pp. 66–8.
6. 'Building Societies', February 1985, pp. 62–5.
7. 'Banks and Building Societies', February 1986, pp. 74–80.
8. 'Building Societies', September 1985, pp. 419–22.
9. 'Building Societies', February 1986, pp. 86–7.
10. 'Insurance', October 1985, pp. 456–63 (*for two people*).
11. 'Covenants for Students', September 1985, pp. 428–30.
12. 'Best Ways to Borrow', April 1985, pp. 172–6.
13. 'Buying and Selling a House', July 1984, pp. 304–13 (*for two people*).
14. 'Mortgages and Mortgage Protection Policies', May 1986, pp. 224–31 (*for two people*).
15. 'Post Office Investments', November 1985, pp. 501–7.
16. 'A Pension from Your Job', October 1984, pp. 450–5.

Students should then combine all the information and present it in the form of a report.

Skills tested:
- Learning and studying.
- Information gathering.
- Communicating.

3
Borrowing

Nearly everyone has to borrow money to buy things at some time in their life. Credit is readily available everywhere – for example, credit cards, hire-purchase and, probably most important, mortgages to buy houses or flats. Remember, we have two alternatives when buying things. We can either

- **save up to buy them** or
- **borrow** (or, to put it another way, **buy on credit**).

As long as we do not borrow more than we can afford, borrowing is very convenient and useful. First of all, it allows us to buy better-quality goods and to enjoy them earlier. If inflation is high, it also avoids the need to pay much higher prices in the future.

Activity

You decide to save £50 a month so that you can buy your own home. How long would it take for you to buy a £40,000 house? (Ignore any interest received on the savings.)

You can see that it would take a very long time to save up £40,000, and you would not have much time to enjoy it!

Later in the chapter we shall look at the different types of borrowing and consider which ones are the cheapest and most suitable for you. First of all, though, we need to introduce some terms which are commonly used in borrowing.

Some terms you should know

Capital and interest

The term **capital** is used to describe the total amount borrowed. You obviously have to repay this money over a certain period of time, i.e. the **repayment period** of the loan. In addition, you

have to pay **interest** on the amount borrowed (unless you are lucky enough to get free credit!).

Creditworthiness

This refers to your ability to repay the interest and capital repayments.

Activity

Think what factors a bank manager would consider before giving you a loan to buy a car.

You should have concluded that your **creditworthiness** is dependent upon

(a) your income,
(b) your expenditure,
(c) your wealth (i.e. the value of things which you own, which could possibly be used as **security** for the loan – see below),
(d) your age (lending institutions such as banks rarely lend money to people under eighteen; this is because, under English law, they cannot sue such a person in the courts, if (s)he fails to repay the loan) and
(e) your past borrowing record (have you always repaid your loans in the past? Lending institutions such as banks can find out this information from firms called **credit reference agencies**).

Security (sometimes called 'collateral')

This is something which you own that the lending institution can sell if you cannot repay the loan. So it must be something which can easily be sold and turned into cash.

Activity

Imagine that you are a bank manager. Which of the following would you use as security for a loan: (a) motor bike, (b) houseboat, (c) flat, (d) house, (e) life-assurance policy or (f) shares? Give reasons for your choices.

Guarantee

This is a document under which someone (called a **guarantor**) agrees to repay the loan if the borrower cannot do so. For example, a parent may act as a guarantor for his or her child who wants to borrow some money.

Annual percentage rate of charge (APR)

This is the standard way of calculating and showing the cost of a particular type of borrowing. It takes into account:

- The interest charged on the loan (this is often called the **flat rate of interest**).
- Any additional costs such as insurance which may have to be taken out with the loan.
- How quickly the loan is repaid.

How is the APR calculated? The simplest and easiest way is to use the **consumer credit tables**, published by Her Majesty's Stationery Office (HMSO). A copy of this can be obtained from your local council.

Example – £156 loan to be repaid over one year in equal weekly instalments. The flat rate of interest is 15 per cent p.a. and there are no additional costs associated with the loan. What is the total weekly instalment and what is the APR?

Interest paid over the year will be 15 per cent of £156, i.e. £23.40. So the total weekly instalment will be:

Loan repayment (£156 ÷ 52) = £3
plus Interest (£23.40 ÷ 52) = £0.45.

The total weekly repayment is £3.45.

We can find out the APR from the consumer credit tables – see Fig. 3.1. The loan is repaid over 52 weeks, and the charge per pound lent is 0.1500 (15 per cent). Therefore the APR is 32.4 per cent.

Activity

A £4,000 loan is repaid over 50 equal weekly instalments. The flat rate of interest is 14.25 per cent, and there are no additional costs. What is the total weekly instalment and the APR?

The APR also provides the best way of comparing different types of borrowing. The higher the APR, the more expensive the loan will be. You should try to choose the one with the lowest APR.

Activity

Visit your local shopping centre and in pairs find out the APRs of credit offered by:

1. Banks.
2. Building societies.
3. Shops (this will include their credit cards, and hire-purchase or credit sales offered by them).

Some loans, such as personal loans from banks, have a fixed APR, i.e. the same rate is charged throughout the repayment period. But the APR on other loans varies with the general level of interest rates in the country. For example, the APR on mortgages (commonly called the **mortgage rate**) goes up and down with other interest rates.

Activity

Which type of loan would be better if rates were going up: one with a fixed rate or one with a variable rate?

Fig. 3.1: Extract from consumer credit tables

| Number of instalments (weeks) | | | | | | | | | |
45	46	47	48	49	50	51	52	53	APR
.1280	.1309	.1338	.1367	.1396	.1425	.1454	.1483	.1513	32.0
.1284	.1313	.1342	.1371	.1400	.1429	.1458	.1488	.1517	32.1
.1287	.1316	.1345	.1375	.1404	.1433	.1463	.1492	.1521	32.2
.1291	.1320	.1349	.1379	.1408	.1437	.1467	.1496	.1526	32.3
.1294	.1324	.1353	.1382	.1412	.1441	.1471	**.1500**	.1530	**32.4**
.1296	.1327	.1357	.1386	.1416	.1445	.1475	.1505	.1534	32.5
.1302	.1331	.1361	.1390	.1420	.1449	.1479	.1509	.1539	32.6
.1305	.1335	.1364	.1394	.1424	.1453	.1483	.1513	.1543	32.7
.1309	.1339	.1368	.1398	.1428	.1457	.1487	.1517	.1547	32.8
.1313	.1342	.1372	.1402	.1432	.1462	.1491	.1521	.1551	32.9

Source: Office of Fair Trading, *Consumer Credit Act 1974 – Credit Charges* (HMSO, 1980).

Borrowing: how it's done

(See Figs. 3.2 and 3.3.)

Credit cards

Credit cards from banks (e.g. Access) and building societies allow you to borrow interest-free for normally a month. Every month a statement is sent to you, asking you to pay off the money you owe by a certain date. If you fail to do this you start to pay interest on the money outstanding. The maximum amount you can borrow is determined by your **credit limit**, which depends upon your earnings – the higher your earnings, the higher the limit.

Charge cards, like American Express, are similar to credit cards, except that:

- you pay annual fees for the privilege of using them;
- you have to pay off in full what you owe each month;
- there is no maximum limit set on what you can spend.

Verdict: convenient (especially for buying things like petrol), but make sure you don't overspend. Good value if you pay off your debts within the agreed time period; expensive if you don't.

Fig. 3.2: Types of borrowing – summary

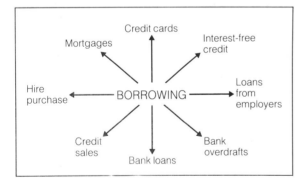

Activity

Make a list of the main credit and charge cards in the UK.

Find out from the government publication *Social Trends* (1986) how many people have a credit card.

Interest-free credit

Sometimes retailers and mail-order firms give interest-free credit (i.e. 0 per cent APR).

Verdict: this obviously has its advantages, but you must check that prices are not set at higher levels to cover the costs of the interest-free credit.

Loans from employers

Cheap or interest-free loans may be given by employers to their employees, so that they can buy certain things like a house, a season ticket or a car.

Verdict: excellent, if you can get them!

Loans and overdrafts from banks

An **overdraft** is the right to overdraw your current account at the bank by a certain amount. For example, if you have nothing in your account, and the bank agrees to allow you a £500 overdraft, you can withdraw cheques up to the value of £500. Interest is calculated on a day-to-day basis, determined by the amount overdrawn at the end of each day.

Verdict: the big advantage is that you don't pay any interest if you don't overdraw. An overdraft is useful to have in case of extra or unexpected expenditures, e.g. when you are moving home.

A **bank loan** gives you a lump sum, and you start to pay interest on that money immediately, whether you spend it or not. A certain amount of the loan is repaid every month. If you can get one, an **ordinary bank loan** is a cheap form of borrowing. If you cannot, a **personal bank loan** is still relatively cheap, although its APR is slightly higher than for an ordinary bank loan.

The factors a bank manager will consider before giving you a loan will be discussed in detail in Chapter 11.

Verdict: ideal for buying a fixed asset like a car, motor bike or stereo. Loans have a slightly lower APR than an overdraft.

Activity

Pick up a leaflet from your local bank on its lending services. Find out what the APR is on its loans and overdrafts (*not* the flat rate of interest on them). Then draw a table, illustrating these rates, and write brief notes on the leaflet.

Hire-purchase and credit sales

You can use these to buy fixed assets like a stereo or a camera. (Are these items of revenue expenditure? Have another look at Chapter 1 if you don't know.)

Under both hire-purchase and credit-sales agreements, a **finance house** lends money to someone, so that (s)he can buy something from a retailer. In return, the buyer pays the finance house (1) a **de-**

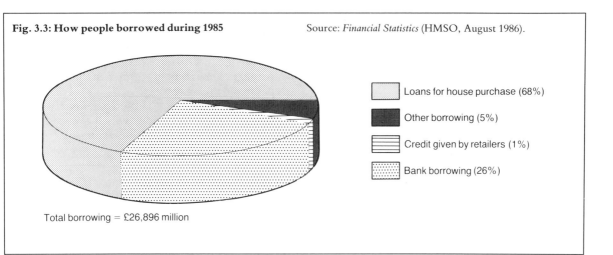

Fig. 3.3: How people borrowed during 1985   Source: *Financial Statistics* (HMSO, August 1986).

- Loans for house purchase (68%)
- Other borrowing (5%)
- Credit given by retailers (1%)
- Bank borrowing (26%)

Total borrowing = £26,896 million

posit and then (2) **monthly instalments**, covering interest and repayments on the loan. With hire purchase, the buyer becomes owner of the goods on **payment of the final instalment**. With credit sales, however, the buyer becomes owner on **payment of the first instalment**.

Verdict: convenient but often more expensive than other forms of borrowing. It is important that you shop around for the lowest APR – rates can vary significantly from one hire-purchase or credit-sales agreement to another.

Activity

Imagine that you are buying a stereo. Compare the APRs on credit offered by retailers in your area for this stereo.

Mortgages from building societies and banks

These are loans given to people so that they can buy their own house or flat. Mortgages are the most important form of borrowing for most people in Britain. By the end of 1985 UK building societies and banks had lent out £97,007 million.

Mortgages are normally repaid over twenty-five years. The interest rate charged on them is commonly called the **mortgage rate**.

The amount you can borrow is calculated on the basis of your **gross income**. The normal guidelines for this are:

- Single people – 2½ × income (can be as high as 3 ×).
- Couples – 2½ × larger income plus 1 × (once) smaller income.

Activity

Visit a local building society or bank and find out:

1. Its mortgage rate.
2. The normal repayment period on its mortgages.
3. How much a person can borrow, on the basis of their income.

Compare your findings with other members of the group; are there any differences?

Also obtain information about the building society or bank's services for home buyers (this is required for the activity on p. 24).

There are two main types of mortgage:

REPAYMENT MORTGAGE

This is where interest and capital (or loan) repayments are both paid to the lender, i.e. to the bank or building society.

ENDOWMENT MORTGAGE

This is where interest is paid to the lender, and premiums are paid to a life-assurance company for a policy which matures at the end of the repayment period to repay the loan. There are two main types of endowment mortgage:

Low-cost endowment mortgage – here the maturity value of the policy, including any profits made from it, just covers the amount of the mortgage. So if the borrower does receive a cash bonus at the end of the mortgage, it is only a relatively small one.

Full endowment mortgage – this pays you a larger cash bonus at the end of the mortgage. The premiums are higher than on a low-cost endowment.

TAX RELIEF

Income tax is not paid on the interest paid on mortgages up to the value of £30,000. Most people now get this tax relief under the system known as MIRAS (Mortgage Interest Relief At Source). Under MIRAS the borrower pays a reduced amount to the lender (i.e. interest paid less tax), and the government makes up the difference.

Example – standard rate of income tax 27 per cent. If the borrower is due to pay total interest payments of £1,000 p.a. on a mortgage, they will pay the lender only £730 (= £1,000 interest *less* tax, i.e. 27 per cent of £1,000). The government then pays the difference (£270) to the lender.

Tax relief is also available for loans which are used to improve your house or flat, e.g. to put in central heating. Such loans can be given by a building society or bank, in addition to your original mortgage.

Activity

Find the 1987 *Which?* publication, *Tax Saving Guide*, in your college or public library. Read and make notes on the section on mortgages and home-improvement loans.

Activity

Read through the information you received from a bank or building society about its services for home buyers. Make notes on it.

Verdict: *repayment or endowment mortgage?* Since life-assurance premiums lost their tax relief in the 1984 Budget, repayment mortgages have become relatively more attractive. The main advantage of a repayment mortgage is that, unlike with an endowment mortgage, you can extend the mortgage repayment period when the mortgage rate rises. This enables you to keep your monthly repayments at the same level.

However, it is essential that you have a **mortgage protection policy** with a repayment mortgage. This gives you life cover, which you automatically get with an endowment mortgage. This means that the mortgage is automatically repaid if you die – very important if you have a family dependent upon you.

The best-value endowment mortgage is probably the **low-cost endowment**. This type of mortgage has become even more popular since in 1986 most building societies and banks abolished the practice of charging people with endowment mortgages ½ per cent more interest than those with repayment mortgages.

Make sure, though, that you get a **with-profits** endowment policy, i.e. one which gives you some of the profits made by the life-assurance company with your money.

Activity

Would you advise someone to buy their own home? Give reasons for your answer. (You will need information about changes in property prices in your area for this. Ask a local building society, bank or estate agent about this.)

Tips about borrowing

The April 1985 issue of *Which?* magazine gave the following tips:

- Use a credit card to receive interest-free credit, but make sure you don't overspend.
- Ask whether a cheap loan is available from your employer.
- Compare APRs before deciding which loans to choose.
- Keep in your bank manager's good books, even if you don't need a bank loan. Other lenders might approach your bank for a reference.
- If you have difficulty getting a loan, find out if credit-reference agencies have files on you. If they do, see what they say – you are entitled under the 1974 Consumer Credit Act to see these files (see below).
- Always find out if there will be any charges for paying off the loan early.
- Take maximum benefit from the tax relief offered on loans, e.g. if you can afford it, get a mortgage of £30,000.

Borrowing and the law

The most important piece of law affecting borrowers is the **1974 Consumer Credit Act**. Its main provisions are:

1. The APR of the credit must be shown on all quotations and advertisements (check your local newspaper and you will see that this is true).

2. If the goods are faulty it will normally be possible to sue the lender as well as the retailer.
3. If the APR is extremely high, you can apply to a court to lower it.
4. If you have paid one-third of the total price under a hire-purchase agreement and you have fallen behind with the payments, the lender (i.e. the finance house) cannot take the goods away from you without your permission or a court order.

Activity

Using books in your library and the April 1985 *Which?* magazine, find out if there are any other provisions in the 1974 Act.

Conclusion

Money makes the world go round, and borrowing makes it go round that much faster! Borrowing is often useful and, when we are buying a house or flat, absolutely essential. The thing to avoid is spending and borrowing too much, or you will end up in the bankruptcy court. To stop this happening, you must be able to record what your financial position is at any particular time. This is the subject we turn to in Chapter 4.

Assignment

You have been asked by your Students' Union to prepare a suitable leaflet for the students in your college, entitled *A Student's Guide to Credit*. This should be presented in an appealing way and should include the following information:

1. The different types of credit available to students over eighteen.
2. Which type of credit is most suitable, bearing in mind its cost and what the credit is used for.
3. Legal protection for borrowers.

The leaflet should not be more than 1,500 words, excluding tables and other visual material used.

Skills tested:
- Numeracy.
- Learning and studying.
- Design and visual discrimination.
- Information gathering.
- Communicating.

4
Personal Accounts

The rest of this book will concentrate on the subject of accounting and how it can be usefully employed in a job. However, as an introduction to this, we need to discuss the documents which can be used to illustrate your personal financial situation. Some of these we have mentioned before (see Fig. 4.1).

Fig. 4.1: Types of personal account

Account	What it contains
● Budget	Your expected receipts and payments
● Receipts and payments statement	Your actual receipts and payments
● Income and expenditure statement	Your income and revenue expenditure
● Sources and application of funds statement	Your sources of cash and how it is spent
● Balance sheet	Your assets (current and fixed), liabilities (current and long-term) and capital

Budget

This states money which you expect to receive and spend in the next week, month or year (see Chapter 2).

Receipts and payments statement

This states money you have actually received and spent in any particular week, month or year (see Chapter 2). This includes all items of capital expenditure, i.e. spending on fixed assets, during that period of time. For example, hire-purchase payments on a motor bike would be included, as would money spent on a new radio or stereo (see Chapter 2). However, depreciation (see below) is *not* included.

Income and expenditure statement

This states your main sources of income and your items of revenue expenditure over a period of time,

e.g. a week, month or year. It does *not* include any items of capital expenditure, although it does include:

1. Depreciation on fixed assets – an amount representing their loss of value due to wear and tear (see Chapter 7 for a more detailed discussion of this).
2. Running expenses of fixed assets, e.g. petrol used in your car or motor bike.
3. Interest paid on any loans which you have been given.

So an income and expenditure statement is equivalent to a profit and loss account in a business (see Chapter 6).

Sources and application of funds statement

This statement (sometimes called a **cash flow** or **funds flow statement**) shows where your cash comes from and how it is spent. To use the language of an accountant, it illustrates your cashflow position.

Balance sheet

This is a 'snapshot' of your financial position on a particular day, showing you how well (or how badly) off you are. It is a statement of the value of your **assets**, **liabilities**, and **capital** on that particular day.

We shall now explain what these terms mean.

Assets

As we mentioned before, an asset is something you own. It can be either **fixed** or **current**.

Fixed assets are items of capital expenditure and are used for a long period of time, e.g. a stereo, motor-bike, camera or car. In the balance sheet they are valued 'at cost' (i.e. according to their purchase price or historical cost), from which depreciation is deducted every year. This then gives the **net value** of the asset (its cost less depreciation).

Current assets are either cash or convertible into cash within one year from the date of the balance sheet – e.g. your bank balance, cash in your wallet or handbag and money owed to you by friends (i.e. your debtors). The current assets which can be least easily turned into cash are placed first. So they would be placed in the following order:

1. Debtors.
2. Building-society deposits.
3. Bank balance.
4. Cash in wallet or handbag.

Liabilities

These include:

- **Longer-term liabilities** – i.e. money owed which is to be repaid at least one year after the date of the balance sheet. These might include a bank loan, a hire-purchase debt or a loan from your parents.
- **Current liabilities** – i.e. money owed which is to be repaid within one year from the date of the balance sheet. These might include a bank overdraft, and your creditors, i.e. people to whom you owe money.

Capital

This is money you have saved and/or received from other people. Your capital in your balance sheet at the end of the year would equal:

- what you had saved during that year (i.e. the excess of your income over your expenditure); *plus*
- the capital you had at the beginning of the year.

As we shall see later in the book, the following relationship is always true for you or for anybody else:

assets = capital + liabilities.

This is why it is called a **balance** sheet, because one side of the equation (assets) *must always* balance with the other side (capital + liabilities). Let us illustrate this with the example of Rebecca Michaels, who has just been born.

Rebecca receives £500 from her grandmother, which is paid into the building society. Rebecca's financial position will be:

assets – building-society deposits (£500)

capital – grandmother's gift (£500)
liabilities – nil
   (i.e. assets £500 = capital + liabilities £500)

Eight years later, assuming nothing else has happened financially to Rebecca...

Rebecca buys a bicycle with £100 withdrawn from her building society. Rebecca's financial position will now be (ignoring any interest):

assets – building-society deposits (£400: £500 less £100)
capital – her capital before the bicycle was bought (£500) less the savings she spent (£100), i.e. £400
liabilities – nil
   (i.e. assets £400 = capital + liabilities £400)

Accountants illustrate this equation in the balance sheet, either vertically or horizontally, as we shall see in the next example.

Example: From the following information, prepare Paul Garcia's personal accounts for the year ended 31 December 1986.

Paul Garcia's financial position on 31 December 1986

	£
Motor bike at cost	600
Stereo at cost	250
Hire-purchase debt on motor bike	550
Bank loan to be repaid during 1988	200
Money owed by a friend, to be repaid during 1987	50
Depreciation on motor bike during 1986	50
Depreciation on stereo during 1986	30
Bank balance	1,000
Building-society deposits	640
Money owed to a friend, to be repaid during 1987	30

Note: His capital on 1 January 1986 was £450.

Paul Garcia's income and expenditures for the year ended 31 December 1986

	£
Net income	3,970
Building-society interest	40
Deposit and six-monthly hire-purchase instalments paid on motor bike (bought on 1 June 1986)	100
Bought stereo with cash	250
Board and lodging	1,500
Entertainment	500
Running expenses of motor bike	200
Holiday	300
Clothing	200
Depreciation on motor bike during 1986	50
Depreciation on stereo during 1986	30

Paul Garcia's personal accounts would be:

Paul Garcia – receipts and payments statement for the year ended 31 December 1986

Payments	£	Receipts	£
Deposit and hire-purchase payments on motor bike	100	Net income	3,970
Stereo	250	Building-society interest	40
Board and lodging	1,500		
Entertainment	500		
Running expenses of motor bike	200		
Holiday	300		
Clothing	200		
Excess of receipts over payments	960		
	£4,010		£4,010

Notice that depreciation is *not* included here, but items of capital expenditure during the year (i.e. the stereo and the motor bike) are.

Activity

Complete your receipts and payments statement for last month.

Paul's sources and application of funds statement would be:

Paul Garcia – sources and application of funds statement for year ended 31 December 1986

	£	£	£	£
Net income		3,970		
Building-society interest		40		
Total income			4,010	
deduct Capital expenditure				
Stereo	250			
Motor bike	100			
		350		
Revenue expenditure				
Board and lodging	1,500			
Entertainment	500			
Motor bike expenses	200			
Holiday	300			
Clothing	200			
Depreciation: stereo	30			
Depreciation: motor bike	50			
		2,780		
Total expenditure			3,130	
Personal saving				880
Assets acquired				
Building-society deposits		600		
Bank deposits		280		
			880	

Notice that depreciation *is* included here as an item of revenue expenditure; and Paul has invested his savings in his bank and building society.

Activity

Complete your sources and application of funds statement for the year just ended.

Paul's income and expenditure statement would be:

Paul Garcia – income and expenditure statement for year ended 31 December 1986

	£		£
Board and lodging	1,500	Net income	3,970
Entertainment	500	Building-society interest	40
Running expenses of motor bike	200		
Holiday	300		
Clothing	200		
Depreciation on motor bike	50		
Depreciation on stereo	30		
	2,780		
Excess of income over expenditure	1,230		
	£4,010		£4,010

Notice that depreciation is again included here, but items of capital expenditure *are not*. In other words, the statement includes only items of revenue expenditure, just like a business's profit and loss account (see Chapter 6).

If Paul's total expenditure had exceeded total income, there would have been an 'excess of expenditure over income' figure on the right-hand side of the account.

Activity

Complete your income and expenditure statement for last month.

The vertical presentation of Paul's balance sheet would be:

Paul Garcia – balance sheet as at 31 December 1986

Net assets employed:	Cost £	Provision for depreciation £	Net £	£	£
Fixed assets					
Motor bike	600	50	550		
Stereo	250	30	220		
	850	80	770		
				770	
Current assets					
Debtors			50		
Building-society deposits			640		
Bank balance			1,000		
			1,690		
less Current liabilities					
Creditors			30		
Net current assets				1,660	
					2,430
Financed by:					
Capital – P. Garcia					
Capital as at 1 Jan. 1986			450		
add Excess of income over expenditure			1,230		
				1,680	
Bank loan				200	
Hire-purchase debt				550	
					2,430

Notice from this that current assets less current liabilities is **net current assets** (or **working capital**, as it is sometimes called). Depreciation is deducted from the value of fixed assets, and Paul's capital on the date of the balance sheet is what he started the year with *plus* the money he has saved (the excess of his income over his expenditure).

The horizontal presentation of this balance sheet would be:

Paul Garcia – balance sheet as at 31 December 1986

Fixed assets	£	£	£	Capital – P. Garcia	£	£
Motor bike at cost	600			Capital as at 1 Jan. 1986	450	
less Depreciation	50					
		550		add Excess of income over expenditure	1,230	
Stereo at cost	250					1,680
less Depreciation	30					
		220		Bank loan		200
			770	Hire-purchase debt		550
Current assets				Current liabilities		
Debtors		50		Creditors		30
Building-society deposits		640				
Bank balance		1,000				
		1,690				
			2,460			2,460

Since the 1981 Companies Act, assets are put on the *left*-hand side of the balance – not the right-hand side, as before.

Activity

Complete your own balance sheet as at today.

Conclusion

This chapter has looked at how accounting can be applied to individuals. In the rest of the book we must see how it can also be used in different types of organisation. We shall start, in Chapter 5, by looking at what an accountant does.

Assignment

Having just left school, Jenny Walker starts working for a bank in your local area on 1 September 1987. She earns £80 gross per week, and benefits from a non-contributory pension scheme. Her only deductions from her gross pay are income tax and National Insurance. She has £1,000 in her building-society account on 1 September 1987, on which she receives 6 per cent p.a. interest. With this money she buys a £250 stereo unit on 1 November 1987 and a £500 motor-scooter on 1 February 1988. Tax and insurance for the bike are £96 per year. The motor-scooter does an average 70 miles to the gallon.

Depreciation is as follows: motor-scooter – £100 per year; stereo – £50 per year.

As from the third week in September Jenny travels to your college for a day each week to do a business studies course. She lives with her parents six miles away from the college. Until 31 January 1988 she goes to college by train (fare: £2 return). Then she uses her motor-scooter as from 1 February 1988 until the end of the college year.

Jenny lives two miles away from the bank where she works. Until 31 January 1988 she goes to the bank by train (£1 return), and then she uses her motor-scooter as from 1 February 1988.

She has four weeks' holiday a year: one week in December, one week in April and two weeks in August. The college year lasts 33 weeks and finishes on 30 June 1988.

Jenny's other expenditures are:

	£
Payment to parents for board and lodging	25 per week
Entertainment	15 per week
Clothes and make-up	20 per month
Other expenses (newspaper, magazines, snacks, etc.)	5 per week

You are required to:

1. Prepare Jenny's receipts and payments statement for the year ending 31 August 1988.
2. Prepare her income and expenditure statement for the same period.
3. Prepare her balance sheet as at 31 August 1988.

Note:

- Assume the tax allowances and National Insurance and tax rates are the same as the ones for 1986–7.
- Assume each month has four weeks except for October, January, March and August, which each have five.
- Ignore public holidays.

Skills tested:

- Numeracy.
- Identifying and tackling problems.
- Learning and studying.
- Communicating.

PART TWO
Accountancy

5
The Role of Accountants

Introducing accountants

Do you want to become a qualified accountant? Then I have some good news and some bad news for you. The good news is that you are likely to earn a lot of money. The bad news is that you will have to become an associate member of an **accountancy body** by obtaining experience in an accountancy firm and passing some more exams!

In fact, there are six major British accountancy bodies which provide virtually all the qualified accountants in the UK (see table below). The members of these bodies are helped in their work by **accounting technicians**. Their professional body is the Association of Accounting Technicians (AAT). It had 11,009 members in 1986.

Activity

Visit your local careers office (or the careers room in your college) and find out what is required to become an associate member of the accountancy bodies mentioned above, including the Association of Accounting Technicians.

Once you have qualified as an accountant, you can work *either*

- in an accountancy firm, similar to the one in which you did your training (normally referred to as **private practice**); *or*
- **in industry or commerce** in a managerial post.

It may surprise you to know that less than half of qualified accountants work for accountancy firms. Those who do are usually either chartered or certified accountants. The firms themselves range in size from small local accountancy firms (which operate as sole traders, partnerships or private limited companies) to large public limited companies like Coopers & Lybrand, which do business all over the world.

	Letters for Associate Members	Number of UK members excluding students (1986)
Institute of Chartered Accountants in England and Wales (ICAEW)	ACA	71,233
Chartered Association of Certified Accountants (CACA)	ACCA	28,500
Institute of Cost and Management Accountants (ICMA)	ACMA	20,048
Institute of Chartered Accountants of Scotland (ICAS)	CA	11,609
Chartered Institute of Public Finance and Accountancy (CIPFA)	IPFA	9,334
Institute of Chartered Accountants in Ireland (ICAI)	ACA	4,280 (in 1982)

Activity

Make a list of accountancy firms from your local Yellow Pages. Identify which ones are sole traders, which are partnerships and which are limited companies.

Accountants in private practice

Chartered and certified accountants in private practice usually offer the following services (see Fig. 5.1).

Fig. 5.1: What accountants do

Book-keeping

Book-keeping means collecting and recording information about an individual's or an organisation's monetary transactions such as the buying and selling of goods. This involves keeping certain documents and using double-entry book-keeping techniques. These will be discussed in Chapter 6.

Financial consultancy

Accountants provide advice on financial matters as consultants to organisations which want to improve their effectiveness. For example, this could involve detailed investigations into how their costs can be reduced, or how they can be more effectively organised. All the major accountancy firms are now extensively involved in such consultancy work.

Taxation

Accountancy firms advise individuals and organisations about how to minimise the amount of tax that they pay (particularly income tax, capital gains tax and capital transfer tax).

Activity

Find out from a management dictionary in your college or public library what capital gains tax and capital transfer tax are.

Investment advice

Accountants give advice to individuals about how they should invest their savings, and which particular investment offers the highest rate of return and the best deal for the investor. Remember, this is what we looked at in Chapter 2 – have you forgotten already?!

Acting as executors, trustees, liquidators, Official Receivers

Accountants are often asked to do these jobs, in which they carry out the following tasks:

- **Executors** – carry out the terms of the deceased's will and make sure that his or her property is given to those who benefit under it.
- **Trustees** – supervise the operation of trusts which look after money for other people (e.g. children who are too young to receive it). The responsibility of the trustee is to make sure that the money is safe and wisely invested.
- **Liquidators** – sell a limited company's assets when it goes out of business, so that its creditors can be repaid as much as possible of the money they are owed.
- **Official Receivers** – do the same as liquidators when individuals, sole traders and partnerships become bankrupt.

Auditing

This is an extremely important part of an accountancy firm's work. It is concerned with preparing every year an organisation's accounts (its balance sheet and profit and loss account), and then checking them to make sure that they give an accurate and fair view of its financial position. In other words, the organisation's accounts must accurately reflect the information contained in its accounting records – ledgers, invoices and so on (see Chapters 6 and 7).

Under the Companies Acts 1948–85, only qualified chartered or certified accountants may audit the accounts of a limited company in this way (see Chapter 9, where this subject is discussed in detail). Partnerships and sole traders also have their accounts prepared by the same accountants, despite the fact that the law does not require them to do so.

Activity

Find out the address of one of the following accountancy companies. Then write a suitable letter to it, requesting a copy of its annual report and accounts:

1. Coopers & Lybrand.
2. Deloitte, Haskins & Sells.
3. Peat Marwick, Mitchell & Co.
4. Price Waterhouse & Co.

Make notes on the services they offer – are they similar to the ones outlined above? Use the accounts for reference purposes when you read through Chapter 9.

Accountants in industry and commerce

Are you keen on tennis? If so, you should thank accountants (yes, them again!) for helping to make Wimbledon the success it is. The reason is that accountants are invaluable members of an organisation's management team (in Wimbledon's case, the All England Tennis Club) who work towards the achievement of its objectives.

Organisations and objectives

As you will see in more detail in Organisation in its Environment I, any organisation must establish what its primary (or main) objectives are to be and then decide upon the secondary objectives necessary to carry out these primary objectives (see Fig. 5.2). For example, the primary objective in a profit-making manufacturing enterprise is likely to be to make as much profit as possible through the satisfaction of its customers' needs and wants. To achieve this, its secondary objectives could be as follows:

Finance objective – to make sure that the organisation's money (or capital) is not being wasted and there is an adequate supply of cash to pay its suppliers and to finance its activities.

Personnel objective – to ensure that the organisation's employees are well motivated, adequately trained and in sufficient numbers to achieve its primary objectives.

Sales and marketing objective – to maximise sales of the organisation, using marketing techniques such as advertising.

Production objective – to produce as many products as possible at the lowest possible cost and at the right price and quality for the product's market.

Purchasing objective – to buy the right quality and correct quantity of the raw materials required for production.

Innovation objective – to develop an adequate number of new products which customers will buy.

Information objective – to make sure that everyone within the organisation has access to every piece of information in an easily understandable form, so that maximum efficiency is achieved.

Activity

Work out what are likely to be the primary and secondary objectives of:

1. The All England Tennis Club.
2. Your college.
3. Your favourite sports team or pop group.

Managers in different departments of the organisation will be more concerned with some objectives than with others. But it is the job of top management to ensure that all their activities are co-ordinated, so that the primary objective(s) can be achieved. Accountants in the finance or accounts department will be primarily concerned with the finance objective, so their main activities will be as follows:

Book-keeping

Accountants in industry and commerce receive, keep and send out financial documents, such as invoices, which affect the running of their organisation. They also use double-entry book-keeping techniques to prepare its accounts before an external accountancy firm audits them (see Chapter 6).

Raising finance (see Chapter 11)

Sometimes this job is given to the organisation's **corporate treasurer**, who is always a qualified accountant.

Fig. 5.2: Objectives of a profit-making manufacturing organisation

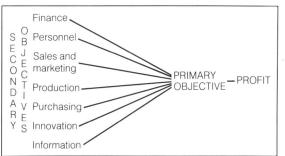

Payments

Accountants are often responsible for paying employees' wages and salaries and for the payment of bills from suppliers.

Management accounting

The purpose of management accounting is to improve managers' performance, so that they are better able to achieve the objectives of the organisation in which they work. Management accounting is concerned with:

- **Cost accounting** – which involves finding out the expenses and revenues of the organisation's product(s). This will then determine the profitability of each product (using techniques such as **break-even analysis** – see Chapter 14) and also provide the basis for calculating the product's price (see also Chapter 14).
- **Budgeting** – which involves preparing an organisation's **budgets** (again see Chapter 14 for more detail on this). These are estimates of its expenses and revenues (e.g. sales) for a given period of time in the future (e.g. the next month or year). In fact, they are very similar to your personal budgets, discussed in Chapter 2.
- **Interpretation of the organisation's accounts** – which has the aim of assessing its profitability and liquidity (i.e. its ability to pay its debts when they become due). This involves the calculation of certain accounting ratios (see Chapter 13).
- **Management of cash flow** – which aims to make sure that the organisation has enough cash to pay off its bills but at the same time does not have cash lying idle which could be more profitably used elsewhere (see also Chapter 13).
- **Investment appraisal** – which assesses whether proposed new products or investment projects (such as building a new factory or buying new machinery) are worth spending money on. In other words, will enough money be made from them to cover the cost of the investment including interest paid on any money borrowed for it? The answer to this question is provided through the use of various investment appraisal techniques, such as **discounted cash flow (DCF)** (see Chapter 12).

Internal auditing

Many organisations have internal auditors (sometimes affectionately called the 'heavy mob') who are employed to examine and improve their methods of accounting, e.g. how they record financial transactions. They will usually do this through occasional 'spot checks' on the organisation's departments or branches (if it is a retailer or financial institution like a bank).

Company secretary's work

Accountants are often employed as the **company secretary** within a limited company. His or her duties include keeping a register of shareholders and ensuring that the company obeys all the laws affecting it, including the Companies Acts.

You should be able to see from this list that the work of accountants affects not only the accounts department but all other departments as well.

Activity

Explain how the work of accountants in a manufacturing organisation would affect:

1. Its production department.
2. Its research and development department.
3. Its marketing department (responsible for sales, market research and advertising).

Conclusion

The difference between financial and management accounting

We have identified two broad categories of an accountant's work:

- Recording financial transactions and preparing accounts from them.
- Identifying ways of increasing an organisation's effectiveness through, for example, the interpretation of these accounts.

The first is the concern of financial accounting, and the second is the subject of management accounting.

Part Three of this book will examine financial accounting, and then in Part Five we shall look at management accounting.

Assignment

Your college principal is keen to make the students more aware of what different types of career have to offer. One of the careers (s)he has chosen for particular attention is accountancy because of its increasing popularity with young people.

Using information from your college library, your public library and your local careers office, prepare a suitable leaflet about accountancy as a career, which includes information about:

1. Pay and qualifications required.
2. Professional bodies and examinations.
3. The activities of accountants and where they work.
4. Career prospects.

The leaflet should not be more than 1,500 words. It should be easy to read and attractive to look at.

Information can be gathered in pairs, but each student must prepare his or her own leaflet.

Skills tested:
- Identifying and tackling problems.
- Learning and studying.
- Design and visual discrimination.
- Information gathering.
- Communicating.
- Working with others.

PART THREE
Financial Accounting

6
Recording
Financial Information I

Sebastian Coe has been one of the most successful British athletes in recent years. To measure his effectiveness and success as a runner, officials have to record his time and his position in each race.

An organisation, believe it or not, is very similar. To measure its success and to increase its effectiveness, information about its performance must be recorded. For example, accountants, within and outside the organisation, must record its **financial transactions**, such as:

- The buying and selling of fixed and current assets which are required to carry out the organisation's activities.
- Money owed to its suppliers.
- Money owed by its customers.
- The buying and selling of its product(s).

Two main methods of recording financial transactions are used:

- Double-entry book-keeping.
- Preparation of other financial documents, such as invoices.

Computers are increasingly being used to help accountants with these tasks, and we shall examine these in Chapter 16. First of all, though, we must have a look at double-entry book-keeping.

Double-entry book-keeping

For hundreds of years this has been the main system which accountants have used to record financial transactions. It was first publicised in a textbook written in 1494 by an Italian, Luca Pacioli, who was a friend of Leonardo da Vinci.

The basis of the double-entry system is that for every financial transaction there is a **debit entry** and a **credit entry** in an organisation's accounts (sometimes called its **ledgers**). As we shall soon see, an organisation has to keep accounts for its capital, its assets (current and fixed) and its liabilities (e.g. loans and creditors).

Therefore, **total credit entries will always be equal to total debit entries**. How these entries are made in an organisation's accounts can be seen by remembering the following rules:

Credit entries (see Fig. 6.1)

Credit entries are always written on the **right**-hand side of the account (see below) and often abbreviated to '**Cr**'. The following are always a credit entry:

1. **An increase in capital** (Rule 1).
2. **An increase in sales or profits** (Rule 2).
3. **An increase in loans** (Rule 3).
4. **An increase in current liabilities**, e.g. creditors (Rule 4).
5. **A decrease in fixed assets**, e.g. motor van, machinery and equipment (Rule 5).
6. **A decrease in current assets**, e.g. cash, bank balance, stocks, debtors (Rule 6).
7. **A decrease in expenses**, e.g. electricity, gas, telephone, wages, rent (Rule 7).

Fig. 6.1: How financial transactions are recorded

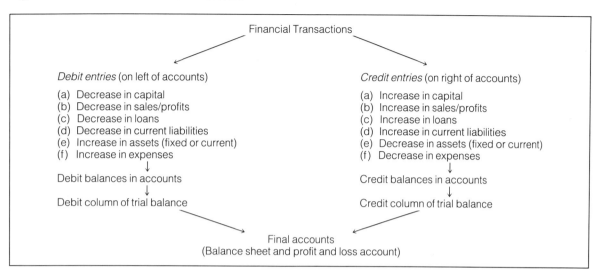

Debit entries (see Fig. 6.1)

Debit entries are always written on the **left**-hand side of the account (see below) and often abbreviated to '**Dr**'. The following are always a debit entry:

1. **A decrease in capital** (Rule 8).
2. **A decrease in sales or profits** (Rule 9).
3. **A decrease in loans** (Rule 10).
4. **A decrease in current liabilities** (Rule 11).
5. **An increase in fixed assets** (Rule 12).
6. **An increase in current assets** (Rule 13).
7. **An increase in expenses** (Rule 14).

Accounting concepts and conventions

How these rules are followed is dependent upon what accountants call **concepts** and **conventions**.

Basic concepts of accounting

COST CONCEPT

Assets are usually valued according to their cost price (although this can cause problems in times of rising prices – see Chapter 12).

MONEY MEASUREMENT CONCEPT

Accounting is concerned only with those things which can be measured in monetary terms; e.g. an organisation's balance sheet or profit and loss account will not tell you directly how good its work-force is, or how good its competitors are.

GOING CONCERN CONCEPT

Accounting will always assume that an organisation will continue to exist for an indefinitely long period of time (unless it is known that it will close down). So little emphasis is placed upon the sale price of assets.

BUSINESS ENTITY CONCEPT

The only transactions that are entered in the accounting records of an organisation are those that affect the organisation itself.

REALISATION CONCEPT

Sales are assumed to be earned on the date the goods or services are passed to the customer. *Example*. Goods worth £500 sold to J. Wilson on credit on 2 December; £500 cash received from J. Wilson in payment on 10 December. The sale takes place on 2 December *not* 10 December.

DUAL ASPECT CONCEPT

There are two aspects to accounting:

- The **assets** of an organisation.
- **Money it owes** to other people including its creditors and owners (the liabilities and capital of an organisation).

Therefore, as we have said, in the balance sheet the following is always true:

assets = liabilities + capital.

Activity

Read through Chapter 4 again to remind you that this is correct.

ACCRUAL CONCEPT

This means that:

profit for a certain period = revenues less expenditures for that period of time.

In accounting, profit is *not* cash receipts less cash expenditures. In other words:

(a) Sales revenue occurs in 1986 if goods are sold on credit in that year but cash is received only for them during 1987.
(b) Expenditures occur in 1986 if goods are bought on credit in that year but cash is paid out for them during 1987.

Conventions of accounting

MATERIALITY

Recording a transaction must be worthwhile, e.g. depreciation of a paperclip is ignored.

CONSERVATISM (OR PRUDENCE)

Whenever possible, an accountant will understate rather than overstate the amount of an organisation's profits and capital. Therefore, there is the rule that stocks should be valued at cost or realisable value, whichever is higher (see Chapter 12).

CONSISTENCY

As far as possible, methods of accounting (e.g. concerning the calculation of depreciation and the valuation of assets) should not be changed from one period of time to another.

Bearing these concepts and conventions in mind, we must now see how entries are made in an organisation's or an individual's accounts, using the fourteen rules outlined on pp. 36–7.

How double entries are made

Example 1. A college student like yourself

BORROWING £100 CASH FROM A BANK ON 1 JUNE 1987

- *Debit cash account* (normally abbreviated a/c). Why? This is an increase in a current asset and so is a debit entry (Rule 13).

- *Credit loan a/c*. Why? This is an increase in a loan and so is a credit entry (Rule 3).

How is this written in the student's accounts? Remember that a debit entry always goes on the left-hand side of the account. So the cash account will look like this:

Debit (Dr)		Cash account	Credit (Cr)
1987		£	
1 June	Loan	100	

Note how we have written the entry:
First: the date of the transaction (1 June 1987).
Second: the name of the account which is to be credited. This is stated to show us where the cash has come from.
Third: the amount of the transaction (£100).

Remember that a credit entry always goes on the right-hand side of the account. So the loan account will look like this:

Debit (Dr)	Loan account		Credit (Cr)
	1987		£
	1 June	Cash	100

Note how we have written this entry:

First: the date of the transaction.
Second: the name of the account which is to be debited. This is stated to show us where the loan has gone to.
Third: the amount of the transaction.

BUYING A £250 STEREO WITH A CHEQUE ON 2 JUNE 1987

- *Debit stereo a/c*. Why? This is an increase in a fixed asset and so is a debit entry (Rule 12).
- *Credit bank a/c*. Why? This is a decrease in a current asset – your bank balance – and so is a credit entry (Rule 6). This may seem rather odd to you. Any money which you draw out of your bank account is always a *debit* entry on your bank statement.

This is because the bank statement is written from your *bank's point of view*. From *your* point of view, any money drawn out of your account is a **credit** entry (as we have said above). So the student's accounts would look like this:

Debit (Dr)		Stereo account	Credit (Cr)
1987		£	
2 June	Bank	250	

Debit (Dr)	Bank account		Credit (Cr)
		1987	£
		2 June Stereo	250

A year later the same student sells the stereo for £200 . . .

SELLING A STEREO FOR £200 ON 2 JUNE 1988 (A CHEQUE IS RECEIVED, WHICH THE STUDENT PAYS INTO HIS OR HER BANK ACCOUNT)

Activity

Answer the following questions:

1. Which two accounts are involved?
2. Which one is credited and which one is debited (from the *student*'s point of view, remember, not the bank's)?
3. How will this be written in the student's accounts?

You should have come up with the following:

- *Debit bank a/c*. Why? This is an increase in a current asset (the student's bank balance) and so is a **debit entry** (Rule 13). You can see again that this is the opposite of what would be written in the student's bank statement.
- *Credit stereo a/c*. Why? This is a decrease in a fixed asset and so is a credit entry (Rule 5).

So, the entries in the student's accounts would look like this:

Debit (Dr)	Bank account		Credit (Cr)
1988	£	1987	£
2 June Stereo	200	2 June Stereo	250

Debit (Dr)	Stereo account		Credit (Cr)
1987	£	1988	£
2 June Bank	250	2 June Bank	200

Notice that we also have the entries for 1987.

BUYING PAPER AND FILES (STATIONERY) WITH £5 CASH ON 10 JULY 1988

Activity

Again try to think of what the entries for this transaction would be in the student's accounts.

You should have come up with:

- *Debit stationery a/c*. Why? This is an increase in an expense (stationery) and so is a debit entry (Rule 14).

- *Credit cash a/c*. Why? This is a decrease in a current asset (cash) and so is a credit entry (Rule 6).

So the entries in the student's accounts would look like this:

Debit (Dr)	Stationery account		Credit (Cr)
1988	£		
10 July Cash	5		

Debit (Dr)	Cash account		Credit (Cr)
1987	£	1988	£
1 June Loan	100	10 June Stationery	5

(Remember that the student borrowed £100 cash on 1 June 1987.)

Activity

What would be the entries in your accounts of the following transactions?

1. Bought your motor bike for £500 with a cheque.
2. Bought some beer with £1 cash.
3. Paid a £20 telephone bill with a cheque.
4. Sold your car for £400 cash.
5. Bought some records with £10 cash.
6. Paid an electricity bill with a £25 cheque.
7. Bought some chocolate with £1 cash.
8. Borrowed £100 from your parents, which you pay directly into your bank account.
9. Bought a meal at the refectory with £1 cash.
10. Bought some clothes with a £20 cheque.

Example 2. Colin Smith, Greengrocer

You will have come across the term **sole trader** in Organisation in its Environment. Well, Colin Smith is one – just like Alf Roberts in *Coronation Street*. We shall be looking at how Colin's business grows in the next few chapters – first into a partnership, with a woman called Helen Baptiste (Chapter 8), and then into a limited company (Chapter 9).

Colin worked for a fruit and vegetable wholesalers and always wanted to run his own business. He wanted to be his own boss and 'do his own thing'. His chance came when his uncle, a greengrocer, unfortunately died and left him £5,000 in his will. His aunt agreed to let him rent the shop.

The transactions in the first week of the business were as follows:

COLIN STARTS HIS BUSINESS WITH £5,000 (HIS INHERITANCE) ON 1 JUNE 1985, WHICH HE PAYS INTO HIS BANK ACCOUNT

This £5,000 is the business's capital. So the entries in Colin's accounts will be:

- *Debit bank a/c.* Why? This is an increase in a current asset (Fred's bank balance) and so is a debit entry (Rule 13).
- *Credit capital a/c.* Why? This is an increase in capital and so is a credit entry (Rule 1).

Colin's accounts would look like this:

Debit (Dr)		Bank account	Credit (Cr)		
1985		£			
1 June	Capital	5,000			

Debit (Dr)		Capital account		Credit (Cr)	
			1985		£
			1 June	Bank	5,000

COLIN CASHES A CHEQUE FOR £100 (I.E. TRANSFERS £100 FROM HIS BANK ACCOUNT INTO HIS CASH ACCOUNT) ON 2 JUNE 1985

The entries are:

- *Debit cash a/c.* Why? This is an increase in a current asset (cash) and so is a debit entry (Rule 13).
- *Credit bank a/c.* Why? This is a decrease in a current asset (Colin's bank balance) and so is a credit entry (Rule 6).

So Colin's accounts would now look like this:

Debit (Dr)		Cash account	Credit (Cr)		
1985		£			
2 June	Bank	100			

Debit (Dr)		Bank account			Credit (Cr)
1985		£	1985		£
1 June	Capital	5,000	2 June	Cash	100

Notice that we also have the entry for capital from the previous day.

COLIN BUYS A MOTOR VAN WITH A £2,000 CHEQUE ON 3 JUNE 1985

The entries are:

- *Debit motor-van a/c.* Why? This is an increase in a fixed asset (the motor van) and so is a debit entry (Rule 12).
- *Credit bank a/c.* Why? This is a decrease in a current asset (Colin's bank balance) and so is a credit entry (Rule 6).

So Colin's accounts would now look like this:

Debit (Dr)		Motor-van account	Credit (Cr)		
1985		£			
3 June	Bank	2,000			

Debit (Dr)		Bank account			Credit (Cr)
1985		£	1985		£
1 June	Capital	5,000	2 June	Cash	100
			3 June	Motor van	2,000

COLIN BUYS STOCKS OF FRUIT AND VEGETABLES WITH A CHEQUE FOR £900 on 4 JUNE 1985

Accountants always put purchases of stocks like this into a **purchases account**. The entries are:

- *Debit purchases a/c.* Why? This is an increase in a current asset (stocks) and so is a debit entry (Rule 13).
- *Credit bank a/c.* Why? This is a decrease in a current asset (Colin's bank balance) and so is a credit entry (Rule 6).

So Colin's accounts would now look like this:

Debit (Dr)		Purchases account	Credit (Cr)		
1985		£			
4 June	Bank	900			

Debit (Dr)		Bank account			Credit (Cr)
1985		£	1985		£
1 June	Capital	5,000	2 June	Cash	100
			3 June	Motor van	2,000
			4 June	Purchases	900

COLIN BUYS £200 WORTH OF FRUIT AND VEGETABLES ON CREDIT FROM W. PRICE ON 5 JUNE 1985

In other words, Colin does not pay for them straight away, and so W. Price becomes one of his creditors. The entries are:

- *Debit purchases a/c.* Why? This is an increase in a current asset (stocks) and so is a debit entry (Rule 13).
- *Credit W. Price a/c.* Why? This is an increase in current liabilities (creditors) and so is a credit entry (Rule 4).

So Colin's accounts would now look like this:

Debit (Dr)		Purchase account	Credit (Cr)		
1985		£			
4 June	Bank	900			
5 June	W. Price	200			

Debit (Dr)		W. Price account			Credit (Cr)
			1985		£
			5 June	Purchases	200

COLIN SELLS £1,250 WORTH OF FRUIT AND VEGETABLES FOR CASH ON 6 JUNE 1985

The entries are:

- *Debit cash a/c.* Why? This is an increase in a current asset (cash) and so is a debit entry (Rule 13).
- *Credit sales a/c.* Why? This is an increase in sales and so is a credit entry (Rule 2).

So Colin's accounts would now look like this:

Debit (Dr)		Cash account	Credit (Cr)
1985		£	
2 June	Bank	100	
6 June	Sales	1,250	

(Remember, Colin transferred £100 from his bank account on 2 June.)

Debit (Dr)	Sales account		Credit (Cr)
	1985		£
	6 June	Cash	1,250

COLIN SELLS £50 WORTH OF FRUIT AND VEGETABLES ON CREDIT TO L. MEHTA ON 7 JUNE 1985

In other words, Colin does not receive cash for them straight away, and so L. Mehta becomes one of his debtors. The entries are:

- *Debit L. Mehta a/c.* Why? This is an increase in a current asset (debtors) and so is a debit entry (Rule 13).
- *Credit sales a/c.* Why? This is an increase in sales and so is a credit entry (Rule 2).

So Colin's accounts would now look like this:

Debit (Dr)		L. Mehta account	Credit (Cr)
1985		£	
7 June	Sales	50	

Debit (Dr)	Sales account		Credit (Cr)
	1985		£
	6 June	Cash	1,250
	7 June	L. Mehta	50

COLIN PAYS A £10 ELECTRICITY BILL WITH A CHEQUE ALSO ON 7 JUNE 1985

The entries are:

- *Debit electricity a/c.* Why? This is an increase in an expense (electricity) and so is a debit entry (Rule 14).
- *Credit bank a/c.* Why? This is a decrease in a current asset (Colin's bank balance) and so is a credit entry (Rule 6).

So Colin's accounts would now look like this:

Debit (Dr)		Electricity account	Credit (Cr)
1985		£	
7 June	Bank	10	

Debit (Dr)		Bank account			Credit (Cr)
1985		£	1985		£
1 June	Capital	5,000	2 June	Cash	100
			3 June	Motor van	2,000
			4 June	Purchases	900
			7 June	Electricity	10

COLIN PAYS A WEEK'S RENT FOR THE SHOP WITH £100 CASH ALSO ON 7 JUNE 1985

The entries are:

- *Debit rent a/c.* Why? This is an increase in an expense (rent) and so is a debit entry (Rule 14).
- *Credit cash a/c.* Why? This is a decrease in a current asset (cash) and so is a credit entry (Rule 6).

So Colin's accounts would now look like this:

Debit (Dr)		Rent account	Credit (Cr)
1985		£	
7 June	Cash	100	

Debit (Dr)		Cash account			Credit (Cr)
1985		£	1985		£
2 June	Bank	100	7 June	Rent	100
6 June	Sales	1,250			

Activity

Sheila starts a newsagency business on 1 January 1986. Prepare her accounts on the basis of the following transactions:

1 Jan. – she starts her business with £6,000, which she puts into her bank account.

2 Jan. – she borrows £1,000 from her bank, which she also puts into her bank account.

2 Jan. – she buys goods for the business with a £1,500 cheque.

3 Jan. – she cashes a cheque for £100.

3 Jan. – she sells goods for £200 cash.

4 Jan. – she sells goods on credit to P. Shooter worth £50.

4 Jan. – she buys goods on credit from B. Lloyd worth £100.

5 Jan. – she pays a gas bill with a £20 cheque.

5 Jan. – she pays an electricity bill with £10 cash.

6 Jan. – she buys a motor van with a £3,000 cheque.

6 Jan. – she sells goods for £300 cash.

7 Jan. – she pays wages to a sales assistant with a £40 cheque (remember, wages are an expense).

Preparation of final accounts

The next important question we must answer is how we prepare an organisation's balance sheet and profit and loss account from all these debit and credit entries. The short answer is that we must do three things (look back to Fig. 6.1 on p. 37):

1. **'balance off'** the organisation's individual accounts on the date of the balance sheet; then
2. prepare what is called a **trial balance**; then
3. prepare the **final accounts**, i.e. the profit and loss account for the period of time being considered and the balance sheet.

We shall now look at each of these in detail, using Colin Smith, Greengrocer, as an example. The period of time we are looking at is the first week of his trading, i.e. 1 June to 7 June. So the balance sheet will be prepared on 7 June.

'Balancing off' the individual accounts

The aim of this is to balance both sides of each individual account on a particular day (in Colin Smith's case, 7 June 1985). The balancing figure on one side of the account is called the **balance to carry down** (abbreviated **balance c/d**) – see the examples below.

This figure is then brought down to the other side of the account on the next day (in Colin's case, 8 June 1985). This is normally abbreviated **balance b/d**, i.e. the **balance brought forward** – see also the examples below.

We shall now see how this is done for each of Colin's accounts. His capital a/c would have looked like this:

Debit (Dr)			Capital account		Credit (Cr)
1985		£	1985		£
7 June	Balance c/d	5,000	1 June	Bank	5,000
			8 June	Balance b/d	5,000

Note:
(a) The 'balance c/d' figure is £5,000 because this amount is required to balance both sides of the account.
(b) The balance is called a **credit balance**, because the 'balance b/d' figure is on the credit (right-hand) side.

His motor-van account would have looked like this:

Debit (Dr)			Motor-van account		Credit (Cr)
1985		£	1985		£
3 June	Bank	2,000	7 June	Balance c/d	2,000
8 June	Balance b/d	2,000			

This balance is called a **debit balance**, because the 'balance b/d' figure is on the debit (left-hand) side.

Activity

'Balance off' Colin's remaining accounts. Are they debit or credit balances?

They should have looked like this:

Debit (Dr)			Cash account		Credit (Cr)
1985		£	1985		£
2 June	Bank	100	7 June	Rent	100
6 June	Sales	1,250	7 June	Balance c/d	1,250
		£1,350			£1,350
8 June	Balance b/d	1,250			

This is a **debit balance**.

Debit (Dr)			Bank account		Credit (Cr)
1985		£	1985		£
1 June	Capital	5,000	2 June	Cash	100
			3 June	Motor van	2,000
			4 June	Purchases	900
			7 June	Electricity	10
			7 June	Balance c/d	1,990
		5,000			5,000
8 June	Balance b/d	1,990			

This is a **debit balance**.

Debit (Dr)			Sales account		Credit (Cr)
1985		£	1985		£
7 June	Balance c/d	1,300	6 June	Cash	1,250
			7 June	L. Mehta	50
		£1,300			£1,300
			8 June	Balance b/d	1,300

This is a **credit balance**.

Debit (Dr)			Purchases account		Credit (Cr)
1985		£	1985		£
4 June	Bank	900	7 June	Balance c/d	1,100
5 June	W. Price	200			
		£1,100			£1,100
8 June	Balance b/d	1,100			

This is a **debit balance**.

Debit (Dr)			W. Price account		Credit (Cr)
1985		£	1985		£
7 June	Balance c/d	200	5 June	Purchases	200
			8 June	Balance b/d	200

This is a **credit balance**.

Debit (Dr)			L. Mehta account		Credit (Cr)
1985		£	1985		£
7 June	Sales	50	7 June	Balance c/d	50
8 June	Balance b/d	50			

This is a **debit balance**.

Debit (Dr)			Electricity account		Credit (Cr)
1985		£	1985		£
7 June	Bank	10	7 June	Balance c/d	10
8 June	Balance b/d	10			

This is a **debit balance**.

Debit (Dr)			Rent account		Credit (Cr)
1985		£	1985		£
7 June	Cash	100	7 June	Balance c/d	100
8 June	Balance b/d	100			

This is a **debit balance**.

Preparing a trial balance (see Fig. 6.1)

This lists all the debit and credit balances on the date of the balance sheet. Debit balances are put in the debit column (abbreviated 'Dr'), and credit balances are put in the credit column ('Cr'). The **totals of both columns should balance**, i.e.

total debit balances = total credit balances.

This results from the fact that, as we noted earlier, for each transaction there is always a debit entry and a credit entry.

Activity

On the left-hand side of a piece of paper list each of Colin's accounts. On the right-hand side draw two columns. Put the debit balances in the debit column and the credit balances in the credit column. Total each column.

Now you have just written Colin's trial balance on 7 June 1985 – your first. Well done! It should have looked like this:

C. Smith, Greengrocer – trial balance as at 7 June 1985

	Dr £	Cr £
Capital		5,000
Motor van	2,000	
Cash	1,250	
Bank	1,990	
Sales		1,300
Purchases	1,100	
W. Price		200
L. Mehta	50	
Electricity	10	
Rent	100	
	£6,500	£6,500

Note:
1. The value of Colin's stocks on 7 June (called **closing stock** – see below) was £200.
2. Depreciation on the motor van up to 7 June was £6.

Activity

1. Balance off the student's accounts mentioned earlier in the chapter (p. 39) and prepare his or her trial balance on 10 July 1988.
2. Balance off Sheila's accounts mentioned earlier in the chapter (p. 41), and prepare her trial balance on 7 January 1986.

Preparing final accounts (see Fig. 6.1)

We can now prepare a balance sheet and a profit and loss account from the information in the trial balance and in the notes to it. We shall see in Chapter 7 how this is done. But first of all we must say a few words about the impact of computers upon double-entry book-keeping.

Computers and double-entry book-keeping

The effects of computers upon accounting will be discussed in detail in Chapter 16. Computers are being used more and more by accountants to carry out double-entry book-keeping. Although the computer does the work, accountants still have to understand the double-entry system, so that they can cope if anything goes wrong.

The style of accounts described in this chapter (i.e. debit on the left-hand side and credit on the right) is not used with computerised book-keeping systems. A three-column account is used, with columns for:
1. Any debit entries in the account.
2. Any credit entries in the account.
3. The balance of the account (a debit balance, Dr, or a credit balance, Cr), which is calculated automatically by the computer after each entry.

For example, Colin Smith's three-column bank account would look like this:

Bank account

1985		Debit	Credit	Balance
		£	£	£
1 June	Capital	5,000		5,000 Dr
2 June	Cash		100	4,900 Dr
3 June	Motor van		2,000	2,900 Dr
4 June	Purchases		900	2,000 Dr
7 June	Electricity		10	1,990 Dr

Notice that all the entries are placed in date order, and the balance at the end of the week has been calculated automatically by the computer. No need for a 'balance c/d' or a 'balance b/d'.

Activity

Convert all of Colin's other accounts into this three-column format.

Activity

Imagine that you are setting up your own mail-order record business on 1 January. On the basis of the following transactions, prepare your trial balance as at the end of January.

1 Jan. – you start your business with £10,000 which you pay directly into your bank account.
2 Jan. – you buy records with a £2,000 cheque.
3 Jan. – you cash a £200 cheque.
4 Jan. – you buy stationery with £100 cash.
4 Jan. – you buy equipment for postage with a £500 cheque.
5 Jan. – you buy a van with a £3,000 cheque.
8 Jan. – sales by cheque £200.
9 Jan. – cash sales £100.
9 Jan. – you pay wages to staff with two £100 cheques.
15 Jan. – sales by cheque £400.
16 Jan. – cash sales £200.
16 Jan. – you pay wages to staff with two £100 cheques.
18 Jan. – you buy £1,000 worth of records from UK Records Ltd on credit.
22 Jan. – sales by cheque £500.
23 Jan. – cash sales £300.
23 Jan. – you pay wages to staff with two £100 cheques.
25 Jan. – you buy records with a £300 cheque.
26 Jan. – you pay rent on the warehouse with a £200 cheque.

27 Jan. – you pay your electricity bill with a £100 cheque.
27 Jan. – you pay your gas bill with a £75 cheque.
29 Jan. – sales by cheque £500.
30 Jan. – cash sales £400.
30 Jan. – you pay wages to staff with two £100 cheques.
31 Jan. – you buy records worth £500 from UK Records Ltd on credit.
31 Jan. – you pay UK Records Ltd £1,000 by cheque.

Activity

M. A. D. Screwloose has decided to set up his own business as a rubber-duck manufacturer on 1 February. His friends think that he is 'quackers', but he wants to sell a revolutionary design. He developed this after many years' work in his bath and his shed, which he had converted into a wind tunnel.

On the basis of the following transactions, prepare Screwloose's trial balance as at the end of February.

1 Feb. – he starts his business with £15,000 which he puts into his bank account.
2 Feb. – he buys rubber and other materials for producing the ducks with a £2,000 cheque.
3 Feb. – he buys manufacturing equipment with a £4,000 cheque.
3 Feb. – he buys a van with a £3,000 cheque.
4 Feb. – he buys a word processor with a £500 cheque.
4 Feb. – he buys stationery with a £100 cheque.
5 Feb. – he cashes a £300 cheque.
8 Feb. – he pays his employees' wages by cheque (£1,000).
9 Feb. – he sells £500 worth of ducks to S. Idiot Ltd on credit.
15 Feb. – he pays his employees' wages by cheque (£1,000).
16 Feb. – cash sales £500.
17 Feb. – sales by cheque £500.
22 Feb. – he pays his employees' wages by cheque (£1,000).
23 Feb. – sales by cheque £1,000.
25 Feb. – he pays rent on his factory with a £1,000 cheque.
26 Feb. – he pays his electricity bill with £300 cash.
27 Feb. – he pays his gas bill with a £200 cheque.
28 Feb. – S. Idiot Ltd pays him a £500 cheque.

7
Recording Financial Information II

This is the second part of 'Recording Financial Information'. This chapter has two main objectives:

- To explain how the final accounts of a sole trader like Colin Smith are prepared from a trial balance.
- To discuss other methods, apart from double-entry book-keeping, which are used by organisations to record financial information.

First of all, we look at how to prepare a sole trader's final accounts. We again use Colin Smith, Greengrocer, as our example, so you will sometimes have to refer back to Chapter 6.

Preparation of final accounts

Organisations prepare final accounts to find out how well they are doing financially. They can do this by using the information in the trial balance and any notes attached to it. The two most important final accounts are an organisation's profit and loss account, and its balance sheet.

Profit and loss account

Activity

Read through the section on income and expenditure statements in Chapter 4.

It was mentioned in Chapter 4 that an organisation's profit and loss account is very similar to an individual's income and expenditure statement. In other words it includes:

- all sources of the organisation's income; and
- any of its items of revenue expenditure over a certain period of time.

Activity

In the week ending 7 June what are Colin Smith's sources of income and items of revenue expenditure?

You should have found out the following:

- Income: sales (£1,300).
- Revenue expenditure: (a) purchases (£1,100), (b) electricity (£10), (c) rent (£100), (d) depreciation (£6).

Notice that the only other item of expenditure, the motor van, is not included, because it is an item of capital expenditure.

A profit and loss account illustrates the organisation's income and revenue expenditures in three sections: the **trading account**, the **profit and loss account** and the **appropriation account**. For example, the vertical presentation of Colin's account would look like this:

C. Smith, Greengrocer – profit and loss account for the week ended 7 June 1985

	£	
Sales	1,300	} 1. Trading account
Cost of sales (see below)	900	
Gross profit	400	} 2. Profit and loss account
Electricity	10	
Rent	100	
Depreciation on motor van	6	
Net profit	284	} 3. Appropriation account
Transferred to C. Smith's capital a/c	284	

We shall now have to make a few comments about each section.

1. TRADING ACCOUNT

As you can see, this section includes sales and the cost of sales. The difference between the two is the organisation's **gross profit**, i.e.

gross profit = sales less cost of sales.

The **cost of sales** (sometimes called the cost of goods sold) is the total of an organisation's direct

---

45

expenses, i.e. expenses directly related to the production of the organisation's product. In Colin's case, his 'product' is the sale of fruit and vegetables, and therefore his direct expenses (i.e. his cost of sales) are the cost of the fruit and vegetables he has sold during the week.

So Colin's cost of sales is calculated as follows:

- **opening stock**, i.e. the value of stocks (fruit and vegetables) at the beginning of the period (1 June 1985, in Colin's case). Colin had no stocks on this day;
- *plus* **purchases**, i.e. the value of stocks (fruit and vegetables) bought during the period (1 June to 7 June). This figure was £1,100 for Colin (see the trial balance on p. 43);
- *less* **closing stock**, i.e. the value of stocks (fruit and vegetables) at the end of the period (7 June). This figure was £200 for Colin (see the trial balance in Chapter 6).

So Colin's cost of sales was:

$$0 + 1,100 - 200 = £900.$$

2. PROFIT AND LOSS ACCOUNT

This section calculates **net profit** by deducting items of revenue expenditure not in the trading account from gross profit, i.e.

net profit = gross profit *less* revenue expenditures not in trading account

So Colin's items of revenue expenditure to be included are rent, electricity and depreciation on the motor van. However, other items which might also have been included here are:

- Interest paid on loans from a bank.
- Bad debts, i.e. money owed to the organisation which cannot be repaid for some reason, e.g. bankruptcy of a customer.
- Provision for doubtful debts, i.e. money put aside to cover the eventuality that some debts may not be repaid in the twelve months after the date of the balance sheet.
- Motor expenses, i.e. the running costs of the motor van including petrol.
- Gas
- Insurance, i.e. premiums paid on any insurance policies.
- Selling and distribution expenses, i.e. the costs of selling and distributing fruit and vegetables to Colin's customers. This could include advertising and costs of delivering to customers' homes.
- Auditor's fees, i.e. fees paid by Colin to prepare and audit his final accounts.

3. APPROPRIATION ACCOUNT

This section shows how the net profit is distributed. As you can see, it is transferred to the sole trader's capital account. Colin can then either spend it himself, reinvest it in the business, or do a bit of both (see below).

Unlike a limited company (see Chapter 9), a sole trader's business is *not* a legal entity separate from its owner. In other words, the sole trader (e.g. Colin Smith) *is the business*. So any profit from the business is the sole trader's personal income. Any of its debts are also his or her own personal debts.

This has two main consequences:

1. **Payment of income tax** – any income tax is paid by the sole trader personally out of his or her capital. In other words, it is **deducted from the sole trader's capital account as drawings**. So unlike for a limited company, tax is *not* included in the appropriation account of the profit and loss account.

   The amount of income tax the sole trader pays is based upon his or her net profit:

   Amount of income tax = percentage of taxable income (i.e. net profit less tax allowances).

   You can see that net profit is looked upon as the sole trader's income, and then tax is calculated just as for any other individual.

Activity

Re-read the section on payment of income tax in Chapter 1.

2. **Distribution of net profit** – as we have just seen, the net profit of a sole trader's business is paid directly into his or her capital account. Sole traders are likely to spend some of this money themselves, and they will reinvest the rest of it in the business.

   These will be shown in the accounts as follows:

   - **Personal share of profit** – this will be deducted from the sole trader's capital account as drawings, which he or she will then spend on him/herself.
   - **Reinvested profit** – this will be transferred from the capital account into the sole trader's cash or bank account and spent on the business.

As we shall see in Chapter 8, a partnership deals with income tax and net profit in a similar way to a sole trader.

Balance sheet

Activity

Read through the section on balance sheets in Chapter 4.

You should have been reminded that a balance sheet is a 'snapshot' of the financial position of an organisation or individual on a particular day. It shows an organisation's

- **assets** (things it owns);
- **liabilities** (money owed to its creditors);
- **capital** (money put in by its owner(s)).

How then do we prepare Colin's balance sheet on 7 June 1985? We should note two things here:

1. *All the trial balance items not in the profit and loss account are included in the balance sheet,* i.e.

   (a) Capital (i.e. £5,000 *plus* Colin's net profit) – note that no tax has been deducted here as drawings because he has not paid any yet.
   (b) Motor van (fixed asset) less depreciation.
   (c) Cash and bank (current assets).
   (d) L. Mehta (debtor, i.e. current asset).
   (e) Closing stock (current asset).
   (f) W. Price (creditor, i.e. current liability).
   (g) Tax to be paid (a current liability).

2. *How the balance sheet is presented* – the vertical presentation of Colin's balance sheet would look like this:

C. Smith, Greengrocer – balance sheet as at 7 June 1985

Net assets employed:	£	£	£	£	£
Fixed assets	Cost	Provision for depreciation	Net		
Motor van	2,000	6	1,994		
	2,000	6	1,994		
				1,994	
Current assets					
Stock		200			
Debtors		50			
Bank balance		1,990			
Cash in hand		1,250	3,490		
less current liabilities					
Creditors			200		
Net current assets				3,290	
					5,284
Financed by					
Capital – C. Smith					
Capital account				5,000	
add net profit				284	
					5,284

You should have noticed the following things from this:

NET ASSETS EMPLOYED

This refers to the net assets used by the organisation. As you can see from the balance sheet, net assets are:

- **fixed assets** (less depreciation); *plus*
- **net current assets** – current assets less current liabilities (sometimes called **working capital**, as we said in Chapter 4).

DEPRECIATION

This is deducted from the cost of a fixed asset to give the **net value** of that asset. As this is an important subject, we shall look at it in greater detail later in the chapter.

CURRENT ASSETS

These are always placed in order of liquidity (i.e. the ones which take the longest to be converted into cash, e.g. stock, are at the top, and cash is placed at the bottom). A few comments need to be made about each of these current assets:

Stock – this is the **closing stock** figure, i.e. the value of stocks on the date of the balance sheet. In a retailing business like Colin's, stocks (sometimes called *inventories*) are goods which are to be sold to the public (in his case fruit and vegetables). In a manufacturing enterprise, however, stocks are (1) **raw materials** (materials used to manufacture its product(s)), (2) **work in progress** (uncompleted products still on the production line), (3) **finished goods** (products in storage, ready to be sold to customers).

Debtors – this is the £50 still owed to Colin by a customer, L. Mehta.

Bank balance – this is the balance of Colin's bank account on 7 June 1985.

Cash in hand – this is the balance of Colin's cash account on 7 June 1985.

CURRENT LIABILITIES

The 'creditors' figure refers to money owed by Colin to his fruit and vegetable wholesaler, W. Price.

SOURCES OF FINANCE

These are in the second half of the balance sheet and show how an organisation finances its spending on net assets (see Fig. 7.1). We shall examine the importance of this relationship in Chapter 13 and look at sources of finance in more detail in Chapter 11.

Fig. 7.1: Sources of finance

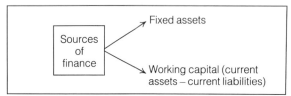

Colin's sources of funds are **his own capital** and the business's **net profit**. Some of this profit will be reinvested in the business.

Activity

1. Prepare the student's income and expenditure statement and balance sheet for the period 1 June 1987 to 10 July 1988 (pp. 38–9). (Note: (s)he has overdrawn her/his bank account, and so this will count as a current liability.)
2. Prepare the balance sheet and profit and loss account of Sheila, the newsagent, for the week ended 7 January 1985 (p. 41).

Depreciation

An important item in both an organisation's profit and loss account and its balance sheet which requires further discussion is **depreciation**. As we have already seen, not only is it an expense in the profit and loss account, but it is also deducted from the cost of fixed assets in the balance sheet.

Depreciation can be defined as a **measure of a fixed asset's loss of value** due to:

(a) **physical 'wear and tear'** (the point we made in Chapter 4); or
(b) **depletion**, if the fixed asset is a natural resource and it is being extracted (e.g. coal and gas); or
(c) **obsolescence**, i.e. a fixed asset becomes out of date because a more efficient replacement has been developed (e.g. adding-machines were replaced by electronic calculators).

Therefore, deducting depreciation can be seen as a way of setting aside money every year to replace a fixed asset at the end of its economic (or useful) life. For example, Colin Smith is putting money aside to replace his motor van when it becomes 'clapped out'.

How we calculate depreciation

Accountants use two main methods to calculate depreciation: the **straight-line method** and the **reducing-balance method**.

STRAIGHT-LINE METHOD

Here the same amount of depreciation is deducted every year. This amount is calculated as follows:

annual depreciation = cost of the fixed asset (£) less its estimated scrap or resale value at the end of its useful life (£) ÷ the fixed asset's expected useful life (in years).

Example – Colin Smith's motor van:
Cost: £2,000.
Scrap or resale value: £200 (a figure estimated by Colin).
Useful life: six years.
Annual depreciation: (2,000−200) ÷ 6 = 1,800 ÷ 6 = £300.

How would this be shown in Colin's accounts?

	Cost £	Provision for depreciation £	Net value £
1st year (entry in balance sheet as at 31/5/86)	2,000	300	1,700
2nd year (entry as at 31/5/87)	2,000	600	1,400
3rd year (entry as at 31/5/88)	2,000	900	1,100
4th year (entry as at 31/5/89)	2,000	1,200	800
5th year (entry as at 31/5/90)	2,000	1,500	500
6th year (entry as at 31/5/91)	2,000	1,800	200

In other words, at the end of the van's life, there will be £2,000 to replace it (£1,800, the depreciation set aside, *plus* £200 from the asset's scrap or resale value). Therefore, the problem with the straight-line method (and the reducing-balance method, for that matter) is that there will not be enough money to replace the fixed asset if prices are rising (see Chapter 12).

In addition, there would be an expense every year in Colin's profit and loss account of £300.

In fact, the straight-line method has been chosen by Colin's accountants to calculate the depreciation n the motor van. So the depreciation figure is £6 in is first week's accounts (£300 ÷ 52 to the nearest ound).

REDUCING-BALANCE METHOD

Here a percentage of the net value of the fixed asset remember, its cost less depreciation) is taken every ear as depreciation. This is done until, at the end of the final year of the asset's life, the net value is approximately equal to its estimated scrap or resale value.

This percentage can be found out either by trial and error, or by use of the formula (for the more mathematically minded):

$$1 - \sqrt[n]{(s \div c)}) \times 100\%$$

where n = the asset's expected useful life (in years), = the estimated scrap or resale value, c = the cost of the asset.

You can find this out by using a calculator.

Example – how to find out $\sqrt[10]{200}$:
. press 200; then
. press 'INV'; then
. press '$x^{1/y}$'; then
. press 10; then
. press 'equals' and you have the answer (1.70).

Example – Colin's motor van:
Cost (c): £2,000.
Estimated scrap or resale value (s): £200.
Expected useful life (n): 6 years.
Percentage depreciation =

$$1 - \sqrt[6]{(200 \div 2,000)}) \times 100$$
$$= (1 - \sqrt[6]{1/10})) \times 100$$
$$= (1 - 0.68) \times 100$$
$$= 0.32 \times 100 = 32.$$

So the depreciation every year would be:

	Cost	Annual depreciation	Net value in balance sheet
	£	£	£
st year (ending 31/5/86)	2,000	640 (32% of 2,000)	1,360
2nd year (ending 31/5/87)	2,000	435 (32% of 1,360)	925
3rd year (ending 31/5/88)	2,000	296 (32% of 925)	629
4th year (ending 31/5/89)	2,000	201 (32% of 629)	428
5th year (ending 31/5/90)	2,000	137 (32% of 428)	291
6th year (ending 31/5/91)	2,000	93 (32% of 291)	198

Note that at the end of the van's useful life we are left with an amount approximately equal to its scrap or resale value.

Activity

Work out what the appropriate entries would be in each year's balance sheet (*i.e.* cost *less* provision for depreciation).

Activity

You decide to buy a car on 1 January 1986. Details are as follows:

Cost: £3,200.
Expected scrap or resale value: £200.
Expected useful life: 6 years.

1. Calculate the annual depreciation using the straight-line method. What are the appropriate entries in your balance sheets as at 31/12/86, 31/12/87, 31/12/88, 31/12/89, 31/12/90 and 31/12/91?
2. Calculate the depreciation each year, using the reducing-balance method. What are the appropriate entries in your balance sheets?

Other documents used to record financial information

So far in this chapter we have discussed in some detail the part that double-entry book-keeping plays in recording an organisation's financial information. Individual **accounts ('ledgers')** are prepared. These are then summarised in the form of a **trial balance**, and from this a **profit and loss account** and a **balance sheet** are worked out.

To finish off this chapter, we must summarise some of the other main documents used to record financial information. They are:

1. **Trading documents –**
   (a) order forms;
   (b) advice notes;
   (c) delivery notes;
   (d) invoices (and possibly credit notes and debit notes);
   (e) statements of account;
   (f) cheques.
2. **Cash book.**
3. **Bank reconciliation statement.**
4. **Petty cash book.**
5. **Sales book.**
6. **Purchases book.**
7. **Returns inwards book.**
8. **Returns outwards book.**
9. **VAT return.**

We shall now look at each of these in turn.

Trading documents

These are the documents which are exchanged between the buyer and seller when goods are bought and sold. You will look at these documents in detail in People in Organisations, but they must be briefly mentioned here.

Example – Colin Smith buying fruit and vegetables from a wholesaler:

```
B    1.───────────Order──────────▶ S
U    2.◀────── Advice note──────── E
Y    3.◀────────Delivery note────── L
E    4.◀──────────Invoice───────── L
R    5.◀────── Statement of account ─── E
(Colin) 6.──────────Cheque─────────▶ R   (Wholesaler)
```

Each of these documents needs a little further explanation.

Order – possibly after receiving a price list from the wholesaler, Colin will send out an order form, indicating the fruit and vegetables he wants.

Advice note – Colin will then receive this after receiving an acknowledgement of the order from the wholesaler. This is often a copy of the invoice (see below) and is sent out to Colin to tell him that he can expect the fruit and vegetables shortly.

Delivery note – this is then sent out by the wholesaler and is again often a copy of the invoice (see below). It is included with the fruit and vegetables, so that Colin can check that they are all there when they arrive.

Invoice – after the fruit and vegetables have been delivered, an invoice (i.e. the bill) will be sent to Colin by the wholesaler, indicating how much he has to pay. Any discounts (e.g. price reductions for prompt payment) will be deducted from the total. If Colin has been overcharged, and/or some fruit and vegetables are missing or rotten, he will receive a **credit note** from the wholesaler. If he has been undercharged, he will receive a **debit note**.

Statement of account – if Colin is a regular customer, he will receive a statement from the wholesaler at regular intervals (e.g. every month). This shows how much money Colin owes.

Cheque – on receipt of the invoice or the statement, Colin will send a cheque to the wholesaler for the amount owed.

Activity

Read about these documents in an Office Practice or World of Work textbook from your library.

Cash book

This simply combines information from an organisation's cash account and bank account into one book.

All debit entries from the cash account are put into the **cash column** on the left-hand side of the cash book. All debit entries from the bank account are put into the **bank column**, also on the left hand side of the cash book. So only money paid into the cash or bank account is put on this side of the cash book.

All credit entries from the two accounts are put into the cash and bank columns on the right-hand side of the cash book. So any money paid out of the cash or bank account is put on this side of the cash book.

All entries in the cash book are made in date order.

EXAMPLE – COLIN SMITH, GREENGROCER

If you remember, Colin's cash and bank accounts at the end of 8 June 1985 looked like this:

Dr			Cash account		Cr
1985		£	1985		£
2 June	Bank	100	7 June	Rent	100
6 June	Sales	1,250	7 June	Balance	
				c/d	1,250
		─────			─────
		£1,350			£1,350
8 June	Balance				
	b/d	1,250			

Dr			Bank account		Cr
1985		£	1985		£
1 June	Capital	5,000	2 June	Cash	100
			3 June	Motor van	2,000
			4 June	Purchases	900
			7 June	Electricity	10
			7 June	Balance	
				c/d	1,990
		─────			─────
		£5,000			£5,000
8 June	Balance				
	b/d	1,990			

50

These are combined into the cash book as follows:

Cash book

1985		Cash £	Bank £	1985		Cash £	Bank £
June	Capital		5,000	2 June	Cash		100
June	Bank	100		3 June	Motor van		2,000
June	Sales	1,250		4 June	Purchases		900
				7 June	Electricity		10
				7 June	Rent	100	
				7 June	Balances c/d	1,250	1,990
		£1,350	£5,000			£1,350	£5,000
June	Balances b/d	1,250	1,990				

This is sometimes called a **two-column** cash book for obvious reasons.

The other type of cash book used today has an additional column for discounts: the **three-column** cash book.

XAMPLE – THREE–COLUMN CASH BOOK

We shall assume Jane, a grocer, pays £100 cash for some goods (£105 total price less £5 discount) on 3 March 1986. She also receives a £30 cheque for goods sold (£32 total price less £2 discount) on 4 March 1986.

Jane's three-column cash book would look like the example shown at the foot of the page.

The amount less discount is shown in either the bank or cash column – on the left-hand side of the cash book, if money has been received. However, the amount is entered on the right-hand side, if money is paid out.

Activity

Prepare the two-column cash books of the student and of Sheila, the newsagent, both introduced in Chapter 6 (pp. 38 and 41).

Bank reconciliation statement

Colin Smith, like any other organisation, will receive a **bank statement** from his bank, showing him how much (or how little) he has in his bank account. Remember that this statement is written from the bank's point of view; i.e. money paid in is a credit entry, and money paid out is a debit.

Colin Smith's bank statement on 8 June 1985

C. Smith

Any Bank plc
10 High Street
Anytown AA1 4BB

STATEMENT OF ACCOUNT

		Debit	Credit	Balance
1985 Sheet: 1	Account Number 22004565			C = Credit D = Debit
4 June	Sundries		5,000	5,000C
5 June	000001	100.00		4,900C
6 June	000002	2,000.00		2,900C
7 June	000003	900.00		2,000C
7 June	Bank charges	1.00		1,999C
8 June	Balance carried forward			1,999C

Note:

1. Each cheque paid into or drawn out of Colin's account takes three days to clear (e.g. the £100 cheque, which was cashed on 2 June, is deducted from the bank balance on 5 June).
2. 000001, etc. are the numbers of Colin's cheques.
3. The 'sheet' number is for Colin's benefit, to tell him how many statements he has received.
4. Colin's account number is 22004565.

However, the bank balance in the cash book is unlikely to be the same as the balance in the bank statement. The main reasons for this are:

- some payments in the bank statement are not in the cash book, e.g. standing orders and bank charges.
- some payments in the cash book are not in the bank statement, e.g. cheques not cleared by the bank.

So the objective of a bank reconciliation statement is to make the necessary adjustments to the cash-book balance, so that it equals the balance in the bank statement.

Cash book

1986		Discount £	Cash £	Bank £	1986		Discount £	Cash £	Bank £
4 March	Sales	2		30	3 March	Purchases	5	100	

EXAMPLE – COLIN SMITH, GREENGROCER

Colin receives his bank statement on 8 June 1985. The balance on this date is £1,999. Bank charges are £1. The £10 cheque for electricity on 7 June is not in the bank statement, because it has not yet been cleared. All the other cheques are in the bank statement (as you see in the statement on p. 51).

Bank reconciliation statement at 8 June 1985

	£
Balance as per cash book	1,990
add Cheque not yet cleared	10
	2,000
deduct Payments not in cash book (bank charges)	1
Balance as per bank statement	£1,999

Activity

Prepare a bank reconciliation statement for Sheila, the newsagent (p. 41), on 8 January. The £40 cheque on 7 January has not been cleared, bank charges are £5, and there is a £10 standing order.

Petty cash book

Small items of expenditure are usually paid out of petty cash; e.g. Colin may want to buy some tea, milk and biscuits for his breaks. In larger organisations petty cash is given out by the cashier only if (s)he has been given a **petty cash voucher** signed by a senior employee and stating on what the money is to be spent.

All the expenditures using petty cash are normally recorded in a petty cash book in date order.

Sales book (sometimes called a 'sales day book' or 'sales journal')

If an organisation sells goods on credit, it will send an invoice to the buyer (known to the seller as a **sales invoice**). The sales book lists the amount of all these sales invoices in date order. The total of these invoices is then transferred to the sales account at the end of each month or week.

EXAMPLE: COLIN SMITH, GREENGROCER

Colin's only credit sale for the week ending 7 June 1985 was the one to L. Mehta on 7 June (assume the number of the invoice sent to L. Mehta is 100). His sales book would look like this:

Sales book

1985		Invoice no.	£
7 June	L. Mehta	100	50
	Transferred to sales account		£50

If Colin had a sales book, this total of £50 would be transferred to the sales account at the end of the week (i.e. 7 June). So his sales account would now look like this:

Sales account

Dr					C
1985		£	1985		£
7 June	Balance c/d	1,300	6 June	Cash	1,250
			7 June	Credit sales for the week	50
		£1,300			£1,300
			8 June	Balance b/d	1,300

Notice that sales for cash are put directly into the sales account. Remember also that L. Mehta's account must be debited £50.

Purchases book (sometimes called the 'purchases day book' or the 'purchases journal')

If an organisation buys goods on credit, the seller will send it an invoice (known to the buyer as a **purchases invoice**). The purchases book lists the amount of all these purchases invoices in date order. The total of these invoices is then transferred to the purchases account at the end of each month or week.

EXAMPLE – COLIN SMITH, GREENGROCER

Colin's only credit purchase for the week ending 7 June 1985 was the one with W. Price on 5 June (assume the number of the invoice sent by W. Price to Colin is 101). His purchases book would look like this:

Purchases book

1985		Invoice no.	£
5 June	W. Price	101	200
	Transferred to purchases account		£200

If Colin had a purchases book, this total of £200 would be transferred to the purchases account at the end of the week (i.e. 7 June). So his purchases account would now look like this:

Purchases account

Dr					C
1985		£	1985		£
4 June	Bank	900	7 June	Balance c/d	1,100
7 June	Credit purchases for the week	200			
		£1,100			£1,100
8 June	Balance b/d	1,100			

notice that purchases with a cheque are put directly to the purchases account. Remember also that W. Price's account must be credited £200.

Returns inwards book

This records, as you might expect, returns inwards in date order. These are goods returned by customers for some reason (e.g. they are faulty).

Returns outwards book

This records returns outwards in date order. These are goods returned to suppliers for some reason.

VAT return

Many businesses have to complete a value added tax (VAT) return, which is then inspected by government officials from the Customs and Excise Department. The return lists the value of goods or services sold by the business, and from this the officials can calculate how much VAT each business must pay.

Conclusion

We have covered a lot in the last two chapters, and I hope that you have understood it all! You should be aware of what the final accounts of a sole trader such as Colin Smith look like and how they are prepared. In Chapter 8 we must look at the accounts of the next biggest type of organisation: a partnership.

Assignment

Liz Collins has just set up a grocer's business near your home. As you buy things there regularly, you have got to know her quite well, and she has asked you to do some book-keeping work for her part-time.

The transactions in the first two weeks of trading were:

1987

1 Feb. – started business with £5,000 paid into the bank.
3 Feb. – cashed a cheque for £200.
4 Feb. – bought goods on credit (£500) from L. Grundy, wholesaler.
6 Feb. – bought a van with a cheque (£2,000).
6 Feb. – cash sales £200.
7 Feb. – put £200 cash in her bank account.
8 Feb. – bought goods on credit (£500) from L. Grundy, wholesaler.
8 Feb. – cash sales £350.
9 Feb. – put £350 cash in her bank account.
9 Feb. – sold goods on credit to A. Marks, £50.
9 Feb. – cash sales £150.
10 Feb. – borrowed £500 from her bank, which was paid into her bank account.
10 Feb. – paid £150 cash into her bank account.
10 Feb. – bought goods on credit (£400) from L. Grundy, wholesaler.
11 Feb. – A. Marks paid her a £50 cheque.
11 Feb. – cash sales £100.
12 Feb. – paid £100 cash into her bank account.
12 Feb. – cash sales £150.
12 Feb. – sold goods on credit to P. Khan, £40.
13 Feb. – cash sales £100.
13 Feb. – paid £150 cash into her bank account.
14 Feb. – paid L. Grundy £500 by cheque.
14 Feb. – sold goods on credit to S. Ross £30.

On 15 February Liz receives her bank statement, stating her bank balance on 14 February. All her payments into and out of her bank account are included, except the cheque paid to L. Grundy, which has not yet been cleared. The only payments in the bank statement but not in the cash book are bank charges (£2) and interest on loan (£4).

Liz wants you to prepare:

1. Her ledgers, balanced off on 14 February.
2. Her trial balance on 14 February.
3. Her profit and loss account and balance sheet for the two weeks ending 14 February.
4. Her cash book, sales book and purchases book.
5. A bank reconciliation statement as at 14 February.

8
Accounts in a Partnership

Introducing partnerships

Colin Smith's greengrocer business has been a big success, and he wants to expand and buy other shops in his area. The problem is that he is short of money. He has decided to borrow some money from his bank, but he does not want to borrow too much, because of the high interest rates presently being charged (see Chapter 11 for a detailed discussion of the factors a business should consider when raising finance).

As a sole trader, Colin has two other major sources of finance apart from borrowing from a bank:

- Reinvested profits.
- Going into partnership with someone else.

His reinvested profits are not high enough to finance his expansion plans, but he knows somebody called Helen Baptiste, who is prepared to go into partnership with him.

They decide that it is to be an **ordinary** partnership.

Activity

Read the section on partnerships in your Organisation in its Environment textbook. Note the characteristics of an ordinary partnership and its advantages and disadvantages as compared with a sole trader.

So Colin and Helen are to become **ordinary partners** (sometimes called **general partners**); i.e. they will both take part in the running of the business and have unlimited liability. In other words, if necessary, all their personal possessions would have to be sold to pay the debts of the partnership.

It could possibly have been a limited partnership, but one of the partners has to be a **limited partner**.

Although such a partner has **limited liability** (i.e. his or her liability for the partnership's debts is limited to how much money (s)he has put into the partnership), s(he) cannot take part in the management of the partnership. Since both Colin and Helen wanted to take an active part, it was impossible for them to form a limited partnership.

Partnership Agreement

A **Partnership Agreement** was drawn up between Helen and Colin, laying down rules for the management of the partnership. The main provisions of the agreement that are of most interest to accountants are outlined below. However, remember that, when any Partnership Agreement does not cover a particular subject, the appropriate section of the **1890 Partnership Act** will apply. For this reason the relevant sections of the 1890 Act are mentioned below.

How much capital is to be contributed by each partner

- Partnership Agreement: both Colin and Helen to contribute £20,000 from their personal savings (Colin was lucky enough to inherit some more money from another relative – he has rich relatives!).

How profits and losses are to be shared

- **Partnership Agreement:** profits and losses to be shared on the basis of capital contributed; i.e. they both receive one-half of the profits and bear one-half of the losses, where appropriate.
- **1890 Act:** profits and losses are shared equally between partners, whatever their capital contribution.

The rate of interest to be given to partners on capital contributed

- **Partnership Agreement:** Colin and Helen to receive 10 per cent p.a. on capital contributed.
- **1890 Act:** no interest to be given on capital.

The rate of interest to be charged on partners' drawings (i.e. withdrawals from their capital)

- **Partnership Agreement:** 5 per cent p.a. to be charged on drawings.
- **1890 Act:** no interest to be charged.

Salaries to be paid to the partners

- **Partnership Agreement:** both Colin and Helen to receive £3,000 p.a., in addition to their share of the profits.
- **1890 Act:** no salaries are allowed.

Money lent to the partnership by partners

- **Partnership Agreement:** 10 per cent p.a. to be paid on any loans.
- **1890 Act:** 5 per cent to be paid on any loans.

The partnership, called Smith & Baptiste, Greengrocers, started trading on 1 June 1986. By 31 May 1987 it had two shops. One is still rented and run by Colin with the help of a part-time sales assistant. However, the other shop has been bought freehold at a cost of £80,000. This is run by Helen with the help of another part-time sales assistant.

Activity

Find out the difference between leasehold and freehold property. What are the advantages to the partnership of having freehold property?

A partnership's final accounts

We must now see what the partnership's accounts for the year ended 31 May 1987 would look like.

Profit and loss account

The vertical presentation of this account would look like this:

Smith & Baptiste, Greengrocers – profit and loss account for the year ended 31 May 1987

	£	£
Sales		200,000
Cost of sales		130,000
Gross profit		70,000
Wages		8,000
Electricity and gas		500
Rent and rates		5,600
Depreciation on motor van		300
Interest on bank loan		1,000
Bad debts		200
Provision for doubtful debts		100
Motor expenses		400
Insurance		200
Advertising		600
Auditor's fees		400
General expenses		200
Net profit		52,500
Interest on loan – C. Smith (10% on £1,000)		100
		52,400
Interest on drawings		
C. Smith (5% on £8,700)	435	
H. Baptiste (5% on £8,700)	435	
		870
		53,270
Salaries		
C. Smith	3,000	
H. Baptiste	3,000	
		6,000
		47,270
Interest on capital		
C. Smith (10% on £20,000)	2,000	
H. Baptiste (10% on £20,000)	2,000	
		4,000
		43,270
Balance of profits shared		
C. Smith (½)	21,635	
H. Baptiste (½)	21,635	
		43,270

So the partners' share of the profit can be summarised as follows:

	Colin Smith £	Helen Baptiste £
Interest on loan	100	
Salaries	3,000	3,000
Interest on capital	2,000	2,000
Balance of profits	21,635	21,635
	26,735	26,635
less Interest on drawings	435	435
	£26,300	£26,200

In comparison with a sole trader's profit and loss account, it is only the appropriation account (the section dealing with the distribution of net profit) which is significantly different in a partnership. So, as far as this is concerned, note the following:

1. Interest on loans from partners is paid out of the partnership's net profit, and interest on drawings is then added (see Fig. 8.1).
2. Partners' salaries and interest on their capital are also paid out of the partnership's net profit (see Fig. 8.1). This may seem rather odd to you, but the reason is that you should look upon both of them as a reward for:

   (a) a partner's efforts in running the business (in the case of salaries);
   (b) the capital a partner has put into the business (in the case of interest on capital).

   The alternative in either case would be to give the partner a greater percentage of the profits. However, at the same time (s)he would also have to bear a larger share of the losses. In other words, (s)he could be penalised for contributing either managerial effort or capital to the partnership. This would be unfair and unsatisfactory.
3. The following things have happened during the year:

   - Colin has lent the partnership £1,000.
   - Both Colin and Helen have £8,700 of drawings, i.e. they have each withdrawn £8,700 from their capital. This includes £7,700 income tax for each of them, which was paid out of partnership funds. In such circumstances, any income tax paid is treated as drawings, just like for a sole trader (see below).
   - Both Colin and Helen have each made a capital contribution of £20,000.
4. Like a sole trader but unlike a limited company (see Chapter 9), tax is *not* included in a partnership's appropriation account. The reason is that the law regards a partnership as a group of individuals working together, *not* as a legal entity which is separate from them. So any partner's income tax paid out of partnership funds is looked upon as his or her own personal debt, and so it is treated as drawings from that partner's capital account.

   The amount of income tax paid by each partner is calculated as a percentage of his or her taxable income, i.e. his or her share of the net profit (including interest on capital, salary and interest on loans) *less* tax allowances.

Some of each partners's share of the profits will obviously be spent on him/herself, and the rest will be reinvested in the business.

We must also look at some of the other terms in Smith & Baptiste's profit and loss account:

Fig. 8.1: Distribution of profits in a partnership

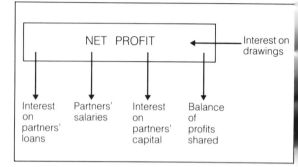

SALES

Accountants sometimes call sales **turnover**. Sales are calculated as follows:

number of units sold × their price.

In the accounts of any type of organisation (sole traders and limited companies as well as partnerships), this sales figure *always* excludes:

- **value added tax (VAT)** on the goods or services sold; and
- **returns inwards** – the value of goods returned by customers (we mentioned this term at the end of Chapter 7).

COST OF SALES

Remember from Chapter 7 that this covers all the organisation's **direct expenses**, i.e. expenses directly related to the production of the organisation's product(s). Remember also that Smith & Baptiste's 'product' is the sale of fruit and vegetables. Retailing businesses like Smith & Baptiste usually define their cost of sales as the cost of goods sold during the year (i.e. opening stock *plus* purchases *less* closing stock: see p. 46).

Smith & Baptiste's figures for the year ended 31 May 1987 were: opening stock £5,000, purchases £128,600 and closing stock £3,600 – the figure in the balance sheet (see later in the chapter). So the business's cost of sales for the year (i.e. the cost of fruit and vegetables it sold during the year) was £130,000.

If Smith & Baptiste had been a manufacturing organisation, its cost of sales would have been:

- cost of raw materials bought to produce its product – i.e. opening stock plus purchases (of raw materials) less closing stock – *plus*
- other direct expenses directly related to manufacturing its product – i.e. all costs related to running its factory, e.g. the wages of people who work there.

In the accounts of any type of organisation, the purchases figure includes **carriage inwards**, i.e. the costs of transporting goods from suppliers. However, it excludes **returns outwards**, i.e. goods returned to suppliers because they are faulty in some way.

WAGES

This refers to the £8,000 paid to the sales assistants during the year.

ELECTRICITY AND GAS

Electricity and gas bills for the year totalled £500.

RENT AND RATES

Rent and rates on the shops totalled £5,600.

DEPRECIATION ON MOTOR VAN

This is the same van that Colin had. Depreciation on it is still calculated on a straight-line basis.

INTEREST ON BANK LOAN

Smith & Baptiste borrowed £10,000 from the bank during the year (see the balance sheet).

BAD DEBTS

Remember from Chapter 7 that these are debts owed to Smith & Baptiste which cannot be repaid for some reason. One of the partnership's customers has become bankrupt, leaving a debt of £200 unpaid.

PROVISION FOR DOUBTFUL DEBTS

We mentioned this in Chapter 7, too. It is money put aside by the partnership to cover the eventuality that some of its debts may not be repaid in the twelve months after the date of the balance sheet, i.e. up to 31 May 1988. As you can see, Smith & Baptiste has put aside £100 for this purpose.

MOTOR EXPENSES

These are the running expenses of the motor van for the year.

INSURANCE

This figure refers to the amount spent on premiums for policies covering fire and theft of the partnership's property, and **employers' liability insurance**, which is compulsory for all employers.

Activity

Look up the term 'employer's liability insurance' in your library. What does it cover?

ADVERTISING

Money spent on advertising.

AUDITOR'S FEES

Smith & Baptiste paid its accountant £400 to prepare and audit its accounts.

GENERAL EXPENSES

This includes £150 spent on the telephone, £20 on stationery and £30 on other items.

Activity

You have decided to go into partnership with one of your fellow students, selling T-shirts. Draw up a suitable **Partnership Agreement** with this other student.

On the basis of this agreement and the following information, complete your partnership's appropriation account for its first year's trading.

1. Net profit £40,000 (you did extremely well!).
2. Drawings £100 by each partner.
3. Each partner receives a salary of £2,000.
4. £100 lent by one partner.
5. Each partner contributed £500 capital.

Summarise each partner's share of the profits, as we did above.

Smith & Baptiste, Greengrocers – balance sheet as at 31 May 1987

Net assets employed:	£	£	£	£	£
Fixed assets	Cost	Provision for depreciation	Net		
Freehold property	80,000	Nil	80,000		
Motor van	2,000	600	1,400		
	82,000	600	81,400		
				81,400	
Current assets					
Stock			3,600		
Debtors			1,000		
Prepayments			200		
Bank balance			400		
Cash in hand			100		
			5,300		
less current liabilities					
Creditors		300			
Accruals		300			
		600			
Net current assets				4,700	
					86,100
Financed by					
Capital accounts:					
Smith			20,000		
Baptiste			20,000		
				40,000	
Loan account: Smith				1,000	
Current accounts:					
Smith			17,600		
Baptiste			17,500		
				35,100	
Bank loan				10,000	
					86,100

Balance sheet

The vertical presentation of Smith & Baptiste's balance sheet would look like the one shown above.

In comparison with a sole trader's balance sheet, the main difference here is that the owners (i.e. the partners) each have a **current account** as well as a capital account.

The amount in each partner's capital account will normally remain the same from one period of time to another. This is because changes in profits or losses, partners' salaries and the interest paid on their capital are all recorded in each partner's current account.

We can illustrate this by seeing what Colin and Helen's capital and current accounts would look like on 31 May 1987 (see p. 59). The balances from each of these accounts on that date are put in the partnership's balance sheet (refer again to the balance sheet).

Activity

Prepare the current and capital accounts for you and your partner in the T-shirt-selling business at the end of its first year's trading.

We must also make some comments about some of the other terms in Smith & Baptiste's balance sheet:

FIXED ASSETS

Remember that the partnership now owns another shop in addition to the motor van, bought by Colin. Notice that no depreciation is deducted from the cost of the shop. This is considered to be realistic because property prices were rising not falling at the time the shop was bought.

STOCK

This is the value of the partnership's stocks at the date of the balance sheet, i.e. the **closing stock** figure.

DEBTORS

Smith & Baptiste sells goods on credit to a few customers. On the date of the balance sheet they owed £1,000.

PREPAYMENTS

These refer to any payments in advance and are always classified as a current asset in any type of organisation, not just a partnership. Smith & Baptiste has paid in advance insurance premiums to the value of £200. They cover the period 1 June 1987 to 31 May 1988.

CREDITORS

This figure refers to money owed by Smith & Baptiste to its fruit and vegetable wholesaler.

ACCRUALS

This refers to **accrued expenses**, the term accountants give to expenses which remain unpaid on the date of the balance sheet. Smith & Baptiste still owes £300, which is the rent to be paid on the shop for May 1987.

CAPITAL AND CURRENT ACCOUNTS

(See p. 58.)

BANK LOAN

Apart from partners' capital contributions and any profits which the partners decide to reinvest, the other major source of finance for the partnership is a £10,000 loan borrowed from its bank.

Activity

Prepare a suitable balance sheet for your T-shirt business.

Conclusion

As you can see, Colin and Helen are doing quite well. However, they are both married with children (not to each other!) and so are worried about their **unlimited liability**. They find out that converting their business into a limited company would solve this problem. We examine the accounts of a limited company in Chapter 9.

Smith & Baptiste, Greengrocers – current and capital accounts as at 31 May 1987

Debit (Dr) — Current accounts — Credit (Cr)

		Smith £	Baptiste £				Smith £	Baptiste £
31 May	Drawings	8,700	8,700	31 May	Interest on loans		100	
31 May	Interests on drawings	435	435	31 May	Salaries		3,000	3,000
31 May	Balances c/d	17,600	17,500	31 May	Interest on capital		2,000	2,000
				31 May	Balance of profits		21,635	21,635
		26,735	26,635				26,735	26,635
				1 June	Balances b/d		17,600	17,500

Debit (Dr) — Capital accounts — Credit (Cr)

		Smith £	Baptiste £				Smith £	Baptiste £
1987 31 May	Balances c/d	20,000	20,000	1986 1 June	Bank		20,000	20,000
				1987 1 June	Balances b/d		20,000	20,000

Note: As we said earlier, each partner started off the partnership by putting £20,000 capital into the business from their own savings.

Assignment (intramodular assignment with Organisation in its Environment I)

In groups of three, you are required to give a talk (maximum twenty minutes) to the rest of your group on 'Setting up a Business as a Partnership'. This must include:

1. The legal and accounting implications of setting up a partnership.
2. The advantages and disadvantages of setting up a partnership.
3. Help provided by the government for new businesses.

Each member of the group is also required to prepare a written report on the subject.

Sources of information:
- Leaflets on new businesses, which can be obtained from your local public library and your local careers office.
- Your textbooks and books from your college library.

Skills tested:
- Learning and studying.
- Information gathering.
- Communicating.
- Working with others.

9
Accounts in a Limited Company

Introducing limited companies

After two years of successfully trading as a partnership, Colin and Helen were again looking for money and were worried by the fact that they both had unlimited liability. Their accountant advised them that the best thing to do was to convert their business into a **private limited company**. They did this on 1 June 1988 by placing the appropriate documents, including the company's **Memorandum and Articles of Association**, with the Registrar of Companies.

Activity

Revise your Organisation in its Environment notes on:

1. Formation of a limited company.
2. The advantages and disadvantages of both a partnership and a private limited company.

Colin bought one half of the shares in the company, and Helen bought the other half. They bought two types of share: ordinary and preference. The difference between these two will be discussed in Chapter 11. They each now own 5,000 preference shares and 42,000 ordinary shares.

As a private limited company, Colin and Helen's business cannot advertise its shares or sell them to the general public. However, it can sell shares privately to any number of people (remember from Organisation in its Environment that, since the 1981 Companies Act, there is no limit to the number of shareholders in a private limited company). This gives Colin and Helen the ability to raise more money to finance any expansion plans they might have.

Remember, too, that another big advantage for them is that as shareholders they now have **limited liability**. In other words, the amount of money they have to contribute towards the debts of their company is limited to the amount they paid for their shares. If the company goes out of business

(what is the legal term for this?), their shares will become worthless, but they will not have to sell any of their personal possessions.

Colin and Helen named their new limited company Fruit & Veg Ltd. Any name of a private limited company must end with the word 'Limited' or its abbreviation 'Ltd' under the 1981 Companies Act. Colin and Helen are the only two directors in the company, and they hope that one day the company will be big enough to 'go public', i.e. become a public limited company.

Activity

Make a list of the advantages and disadvantages of Fruit & Veg Ltd 'going public'.

A limited company's final accounts

You will probably have guessed already that the main laws affecting companies are the Companies Acts 1948–85. The ones which are relevant today were passed in 1948, 1967, 1976, 1980 and 1981. The 1985 Act is extremely useful because it contains all the provisions of the five previous Acts which are legally binding today. Under these Acts, every limited company, like Fruit & Veg Ltd, should prepare (1) a **balance sheet**, (2) a **profit and loss account**, (3) a **directors' report** and (4) an **auditor's report** (see Fig. 9.1)

Fig. 9.1: Documents a limited company should prepare – summary

1. Balance sheet.
2. Profit and loss account.
3. Directors' report.
4. Auditor's report.
5. Sources and application of funds statement
6. Value added statement. } *Sometimes optional*
7. Chairman's statement.

Balance sheet

This is a statement of the company's assets and liabilities on the last day of the accounting year (31 May 1989 in our example on p. 65).

Profit and loss account

This is a statement of the company's revenue expenditures and income during the accounting year (in our example, the year ended 31 May 1989 on p. 63).

Directors' report

This must give details about the company's present and future activities, including information about:

- The sales revenue (i.e. turnover) and profits by geographical region (this is not required for Fruit & Veg Ltd, but only for public limited companies quoted on the Stock Exchange).
- The number of its employees.
- Charitable and political donations made by it over £200.
- The names of its directors.
- Those people who own more than 5 per cent of its shares.

Auditor's report

This must be written by a qualified certified or chartered accountant who is independent of the company and appointed by the company's shareholders. It must state whether or not the company's balance sheet and profit and loss account for the year give a 'true (i.e. accurate) and fair view' of the company's financial position. In other words, do the accounts accurately reflect the information contained in the company's accounting records, e.g. invoices and ledgers?

In addition, a company may publish (1) a **sources and application of funds statement**, (2) a **value added statement** and (3) a **chairman's statement**.

Sources and application of funds statement

This is sometimes called a **funds flow statement** or a **cash flow statement**. We looked at one of these for an individual in Chapter 4. It is similar for a limited company. It shows what changes have taken place during the accounting year in the company's sources of funds and how it has spent or applied that money. For example, extra funds can be generated from its sales revenue which can then be spent on buying new fixed assets.

We shall see later in the chapter how one of these statements is presented for a limited company.

Value added statement

This shows a company's **value added** and how it is spent. This is the sales revenue of the product(s) *less* the cost of materials and services bought in by the company from outside to produce those product(s), e.g. raw materials, heating and lighting.

Example. You buy a Mars Bar for 18p, and 5p worth of materials and services are bought in by the Mars Company to make every bar. So the value added for each bar is 18p *less* 5p = 13p.

We shall see later in the chapter how one of these value added statements is presented.

Activity

Try to identify how a company's value added is spent, i.e. who receives the value added.

You should have come up with the following:

1. Employees' pay.
2. Interest paid on borrowings, e.g. bank loans.
3. Depreciation of fixed assets.
4. Net profit which is allocated to (a) taxation, (b) dividends to shareholders and (c) reinvested profits.

See Fig. 9.2.

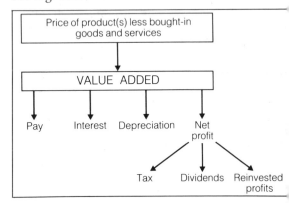

Fig. 9.2: A limited company's value added and its distribution

Chairman's statement

This is a general statement by the company's chairman about its performance during the past year and how it is likely to develop in the future.

Disclosure of accounting information: large versus small companies

Every company has to give its shareholders a copy of its annual balance sheet, profit and loss account, directors' report and auditor's report. However, smaller companies do not have to publish as much information as larger companies. This means that they can keep quite a lot of accounting information secret.

For example, under the 1981 Companies Act, small companies like Fruit & Veg Ltd do *not* have to publish:

1. A profit and loss account for the year (although they obviously have to prepare one).
2. A directors' report.
3. Certain details in the balance sheet.

However, they still have to publish a detailed auditor's report.

On the other hand, the largest companies, e.g. those which are quoted on the Stock Exchange, have to publish all the above documents (see Fig. 9.3).

Fig. 9.3: Publication requirements of limited companies

	Need to be published?	
	Large companies	Small companies
1. Balance sheet.	Yes	Yes, in part
2. Profit and loss account.	Yes	No
3. Directors' report.	Yes	No
4. Chairman's statement.	Yes	No
5. Auditor's report.	Yes	Yes
6. Sources and application of funds statement.	Yes	Yes*
7. Value added statement.	No	No

*Only for companies with a turnover greater than £25,000.

Note: The 1981 Companies Act defines a 'small' company as one which during any accounting year does not exceed two of the following criteria:

1. Turnover – £1.4 million.
2. Total assets – £0.7 million.
3. Employees – 50.

Statements of Standard Accounting Practice (SSAPs)

In addition to the Companies Acts, the professional accountancy bodies (such as the Institute of Chartered Accountants in England and Wales) lay down certain rules for the preparation of a company's accounts. These are contained in **Statements of Standard Accounting Practice** (SSAPs).

For example, although it is not required by the Companies Acts, a sources and application funds statement must be published by every company (public and private) with a turnover greater than £25,000. As we shall soon see, Fruit & Veg Ltd is such a company and so has to publish one.

The value added statement, though, is required neither by law nor by SSAPs. However, some British companies, mostly large public limited companies, publish one voluntarily every year. One such company is H. P. Bulmer's, the cidermakers, whose accounts are looked at later in the chapter.

Fruit & Veg Ltd's accounts for the year ended 31 May 1989

It is important to note that the 1981 Companies Act specifies guidelines about how a limited company's profit and loss account and balance sheet should be laid out. It identifies four alternative formats for the profit and loss account, and two alternative formats for the balance sheet. The most commonly used of these are shown below.

Profit and loss account

Like H. P. Bulmer's profit and loss account shown later in the chapter, this is based upon Format 1 in the 1981 Act, which is vertically presented. It is the most common format used today.

Fruit & Veg Ltd – profit and loss account for the year ended 31 May 1989

	£
Turnover	268,000
Cost of sales	228,600
Gross profit	39,400
Distribution costs	2,000
Administration expenses	28,600
	8,800
Share of profits (or losses) of related companies	—
Operating profit	8,800
Interest payable, less receivable	1,400
Employees' profit share	—
	7,400
Reorganisation costs	—
Profit on ordinary activities before tax	7,400
Tax on profit on ordinary activities	1,700
Profit on ordinary activities after tax	5,700
Extraordinary items	—
Profit for the financial year	5,700
Preference dividends (10% on 10,000 £1 shares)	1,000
Ordinary dividends	—
Profit retained transferred to reserves	4,700

The following points need to be made about Fruit & Veg Ltd's profit and loss account:

TURNOVER

Remember, this is just another term for sales revenue which has been earned during the year by Fruit & Veg Ltd. VAT, charged to customers, is always excluded from this figure.

COST OF SALES

Remember from Chapter 6 that this covers all *direct* expenses, i.e. expenses directly related to the production of the company's product(s). So under the 1981 Companies Act this figure will usually include:

1. **Cost of goods sold** – i.e. opening stock plus purchases less closing stock. Purchases are often called **direct materials**, i.e. materials used for production purposes. For Fruit & Veg Ltd this refers, of course, to the cost of fruit and vegetables it has bought during the year.
2. **Direct labour** – i.e. the wages and salaries of employees directly involved in the production process. For Fruit & Veg Ltd these employees now total four sales assistants, whose total wages are £34,000 p.a. As Helen and Colin are both directors of the company, their salaries are included in administrative expenses (see below).
3. **Depreciation of fixed assets** which are directly involved in the production process – for Fruit & Veg Ltd this refers to the depreciation on the motor van.
4. **Resource and development costs** – Fruit & Veg Ltd has none.

You will have noticed that this is different from how we calculated cost of sales in Chapters 7 and 8. As you can see, direct labour and depreciation on the van are included, in addition to the cost of goods sold. This is because these are sometimes included in the cost of sales, and they are always included for manufacturing organisations.

DISTRIBUTION COSTS

This includes all the company's costs associated with distributing, marketing and selling its product(s) to its customers. As far as Fruit & Veg Ltd is concerned, distribution costs cover the costs of delivering fruit and vegetables to a few of its customers. Its major item of expenditure on marketing and selling is advertising.

ADMINISTRATIVE EXPENSES

These are defined as all costs not included in either cost of sales or distribution costs. They include:

1. **Directors' salaries.**
2. **Salaries of administrative staff** – Fruit & Veg Ltd has none.
3. **Auditor's fees** – Fruit & Veg Ltd employs a local firm of chartered accountants to audit its accounts.
4. **Money set aside to cover bad debts** – i.e. debts which will never be repaid. Fruit & Veg Ltd has none because nearly all of its customers pay immediately by cash. So it has not set aside money for this purpose.

Fruit & Veg Ltd paid its auditors £600, and Colin and Helen were each paid a salary of £14,000 p.a. This gives the total of £28,600 in the profit and loss account.

SHARE OF PROFITS (OR LOSSES) OF RELATED COMPANIES

This refers to any dividends received from either the company's subsidiaries or companies in which it owns more than 20 per cent of the ordinary shares. Any losses from them are deducted as an expense in the profit and loss account. Any dividends are added on as income. Fruit & Veg Ltd obviously has no such income or expenditure.

OPERATING PROFIT

This is the term given to what is left of gross profit after taking into account distribution costs, administration expenses, and profits or losses from related companies.

INTEREST PAYABLE, LESS RECEIVABLE

Interest payable refers to interest paid by the company on any borrowings and is obviously counted as an expense. Consequently interest receivable, i.e. money received from any company investments, other than those in related companies, will be deducted from the interest payable figure. Fruit & Veg Ltd has no such investments but it does pay interest on three loans:

- Debenture – £200 p.a. (10 per cent p.a. on a £2,000 debenture).
- Bank loan – £1,000 p.a. (10 per cent on a £10,000 loan).
- Bank overdraft – £200 p.a. (10 per cent on a £2,000 overdraft).

These borrowings can be seen clearly in the company's balance sheet under the heading of 'creditors'.

Accounts in a Limited Company

Fruit & Veg Ltd – balance sheet as at 31 May 1989

Net assets employed:	£		
Fixed assets			
Intangible assets			
Tangible assets			
Investments			
Current assets			
Stocks		3,000	
Debtors		1,643	
Investments		—	
Cash at bank and in hand		6,400	
		11,043	
Creditors: amounts falling due within one year:			
Debenture loans		—	
Bank loans and overdrafts	2,000		
Other creditors	500		
Corporation tax	1,700		
Proposed dividends	1,000		
Accruals	143		
		5,343	
Net current assets			5,700
Total assets less current liabilities			196,500
Creditors: amounts falling due after more than one year:			
Debenture loans		2,000	
Bank loans and overdrafts		10,000	
Other creditors		—	
			12,000
Provisions for liabilities and charges			85,800
			98,700
Financed by:			
Capital and reserves			
Called-up share capital		94,000	
Revaluation reserve		—	
Other reserves		—	
Profit and loss account		4,700	
			98,700

Like H. P. Bulmer's balance sheet later in the chapter, this is based upon Format 1 in the 1981 Act, which is vertically presented. The only other alternative format, which is much less commonly used, is horizontally presented with assets on the *left*-hand side and capital and liabilities on the right (the opposite to what was the normal practice in the United Kingdom for many years).

EMPLOYEES' PROFIT SHARE

Some companies, like H. P. Bulmer's the cider-makers (see later in the chapter), give their employees a share of the profits. Fruit & Veg Ltd has no such scheme.

Activity

Make a list of organisations which have a profit-sharing scheme.

REORGANISATION COSTS

These cover the costs of making employees redundant, if this is necessary. The most important is, of course, redundancy pay. Fortunately Fruit & Veg Ltd has had no such costs.

Activity

Find out from your library how redundancy payments are presently calculated.

...N ORDINARY ACTIVITIES BEFORE TAX

...the company's net profit, excluding tax-... ...nd extraordinary items. Limited companies ...orporation tax on their profits.

Activity

Find out from your library what the present rates of corporation tax are.

Notice also that a limited company is taxed as a separate legal entity, separate from its owners (i.e. its shareholders). It is the *company* which is taxed, *not* the shareholders. So, unlike in a sole trader or partnership, tax is paid out of the company's net profit and is therefore included in the appropriation account of its profit and loss account.

PROFIT ON ORDINARY ACTIVITIES AFTER TAX

This is the company's net profit after tax *before* the extraordinary items are taken into account.

EXTRAORDINARY ITEMS

These are incomes (called, unsurprisingly, **extraordinary income**) and expenditures (called **extraordinary charges**) which arise from events or transactions outside the ordinary activities of the business and are not expected to occur frequently or regularly. Fruit & Veg Ltd has no such items.

PROFIT FOR THE FINANCIAL YEAR

This is the company's net profit before tax *after* extraordinary items have been taken into account.

PREFERENCE AND ORDINARY DIVIDENDS

The preference dividends are calculated on the basis of the shares' **nominal value**, i.e. 10 per cent of £1 for every share. The nominal value is specified in the company's Memorandum of Association and bears no relation to the shares' market price. Note that Fruit & Veg Ltd has issued 84,000 ordinary shares (nominal value £1), in addition to the 10,000 preference shares.

PROFIT RETAINED

This is the amount of the profits which is reinvested back into the company. Fruit & Veg Ltd will use this money to finance an expansion of the business.

Balance sheet

Activity

Have another look at Paul Garcia's accounts in Chapter 4 (p. 29) to see what a horizontally presented balance sheet can look like.

The following points need to be made about Fruit & Veg Ltd's balance sheet on p. 65.

FIXED ASSETS

Fixed assets are divided up into:

1. **Intangible assets** – these are fixed assets which you cannot touch and may include:

   (a) **goodwill** (an estimate of how much the total value of the company's business exceeds the value of its assets; it is largely dependent upon the company's relationship with its customers).
   (b) **patents, trade marks and copyright, owned by the company.**

Activity

Find out from your library what these terms mean, the main Acts of Parliament affecting them, and how long they last for.

Fruit & Veg Ltd did not include any intangible assets in its balance sheet.

2. **Tangible assets** – this figure represents the total net value (i.e. their cost *less* depreciation) of all the company's fixed assets which you can touch. In Fruit & Veg Ltd's case they now are:

	Cost	Provision for depreciation (i.e. total depreciation to date)	Net
Freehold property (old shop)	80,000	Nil	80,000
Freehold property (new shop)	110,000	Nil	110,000
Motor van	2,000	1,200	800
	£192,000	£1,200	£190,800

The depreciation for the year on the motor van is £300 (remember, Colin bought the van in Chapters 6 and 7).

Activity

Have another look at Chapter 7 to see how we calculated this depreciation, using the straight-line method.

In a manufacturing enterprise, factories and equipment would be included as a tangible asset here. Note also that Fruit & Veg Ltd bought a new shop on 10 June 1988.

3. **Investments** – this refers to long-term investments made by the company. For example, they include shares in related companies (see above for what these are) and loans made to them. Under the 1981 Companies Act, the market value of these investments on the date of the balance sheet must be stated in a note after it. Fruit & Veg Ltd have no such investments.

CURRENT ASSETS

1. **Stocks** – remember, this is the closing stock figure, i.e. the value of stocks held by the company on the date of the balance sheet. As far as Fruit & Veg Ltd is concerned, it refers to the value of unsold fruit and vegetables on that day.
2. **Debtors** – this figure includes not only **trade debtors**, i.e. customers who have not yet paid for products received from the company, but also (a) **prepayments** – payments in advance by the company (see Chapter 8) – and (b) **accrued income** – income from the year's activities which has not yet been received.

   Fruit & Veg Ltd has trade debtors of £1,443 (money owed by a few customers who were given credit) and prepayments of £200 (a prepaid insurance premium).

Activity

From the following information calculate a limited company's prepayments and accrued income as at 31 December 1986:

(a) Paid the rent on its factory for year beginning 1 July 1986 (£5,000).
(b) Paid insurance premium for the year beginning 1 October 1986 (£100).
(c) Building-society interest still to be paid for the last three months of the year. (The company has a £5,000 investment and receives 10 per cent p.a. net.)

3. **Investments** – these are short-term investments made by the company which can be converted into cash within a year from the date of the balance sheet, e.g. money invested by the company in a building society or a bank deposit account. Fruit & Veg Ltd has no such investments.
4. **Cash at bank and in hand** – this refers to cash held by the company and the balance of its current account at the bank. Fruit & Veg Ltd has £100 in hand and £6,300 in the bank on the date of the balance sheet.

CREDITORS: AMOUNTS FALLING DUE WITHIN ONE YEAR

This is just another term for **current liabilities**, i.e. debts which will have to be repaid within a year from the date of the balance sheet. These may include:

1. **Debenture loans, and bank loans and overdrafts** (which are due for repayment during the twelve months after the date of the balance sheet) – these types of borrowing will be discussed in Chapter 11. All you need to know at this stage is that a debenture is a special type of loan to a company. Fruit & Veg Ltd has a £2,000 bank overdraft due to be repaid on 1 February 1990.
2. **Other creditors** – this figure includes **trade creditors**, i.e. suppliers who have not yet been paid. Fruit & Veg Ltd owes its fruit and vegetable wholesalers £500 on the date of the balance sheet.
3. **Corporation tax** – i.e. corporation tax to be paid on the year's profits; in Fruit & Veg Ltd's case, £1,700 to be paid on the profits for the year ended 31 May 1989.
4. **Proposed dividends** – dividends to be paid; in Fruit & Veg Ltd's case, £1,000 preference dividends.
5. **Accruals** – i.e. expenses arising from the company's activities in the year up to the date of the balance sheet, which have not yet been paid (see Chapter 7). Fruit & Veg Ltd's £143 is an unpaid property insurance premium.

Activity

From the following information, calculate a limited company's accruals as at 31 December 1986.

(a) Rent on the factory paid up to 30 September 1986 (annual rent is £1,500).
(b) Property insurance premiums paid up to 31 March 1986 (annual premium is £200).

CREDITORS: AMOUNTS FALLING DUE AFTER MORE THAN ONE YEAR

These are debenture loans, bank loans and overdrafts, and other debts which have to be repaid after more than one year from the date of the balance sheet. Fruit & Veg Ltd has a £2,000 debenture and a £10,000 bank loan falling into this category. This figure is **deducted** from the 'total assets less current liabilities' figure in the balance sheet.

PROVISIONS FOR LIABILITIES AND CHARGES

These are amounts of money put aside by the company for future expenditure, where there is uncertainty about their amount or the date on which they have to be paid. For example, provisions are often made for employees' pensions and taxation. Fruit & Veg Ltd has put £85,800 aside for the future payments of taxation and pensions for its employees. This figure is also **deducted** from the 'total assets less current liabilities' figure in the balance sheet.

CALLED-UP SHARE CAPITAL

Sometimes called **issued share capital**, this refers to the value of ordinary and preference shares which the company has issued. This is based upon the shares' **nominal value** (usually £1), *not* their market value (i.e. the price you could buy them for). The nominal value is specified in the company's Memorandum of Association and bears no relation to the market price.

Issued share capital should be distinguished from a company's **authorised share capital**, which is the maximum value of shares that it can issue. This must be stated in a note after the balance sheet. Fruit & Veg Ltd's called-up share capital is £94,000 (10,000 £1 preference shares and 84,000 £1 ordinary shares). Its authorised share capital is £150,000.

REVALUATION RESERVE

If a fixed asset is revalued, the increase in its value above its cost (less depreciation) is put into a revaluation reserve.

Example – machinery:

Cost (less depreciation)	£100,000
Value of asset after revaluation	£120,000
Amount to revaluation reserve	£ 20,000
	(£120,000 less £100,000)

Assets can be revalued in this way if current cost accounting methods are used (see Chapter 12). Fruit & Veg Ltd has not revalued its fixed assets in this way, and so there is nothing in the revaluation reserve.

OTHER RESERVES

These are reserves kept for purposes other than those mentioned above. The reasons why they are kept will be stated in the company's Articles of Association. Fruit & Veg Ltd has no such reserves.

PROFIT AND LOSS ACCOUNT

This is the total amount up to the date of the balance sheet which has been transferred from the profit and loss account to reserves as reinvested profits. As Fruit & Veg Ltd has been trading for only one year, this figure is the total transferred from the year's profit and loss account, i.e. £4,700.

In Chapters 7 and 8 we discovered that sole traders and partnerships do not include reserves (including reinvested profit) in their balance sheets. Limited companies always do.

Value added statement

Fruit & Veg Ltd's statement would look something like this (see also Fig. 9.2):

Fruit & Veg Ltd – value added statement for the year ended 31 May 1989

	£
Sales	268,000
Bought-in goods and services	196,900
Total value added	71,100
Comprising the following:	
Employees' pay	62,000
Interest on borrowings	1,400
Depreciation of fixed assets	300
Profit on ordinary activities before tax	7,400
	71,100
Profit on ordinary activities before tax	7,400
Extraordinary items	—
Total profit:	7,400
This total profit has been applied:	
To pay taxation	1,700
To pay dividends to shareholders	1,000
Retained to maintain and develop the business	4,700
	7,400

Note:
1. £196,900 is the total value of goods and services bought in by the company.
2. Employees' pay includes directors' salaries (£28,000) and the wages of the four sales assistants (£34,000).
3. Depreciation of fixed assets refers to the depreciation on the motor van.
4. All other figures are taken from the company's profit and loss account for the year. (Refer to this again and check the figures on p. 63.)

Activity

On the basis of the following figures, prepare XYZ Ltd's value added statement for the year ended 31 December 1986.

	£
Sales	200,000
Depreciation of fixed assets	5,000
Taxation on profits	10,000
Dividends	20,000
Net profit before tax	45,000
Interest on borrowings	10,000
Bought-in goods and services	120,000
Employees' pay	20,000
Reinvested profits	20,000
Extraordinary items	5,000

Sources and application of funds statement

Fruit & Veg Ltd's statement would look something like this:

Fruit & Veg Ltd – sources and application of funds statement for year ended 31 May 1989

Sources of funds

	£
Profit	7,400
Depreciation of tangible fixed assets	300
Sales of fixed assets (tangible and intangible)	—
Borrowing	14,000
Issues of shares	94,000
	115,700

Application of funds

	£
Purchase of fixed assets (tangible and intangible)	110,000
Investments in related companies	—
Increase in working capital	5,700
Dividends paid	—
Taxation paid	—
	115,700

We can explain this statement using the example of a water tank with taps on the bottom. The 'water' coming into the tank is the company's sources of funds. These funds are then released from the tank via the taps and spent on various things, i.e. the application of funds – see Fig. 9.4.

One or two points need to be made about these sources and application of funds.

SOURCES OF FUNDS

1. **Profit** – this is the net profit (or profit on ordinary activities) before tax but *after* extraordinary items have been taken into account. This is £7,400 for Fruit & Veg Ltd (see its profit and loss account earlier in the chapter).
2. **Depreciation** – this is, of course, money deducted during the year from the value of fixed assets, so that it can be put on one side and used to replace the assets at the end of their useful life (see Chapter 7). For Fruit & Veg Ltd this is £300, the depreciation deducted every year from the value of the motor van.
3. **Sales of fixed assets** – this is money raised during the year from the sale of fixed assets, tangible and intangible. Fruit & Veg Ltd did not sell any.
4. **Borrowing** – Fruit & Veg Ltd borrowed £14,000 in the year up to 31 May 1989: a £2,000 overdraft, £10,000 in a longer-term bank loan and £2,000 in debenture loans (refer to the balance sheet on p. 65).
5. **Issues of shares** – if you remember, Colin and Helen bought £94,000 worth of shares in the company.

APPLICATION OF FUNDS

1. **Purchase of fixed assets (tangible and intangible)** – this is money spent during the year on buying fixed assets. If you remember, Fruit & Veg Ltd bought a new shop for £110,000 (see the balance sheet on p. 65).
2. **Investments in related companies** – this refers to any money invested in other companies. Fruit & Veg Ltd has no such investments.
3. **Increase in working capital** – this refers to how much working capital (current assets less current liabilities) has increased during the year. Fruit & Veg Ltd increased its working capital by £5,700. If there had been a decrease in working capital, it would have been *deducted* here.
4. **Dividends paid** – this refers to dividends paid to shareholders. Remember, Fruit & Veg Ltd has not yet paid its preference dividend (£1,000),

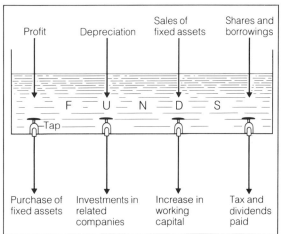

Fig. 9.4: A limited company's sources and application of funds

and so it is not included. However, it will be included in next year's sources and application of funds statement, after the company has paid the dividend.

5. **Taxation paid** – Fruit & Veg Ltd has also not yet paid its corporation tax (£1,700), and so this figure is not included. However, it will be included in next year's sources and application of funds statement, after the company has paid the tax.

Activity

On the basis of the following figures, prepare XYZ Ltd's sources and application of funds statement for the year ended 31 December 1986.

	£
Taxation paid	7,000
Borrowing	1,000
Investments in related companies	2,000
Net profit before tax	20,000
Increase in working capital	5,000
Issues of shares	5,000
Dividends paid	10,000
Sales of fixed assets	2,000
Depreciation of tangible fixed assets	1,000
Purchase of fixed assets	5,000

Case study: H. P. Bulmer Holdings plc

Introduction

The objective of this section is to see what the accounts of a real company look like. First of all, some background information must be given about the company, H. P. Bulmer Holdings plc, which makes Woodpecker and Strongbow ciders.

The company was started in 1887 as a cider-making business by H. P. Bulmer near Hereford. Two years later he was joined by his brother, and it has remained a family business ever since (today over one-half of the company's shares are owned by the Bulmer family). After many years as a private limited company it became a public limited company in 1970, so that it could raise more cash, expand and establish itself as the dominant force in the United Kingdom cider market.

It has certainly done this. Bulmer's accounts for half of the UK cider sales – over 30 million gallons of the stuff! The company has also been keen to reduce its dependence upon cider as a source of revenue and, as you can see from the list of its products below, it now has interests in other alcoholic and soft-drinks products.

BULMER'S PRODUCTS, 1985

- **Cider** – Strongbow, Woodpecker, Bulmer's Original and Pomagne. (Its cider is also manufactured and sold in Australia.)

- **Soft drinks** – Kiri (a sparkling apple juice) and Red Cheek (an apple juice sold in the USA). It is also the agent for the sale and distribution of Perrier mineral water in the UK.
- **Wine, spirits and other drinks** – the company is responsible for the sale and distribution of Domecq Sherry in the UK.
- **Pectin** – Bulmer's is the sole manufacturer of pectin in the UK. This is extracted from fruit and used as a gelling agent (i.e. to bind things together) in the food industry.

We shall now look at the company's profit and loss account and balance sheet for the year ended 26 April 1985 (its accounting year).

Profit and loss account

H. P. Bulmer Holdings plc – profit and loss account for the year ended 26 April 1985

	Year ended 26 April 1985 (52 weeks) £000	Year ended 27 April 1984 (52 weeks) £000
Turnover	155,204	127,402
Excise duty	30,539	24,619
Net sales	124,665	102,783
Cost of sales	75,650	57,830
Gross profit	49,015	44,953
Distribution costs (including selling and marketing costs)	27,863	21,361
Administrative expenses	6,989	5,831
	14,163	17,761
Share of profits or (losses) of related companies	(29)	—
Operating profit	14,134	17,761
Interest payable, less receivable	(2,892)	(964)
Employees' profit share	(386)	(708)
	10,856	16,089
Reorganisation costs	3,339	—
Profit on ordinary activities before tax	7,517	16,089
Taxation on profit on ordinary activities	572	4,616
Profit on ordinary activities after tax	6,945	11,473
Extraordinary items	—	4,662
Profit for the financial year	6,945	6,811
Preference dividends	1,945	533
Ordinary dividends	2,541	2,541
Profit retained transferred to reserves	2,459	3,737
Earnings per ordinary share	9.64p	21.09p

Source: Annual Report and Accounts, 1985.

A number of points need to be made about the profit and loss account:

PREVIOUS YEAR'S FIGURES

As with the balance sheet, it is normal practice to show the previous year's figures as well, in this case for the year ended 27 April 1984. This makes it easier to see if there have been any dramatic changes in the company's financial position.

EXCISE DUTY

This is paid to the government on any cider sold and must be deducted from turnover to obtain the 'net sales' figure.

Activity

Find out which government department deals with the payment of excise duty.

ADMINISTRATIVE EXPENSES

This includes depreciation of tangible fixed assets, which the company calculates on a straight-line basis.

Activity

Have another look at Chapter 7 and remind yourself of the two main methods of calculating depreciation.

INTEREST PAYABLE ON LOANS AND OVERDRAFTS

This was £3,058,000 in 1984–5 and £1,006,000 in 1983–4.

INTEREST RECEIVABLE

This was £166,000 in 1984–5 and £42,000 in 1983–4.

EMPLOYEES' PROFIT SHARE

This is the amount of profits distributed to employees. This money is then used to buy ordinary shares in the company for them.

REORGANISATION COSTS

These resulted from 300 redundancies which had to be made during the year ended 26 April 1985. The main reasons for them were:

- heavy duty increases on cider, which had reduced UK cider sales; and
- increased competition from new entrants into the UK cider market.

TAXATION

The amount of tax paid fell substantially during 1984–5 because the purchase of Red Cheek's fixed assets resulted in a large tax allowance, i.e. Bulmer's did not have to pay tax on a significant proportion of its profits.

EXTRAORDINARY ITEMS

In 1983–4 these included the goodwill and trade marks of certain cider and apple juice brands in Australia, and the costs associated with a bonus issue of preference shares.

Activity

Refer to Chapter 11 and find out what a bonus issue is.

EARNINGS PER ORDINARY SHARE

This is calculated as follows:

$$\frac{\text{net profit after tax less preference dividends}}{\text{number of ordinary shares}} \times 100 \text{ (pence)}.$$

We shall look at this again in Chapter 13.

Under SSAP 3 all public companies listed on the Stock Exchange, like Bulmer's, must show this in their profit and loss account.

Activity

Calculate Fruit & Veg Ltd's earnings per ordinary share, and check H. P. Bulmer's figures (it had 51,865,000 ordinary shares in both years).

Balance sheet

H. P. Bulmer Holdings plc – balance sheet as at 26 April 1985

	26 April 1985 £000	27 April 1984 £000
Net assets employed:		
Fixed assets		
Tangible assets	57,656	42,734
Investments	2,789	5
	60,445	42,739
Current assets		
Stocks	33,206	19,610
Debtors	20,884	18,371
Certificate of tax deposit	1,500	—
Cash at bank and in hand	3,442	5,351
	59,032	43,332
Creditors: amounts falling due within one year	47,734	26,826
Net current assets	11,298	16,506
Total assets less current liabilities	71,743	59,245
Creditors: amounts falling due after more than one year	14,319	3,694
Provisions for liabilities and charges	4,428	4,428
	52,996	51,123
Financed by:		
Capital and reserves		
Called-up share capital	24,705	24,705
Revaluation reserve	9,866	10,085
Other reserves	715	1,235
Profit and loss account	17,755	15,098
Related companies' reserves	(45)	—
	52,996	51,123

Source: Annual Report and Accounts, 1985.

Various points should also be made about this:

TANGIBLE FIXED ASSETS

The total value of these assets at cost was £72,613,000 on 26 April 1985, and total depreciation up until this date was £14,957,000. So the total net book value of these assets was £57,656,000 – the figure in the balance sheet. There were no intangible fixed assets included in the balance sheet.

FIXED ASSET INVESTMENTS

On 26 April 1985 this included £2,784,000 invested in other companies.

DEBTORS

On 26 April 1985 this included prepayments and accrued income of £683,000 and trade debtors of £17,295,000.

CERTIFICATE OF TAX DEPOSIT

This refers to money deposited by the company for the purpose of paying tax in the future.

CREDITORS: AMOUNTS FALLING DUE WITHIN ONE YEAR

On 26 April 1985 this included trade creditors of £13,059,000.

CREDITORS: AMOUNTS FALLING DUE AFTER MORE THAN ONE YEAR

On 26 April 1985 this included:

1. Debentures (interest 6⅝ per cent p.a. and repayable in November 1989).
2. US dollar bank loan repayable by twelve half-yearly instalments from 1 May 1986 to 1 November 1991.

PROVISIONS FOR LIABILITIES AND CHARGES

As you can see, these totalled £4,428,000 for the year.

CALLED-UP (ISSUED) SHARE CAPITAL

On 26 April 1985 this was as follows:

	000s (£)
51,865,000 ordinary shares of 5p each	2,593
1,365,781 9½% cumulative preference shares of £1 each	1,366
20,746,000 8¾% cumulative preference shares of £1 each	20,746
Total called-up share capital	24,705

The company's authorised share capital was as follows:

	000s (£)
72,500,000 ordinary shares of 5p each	3,625
1,375,000 9½% cumulative preference shares of £1 each	1,375
20,746,000 8¾% cumulative preference shares of £1 each	20,746
Total authorised share capital	25,746

Activity

1. Look up the terms **cumulative preference share** and **authorised share capital** in your library. We shall come across these terms again in Chapter 11.
2. Calculate the **total** dividend that preference shareholders are entitled to every year. (Note: the dividend on a 9½ per cent £1 share is 9½p.)

RESERVES

As you can see from the balance sheet, the company had substantial reserves, primarily resulting from the revaluation of assets (revaluation reserve) and reinvested profits (profit and loss account).

Conclusion

This has been an important chapter because, in terms of goods and services produced, the limited company is the most important type of organisation in the United Kingdom. So a large part of a financial accountant's time is spent on preparing and auditing companies' accounts. In Chapter 10 we shall need to look at the accounts of other organisations such as clubs, local authorities and nationalised industries.

> *Assignment (intramodular assignment with Organisation in its Environment I and People in Organisations I)*

You work for a financial newspaper, and you have been asked by your boss to carry out an 'information search' on the leading public limited companies in the United Kingdom.

You are required to write to one of these companies, asking for a copy of its latest annual report and accounts. From this, and any other information you can obtain, you are asked to summarise in report form the following:

1. The company's main activities.
2. Its future prospects.
3. A detailed comparison between the company and other types of organisation in terms of:
   (a) Objectives.
   (b) Sources of finance.
   (c) Organisational structure.
   (d) How profits are distributed and how losses are paid for.

Note: Each student in a group should choose a different company if possible.

Skills tested:
- Numeracy.
- Learning and studying.
- Information gathering.
- Communicating.

> *Assignment (intramodular assignment with People in Organisations I and Organisation in its Environment I)*

British Pullover Ltd is a manufacturer of knitwear near Sunderland in the north-east of England. It sells 50 per cent of its output to a well-known high street store. At present it has 300 employees with four main departments: finance, production, marketing and sales, and personnel. However, its young management team is very ambitious for the company. One of its main objectives is to expand the company as rapidly as possible, so that by the year 2000 it will become one of the leading companies in Britain. As part of this strategy, it is planning to 'go public' and become a public limited company.

The board of the company has therefore asked you to prepare a report on:

1. The legal and accounting implications of setting up a public limited company.
2. Its possible effects upon the company's organisation structure, financial position and profitability.
3. What the company should be doing in five years' time.

Skills tested:
- Identifying and tackling problems.
- Learning and studying.
- Information gathering.
- Communicating.

10
Accounts in Other Organisations

Activity

Make a list of **ten** organisations which directly affect you in your everyday life.

I would guess that not all of these are organisations which have already been discussed in this book – i.e. sole traders, partnerships and limited companies. Your list is likely to include other types of organisation, like social and sports clubs, your college, local authorities and nationalised industries like the National Coal Board and British Rail.

The purpose of this chapter is to have a look at the accounts of these organisations in the following order:

1. Clubs.
2. Nationalised industries.
3. Local authorities.
4. Your college.

Clubs

These can be defined as non-profit-making organisations which are run by private groups and individuals (in other words, not run by the government). They include social clubs, sports clubs, trade unions, political parties, churches and charities.

Although their main objective is not to make a profit, clubs must still prepare accounts. The reason is that a club must show every year how it has financed its activities and how its money has been spent. This is the responsibility of the club's **treasurer**. The accounts (s)he prepares are checked by independent auditors and then presented to the club's **annual general meeting**. These accounts are normally an income and expenditure statement and a balance sheet.

Income and expenditure statement

This is exactly like the profit and loss account of a sole trader (see Chapter 7), except that the final result is called a **surplus** or a **deficiency**, not a net profit or net loss. It is also almost identical to an individual's income and expenditure statement, outlined in Chapters 2 and 4. The only points to note are:

1. A club's **surplus** is equivalent to the 'excess of income over expenditure' figure.
2. Any 'excess of expenditure over income' by the club is called a **deficiency**.

A club's income and expenditure statement would look something like this:

College Badminton Club – income and expenditure statement for the year ended 31 December 1986

Expenditure	£	Income	£
Rent of sports hall	1,000	Subscriptions	2,000
Refreshments for players	150	Hire of rackets	200
Travelling expenses	250	Profit on social events	200
Depreciation: sports equipment	50		
Surplus (transferred to accumulated fund)	950		
	£2,400		£2,400

Balance sheet

This is exactly like the balance sheet of a sole trader, except that a club's capital is referred to as its **accumulated fund**. Therefore:

1. Any surplus it makes is added to its accumulated fund (just as a sole trader's net profit is added to his/her capital).
2. Any deficiency it makes is *deducted* from its accumulated fund (just as a sole trader's net loss is deducted from his/her capital).

Horizontally presented, the College Badminton Club's balance sheet might look like this:

College Badminton Club – balance sheet as at 31 December 1986

Fixed assets	£	£	Accumulated fund	£	£
Sports equipment at cost	1,000		Balance as at 1/1/86	100	
less Depreciation (to date)	100		*add* Surplus	950	
		900			1,050
Current assets			**Current liabilities**		
Cash at bank	150		Money owed for refreshments		20
Cash in hand	20				
		170			
		£1,070			£1,070

Activity

Prepare the vertical presentation of this balance sheet.

Activity

Choose one organisation in which you are involved outside the college. Find out the following about this organisation:

1. Its main items of income and expenditure during the last year.
2. Its fixed and current assets.

If possible, try to get a copy of its last year's accounts.

Nationalised industries

You have probably come across these already in Organisation in its Environment, but your memory might need jogging a little. So . . .

Activity

Have another look at your Organisation in its Environment notes on nationalised industries.

You will have noticed that nationalised industries are owned and run by the government. This means that, although their published accounts are very similar to those of a limited company, they are different in two major ways:

1. In the profit and loss account an excess of revenue over expenditure is sometimes called a **surplus** rather than a profit.
2. Government grants and loans are a major source of finance for them (remember that certain nationalised industries like British Rail are given money to keep loss-making services going for the good of the community – this is examined further in Chapter 15).

In fact, we shall use the example of British Rail to see what the profit and loss account and balance sheet of one nationalised industry looks like.

Profit and loss account

British Rail's profit and loss account for the fifteen months to 31 March 1985 looked like Fig. 10.1. Several things need to be noted about this.

Fig. 10.1: British Rail – profit and loss account for the fifteen months to 31 March 1985

Year ended 31 Dec. 1983

£ million		£ million
	Turnover	
	Turnover excluding government	
2,260.0	grant	2,384.8
933.4	Government grant	1,172.7
3,193.4		3,557.5
3,113.2	**Operating expenditure**	3,789.1
	Total operating surplus/(loss)	
	Notional surplus before the	
80.2	estimated effect of the coal strike	18.4
—	Estimated effect of the coal strike	(250.0)
80.2		(231.6)
	Share of net *(loss)* of associated	
(2.4)	companies	—
8.8	Other income	16.7
	Surplus/(loss) before interest	
	Notional surplus before the	
86.6	estimated effect of the coal strike	35.1
—	Estimated effect of the coal strike	(250.0)
86.6		(214.9)
75.2	Interest payable and similar charges	73.2
0.1	Taxation	—
11.3	**Surplus/(loss) on ordinary activities**	(288.1)
0.4	Extraordinary surplus/*(loss)*	(131.8)
	Group surplus/(loss) for the	
11.7	**financial period**	(419.9)
	Amounts transferred *(to)*/from	
(3.9)	reserves	11.6
	Group surplus/(loss) after transfers	
7.8	**to/from reserves**	(408.3)

Source: Annual Report and Accounts, 1985.

GOVERNMENT GRANT

This is money given to British Rail by the government and is added to turnover as an extra source of income.

OPERATING EXPENDITURE

This refers to *all* items of revenue expenditure incurred by British Rail except interest payable on loans. For example, it included wages and salaries (nearly £2,000 million) and depreciation (just over £200 million).

TOTAL OPERATING SURPLUS/LOSS

This surplus is the profit of the organisation during the last fifteen months, i.e. income (turnover and government grant but excluding other income) *less* operating expenditure. A loss is made when expenditure is greater than income.

In fact, British Rail made a loss of £231.6 million after taking into account the cost of the coal strike through lost freight business. As you can see, these costs were estimated at £250 million.

Without taking the coal strike into account, British Rail made a 'notional' surplus of £18.4 million:

	£ million
Total income (turnover + grant)	3,557.5
less Total operating expenditure (excluding £250 m. for coal strike), i.e. £3,789.1 m. less £250 m.	3,539.1
'Notional' surplus before taking into account coal strike	18.4
less Costs of coal strike	250.0
Total operating loss	231.6

OTHER INCOME

Almost of all this income came from the 'recovery of administration and financing costs from third parties'. This refers to money recovered from people outside the organisation.

SURPLUS/LOSS BEFORE INTEREST

This is British Rail's surplus/loss *after* other income has been added but *before* interest payable and similar charges have been deducted. British Rail made a loss before interest of £214.9 million, after taking into account the effects of the coal strike. However, if the £250 million cost of the strike is ignored, British Rail made a 'notional' surplus before interest of £35.1 million.

INTEREST PAYABLE AND SIMILAR CHARGES

This included £59.7 million of interest paid to the government on loans received from it.

TAXATION

British Rail had no taxation to pay because there was no surplus.

SURPLUS LOSS ON ORDINARY ACTIVITIES

This is the equivalent of a limited company's net profit (or loss) after tax but before extraordinary items have been taken into account. Note that interest payable, as an expense, obviously makes the loss even greater, i.e. it is added *not* subtracted.

EXTRAORDINARY SURPLUS/LOSS

This is calculated by deducting extraordinary charges (i.e. expenses) from extraordinary income. In the period ended 31 March 1985, charges exceeded income, and so an extraordinary loss was made. The only item of extraordinary income was 'surplus sales of scrap assets'. The main extraordinary charge was £102 million provided for the reorganisation of the engineering subsidiary of British Rail, British Rail Engineering Ltd (BREL).

GROUP SURPLUS/LOSS FOR THE FINANCIAL PERIOD

This is the equivalent of a limited company's net profit (or loss) after tax and after extraordinary items have been taken into account.

AMOUNTS TRANSFERRED TO/FROM RESERVES

£11.6 million has been transferred from its reserves by British Rail to reduce the size of its loss to £408.3 million (i.e. £419.9 million less £11.6 million). Note that in 1983 British Rail made a surplus of £11.7 million and of this £3.9 million was transferred to its reserves.

Balance sheet

The vertical presentation of British Rail's balance sheet as at 31 March 1985 looked like Fig. 10.2. Several things need to be noted about this.

Fig. 10.2: British Rail – balance sheet as at 31 March 1985

31 December 1983 £ million		£ million
	Net assets employed:	
	Fixed assets	
	Tangible assets	
359.0	Buildings, way and structures	415.9
775.3	Rolling stock, plant and equipment	812.4
1,134.3		1,228.3
0.7	**Investments**	0.9
0.7		0.9
	Current assets	
174.3	Stocks	213.4
262.6	Debtors	311.4
	Investments	
396.4	Interest in: Non-rail businesses	168.0
	Other transport undertakings	26.0
—		
27.1	Cash at bank and in hand	26.7
860.4		745.5
555.3	**Less creditors:** amounts falling due within one year	652.0
305.1	**Net current assets**	93.5
1,440.1	**Total assets less current liabilities**	1,322.7
20.0	**Less creditors:** amounts falling due after more than one year	25.8
1,420.1		1,296.9
—	**Provisions for liabilities and charges**	102.0
	Financed by:	1,194.9
	Capital and reserves	
435.0	Capital liabilities to Secretary of State	406.3
214.1	Loans and leasing liabilities	275.2
225.9	Revaluation reserve	263.2
786.8	Other reserves	900.2
(241.7)	Profit and loss account	(650.0)
1,420.1		1,194.9

Source: Annual Report and Accounts, 1985.

BUILDINGS, WAY AND STRUCTURES

This covers buildings and new railway lines owned by the organisation. The total cost of these assets was £521.2 million, and the total depreciation on these to date was £105.3 million. So their total net value (cost less depreciation) was £521.2 million less £105.3 million, i.e. £415.9 million – the figure in the balance sheet.

ROLLING STOCK, PLANT AND EQUIPMENT

This includes trains, carriages and equipment owned by the organisation. The total cost of these assets was £1,543 million, and the total depreciation on them to date was £730.6 million. So their total net value was £812.4 million.

INVESTMENTS (UNDER FIXED ASSETS)

This refers to money invested in other transport companies, including Container Base Ltd, a freight company.

DEBTORS

This figure includes £9.7 million of prepayments and accrued income.

INVESTMENTS (CURRENT ASSETS)

This covers money invested in British Rail's non-rail subsidiaries, including British Transport Ltd (which used to own the famous Scottish hotel, Gleneagles). The investments in 'other transport undertakings' refer to money invested in Sealink UK Ltd, the ferry company, which was sold by British Rail in July 1984.

CAPITAL LIABILITIES TO SECRETARY OF STATE

These are loans owed to the Secretary of State for Transport (i.e. the government).

LOANS AND LEASING LIABILITIES

This refers to other loans owed by the organisation and the value of assets which have been leased (i.e. rented) from leasing companies. (We shall mention more about leasing in Chapter 11.)

REVALUATION RESERVE AND OTHER RESERVES

If you remember from Chapter 9, these are reserves for the revaluation of assets and other purposes (have another look at the comments about Fruit & Veg Ltd's balance sheet in Chapter 9, if you have forgotten).

PROFIT AND LOSS ACCOUNT

As you can see, over the years more money has been taken out of reserves from the profit and loss account than put in. This figure of £650 million takes into account the £11.6 million transferred from reserves in the profit and loss account.

Activity

Choose **one** nationalised industry (apart from British Rail) and then look up the address of its local head office in the Yellow Pages. Write a suitable letter to it, asking for a copy of the organisation's annual report and accounts.

When you have received these, compare them with the accounts of:

(a) H. P. Bulmer's (see Chapter 9).
(b) British Rail.
(c) West Sussex County Council (see below).
(d) The accountancy firm which you found out about in Chapter 5.

Local authorities

You have probably also come across these in Organisation in its Environment.

Activity

Find out the name of your local authority. From your Organisation in its Environment notes or textbook, make a list of local authorities' activities and sources of income. Then make a list of what you think their major items of revenue and capital expenditure are.

Having completed this activity, you should be well on the way to understanding a local authority's accounts. All local authorities have to prepare and publish:

1. an income and expenditure statement (called a **revenue account**); and
2. a balance sheet.

We shall use the example of West Sussex County Council to see how these accounts are presented.

Revenue account

West Sussex County Council's revenue account for the year ended 31 March 1985 looked like Fig. 10.3. Note the following points.

NET EXPENDITURE 1984–5

This column shows the net expenditure for the year ended 31 March 1985 for each of the council's activities, i.e. its total or gross expenditure less the total income generated from its activities (see below). As you can see, the net expenditure figures have also been included for the previous year which ended on 31 March 1984.

Fig. 10.3: West Sussex County Council – revenue account for the year ended 31 March 1985

Service	Net expenditure 1983–4 £	Gross expenditure 1984–5 £	Income from Fees and charges £	Income from Specific government grants £	Net expenditure 1984–5 £
Coast and Countryside	493,855	524,197	39,552	—	484,645
Education	115,609,156	143,349,989	13,566,652	9,393,487	120,389,850
Fire and public protection	7,532,952	8,721,541	507,915	72,178	8,141,448
General purposes	2,795,488	3,984,315	763,444	—	3,220,871
Library and archives	4,075,150	4,550,260	306,686	—	4,243,574
Magistrates' courts	323,812	1,777,612	76,171	1,348,736	352,705
Personnel and finance	Cr 707,905	3,569,426	4,864,828	—	Cr 1,295,402
Planning	1,051,243	1,100,052	31,871	—	1,068,181
Police	13,475,803	28,337,523	—	13,971,000	14,366,523
Probation	219,515	1,184,469	86,337	861,304	236,828
Property	613,551	1,328,351	1,081,739	4,171	242,441
Roads and transportation	17,196,906	22,762,575	4,556,592	3,753,571	14,452,412
Social services	21,058,710	27,617,005	5,296,881	24,565	22,295,559
Reserve fund contribution	6,382,764	1,900,000	—	—	1,900,000
	190,121,000	250,707,315	31,178,668	29,429,012	190,099,635
Income from rate support grant – block grant	54,835,361				59,175,625
	135,285,639				130,924,010
Income from rates	127,113,393				135,331,192
Taken from balances	8,172,246				—
Taken to balances	—				4,407,182

Source: Annual Report and Accounts, 1985.

INCOME

This column shows the total income generated from each of the council's activities, for the year ended 31 March 1985. As you can see, there are two main sources of income:

1. fees and charges made by the council; and
2. specific government grants; this is money received from the government in addition to the rate support grant.

RATE SUPPORT GRANT

This is money given to the council by the central government in Whitehall to help finance its activities. As you can see, it is a major source of income for the council but not as important as rates.

RATES

As you probably already know, rates are a property tax. They are paid on property, owned by individuals and organisations, according to its **rateable value**. Each property is given a rateable value, based upon how much it would cost to rent it, i.e. the more valuable the property the higher the rateable value. Then the council works out how much money it needs to raise from rates and on this basis orders each property-owner in the county to pay a certain amount for every £1 of rateable value.

In 1984–5 West Sussex ratepayers paid 131p in the £ – the lowest rate in the country (the highest, by the way, was Cleveland in the north-east of England: 190p in the £).

ITS SERVICES

Most of these are self-explanatory except for:

1. **Coast and countryside** – this refers to money spent on nature conservation and recreational facilities such as picnic sites, footpaths and nature reserves.
2. **Education** – net expenditure for 1984–5 was £80,247,000 on schools and £21,934,000 on further and higher education (including the three technical colleges in the county).
3. **Fire and public protection** – this includes spending on consumer protection (£706,000 for 1984–5). Total spending on the fire service was £7,378,000.

Activity

Find out from your Organisation in its Environment textbook what a local authority does to protect consumers.

4. **General purposes** – this includes spending on waste disposal, county council elections, and registration of births, deaths and marriages.
5. **Personnel and finance** – this refers to the cost of central management services provided by the council to carry out its activities. They include computer services, printing, and full-time managers such as the council's chief executive and treasurer.

   The high figure for fees and charges here is explained by the fact that these services are paid for by each department which uses them.
6. **Planning** – the council's planning department aims to develop the area to provide jobs (Gatwick Airport is in the county) as well as to preserve the beautiful countryside.
7. **Property** – expenditure here includes maintaining the council's property. Its major source of income from property is rent from council houses.
8. **Roads and transportation** – expenditure here includes financial support to bus operators to provide an adequate bus service throughout the county.
9. **Social services** – this includes spending on caring for children in need, old people and the mentally ill.

RESERVE FUND CONTRIBUTION

This is the amount transferred from the council's reserves to help to finance its expenditure.

TAKEN TO/FROM BALANCES

This is the amount which is either added to or subtracted from the council's other reserves. Any excess of income over expenditure is added, as £4,407,182 was in 1984–5. Any excess of expenditure over income is subtracted, as £8,172,246 was in 1983–4.

Balance sheet

West Sussex County Council's balance sheet as at 31 March 1985 looked like Fig. 10.4 on p. 80.

Fig. 10.4: West Sussex County Council – balance sheet as at 31 March 1985

Net assets

	£	£	£
employed:			
Fixed assets			30,050,127
Current assets			
Works in progress	547,599		
Stocks in hand	1,500,286		
Temporary loans	16,952,604		
Other investments	37,234		
Debtors and prepayments	8,035,100		
		27,072,823	
less **Current liabilities**			
Temporary loans	405,000		
Creditors	15,990,704		
Capital fund advances	350		
Cash overdrawn	4,207,243		
		20,603,297	
Net current assets			6,469,526
			£36,519,653
Financed by:			
Loans			8,983,814
Other capital and reserves			27,535,839
			£36,519,653

Source: Annual Report and Accounts, 1985.

Several comments can be made about this balance sheet:

FIXED ASSETS

These include land, buildings, furniture and equipment.

WORKS IN PROGRESS

The major part of this is accounted for by unfinished roadworks.

STOCKS IN HAND

The major part of this was accounted for by road-building materials.

TEMPORARY LOANS

In the current assets section these refer to short-term loans given out by the council. Under current liabilities they refer to money borrowed by the council on a short-term basis.

CAPITAL FUND ADVANCES

This is money borrowed from the capital fund (see below, under 'other capital and reserves') to buy fixed assets such as land and buildings.

CASH OVERDRAWN

Because the council has spent more cash than it has received, the amount overdrawn is a current liability.

LOANS

This refers to money borrowed by the council on a long-term basis.

OTHER CAPITAL AND RESERVES

This includes the money transferred from the revenue account for the year, i.e. £4,407,182 (see above). It also includes the following reserves which have to be kept under the 1972 Local Government Act:

1. **General reserve fund** – this is used to pay any unexpected or unavoidable expenditures.
2. **Capital fund** – this is used to finance the purchase of fixed assets.

Activity

Visit your local council and try to obtain a copy of its annual report and accounts (one between two will do). Compare its accounts with those of West Sussex County Council. (If you live in West Sussex, try to get a copy of the annual report all the same, and study it.) *Note:* A copy of the annual report can be obtained from your local library.

Your college

To find out about your college's accounts, *you* will have to do some work!

Activity

In conjunction with your lecturer, try to arrange for one of the administrative officers in your college to give a talk about 'The Accounts of Your College'. From this talk and any other information you can get hold of (e.g. from the college prospectus or the local council), make a note of the following:

1. Your college's accounting year.
2. Which accounts it has to prepare every year.

3. Your college's main items of income and expenditure.
4. Your college's main assets and liabilities.

Conclusion

You should have seen from this chapter that accounting is relevant to all types of organisation. In particular, one thing we have come across time and time again is the importance of finance for all these organisations. Chapter 11 will summarise what these main sources of finance are.

Assignment

In groups of three, you are asked to organise a 'Charities Week'. With this in mind you are asked to:

1. Illustrate the income and expenditure of the UK's leading charities in whatever way you think best (see Fig. 10.5).
2. Make a list of other charities (local or national) which you either know or can find out about.
3. Choose **one** of the charities mentioned in tasks 1 and 2.

4. Find out its address from the Yellow Pages or telephone directory (look at the London one first). Then write a suitable letter to it, asking for information about the charity and explaining that you might be raising money for it (see task 7 below).
5. With the information you received from task 4 and any other information you can obtain, prepare a publicity leaflet for the charity (maximum 1,000 words).
6. **All** of your group should then pick one of the charities chosen by the smaller groups.
7. Prepare and organise a suitable fund-raising event for this charity. Suitable publicity material must be prepared.

Skills tested:
- Numeracy.
- Identifying and tackling problems.
- Learning and studying.
- Design and visual discrimination.
- Information gathering.
- Communicating.
- Working with others.

Fig. 10.5: Income and expenditure of charities with over £7 million voluntary income in the UK, 1984

£s million cash

	Income						Expenditure			
	Voluntary income			Rents, invest- ments	All other income	Total income	Charit- able	Fund- raising	Other	Total expen- diture
	Legacies	Other	Total							
Oxfam	1.9	23.7	25.6	0.4	3.2	29.1	18.2	3.4	6.1	27.7
National Trust	12.1	12.6	24.7	13.3	20.4	58.3	42.7	2.4	4.3	49.4
Royal National Lifeboat Institution	11.6	9.4	21.0	1.0	0.7	22.7	15.2	1.3	1.2	17.6
Cancer Research Campaign	13.9	6.2	20.1	1.6	0.1	21.8	18.5	1.2	0.4	20.1
Imperial Cancer Research Fund	13.6	4.2	17.8	5.7	4.4	27.8	16.4	0.9	0.5	17.8
Salvation Army	6.6	10.5	17.1	5.4	13.8	36.3	23.9	0.5	2.8	27.2
Dr Barnardo's	7.4	9.5	16.9	2.1	19.6	38.6	23.7	4.0	2.1	29.9
Save the Children Fund	1.4	10.6	12.0	0.6	4.5	17.1	12.8	1.9	0.5	15.3
National Society for the Prevention of Cruelty to Children	2.6	9.1	11.7	0.3	2.1	14.2	9.6	1.3	0.7	11.6
Help the Aged	2.9	8.6	11.5	0.3	1.3	13.2	7.1	3.0	0.5	10.6
Royal National Institute for the Blind	7.8	3.5	11.2	1.3	8.2	20.8	14.6	1.8	0.7	17.1
Spastics Society	2.4	8.8	11.2	1.0	15.4	27.6	22.5	3.0	1.3	26.8
Guide Dogs for the Blind Association	6.2	4.5	10.6	3.2	3.2	17.0	6.4	1.4	0.5	8.4
Christian Aid	1.0	8.9	9.9	0.3	0.9	11.2	10.1	1.2	0.4	11.7
Actionaid	0.1	9.8	9.9	0.1	0.4	10.3	8.5	0.7	0.8	9.9
Jewish Philanthropic Association	0.0	8.7	8.7	0.2	0.0	8.8	6.2	—	2.1	8.4
Marie Curie Memorial Foundation	2.3	5.4	7.7	0.4	0.4	8.5	6.9	0.6	0.2	7.7
Royal British Legion	0.4	6.7	7.1	1.1	1.8	10.0	7.5	0.5	0.9	8.9
Church of England Children's Society	2.5	4.5	7.0	1.0	5.6	13.6	10.2	1.5	0.9	12.6

Source: *Charities Statistics 1985/86.*

PART FOUR
Raising Finance

11
Raising Finance

Any organisation, such as Fruit & Veg Ltd, must raise money (i.e. capital) to carry on its business. The balance sheet shows that this money is spent on:

1. **fixed assets**, e.g. Fruit & Veg's shop and motor van, and
2. **working capital**, i.e. current assets less current liabilities (see Fig. 11.1).

Fig. 11.1: What a balance sheet shows us

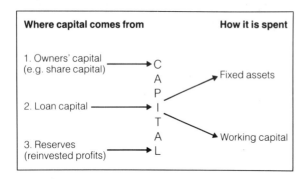

Activity

Compare the fixed assets and working capital of Fruit & Veg Ltd, West Sussex County Council (Chapter 10), British Rail (Chapter 10) and H. P. Bulmer Holdings PLC (Chapter 9).

Factors to consider

In Chapter 12 we shall examine the accounting techniques (called **investment appraisal** techniques) which are used to help to determine whether a fixed asset is bought or not. In Chapter 13 we shall see how important working capital is in providing an organisation with cash to pay off its bills.

However, first of all we need to discuss the factors that any organisation (including non-profit making ones like sports clubs) must consider when raising money. Which source of finance is chosen will be dependent upon an examination of the following factors (see Fig. 11.2):

1. **Cost.**
2. **Taxation.**
3. **Flexibility.**
4. **Availability.**
5. **Organisational objectives.**
6. **Term of the finance.**

Fig. 11.2: Factors to consider when raising finance

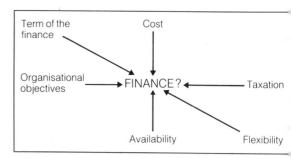

Each of these will now be examined in turn.

Cost

This will include:

1. The **administrative costs** of raising the money.

- The **opportunity cost** (see Chapter 1) of the finance, e.g. the interest the money could have earned if it had been invested elsewhere.
- **Interest paid** (for loans), or **dividends paid** (for shares). The interest paid on loans will be affected by government policy and the general state of the UK economy. This will be explained further in the second year of your Organisation in its Environment course.

Banks use their **base rates** as the basis for calculating their lending rates. In other words, both individuals and businesses are charged a certain percentage above each bank's base rate for loans and overdrafts.

Activity

Choose one of the main high-street banks. Find out how much it charges different customers for loans and overdrafts.

Taxation

As we saw when looking at a limited company's balance sheet, interest paid on loans, unlike dividends to shareholders, is deducted from net profit and so reduces how much corporation tax the company has to pay.

Activity

Find out from your library how the rate of corporation tax has changed over the last ten years.

Flexibility

An organisation's financial requirements may vary from one period of time to another, because of unexpected expenses and/or delayed payment by its customers. In such circumstances an organisation will want a flexible type of borrowing which allows it to change the amount it can borrow from one day to the next. This happens with a **bank overdraft** (see pp. 22 and 87).

Availability

Activity

Imagine that you are a bank manager, and a manufacturing firm in your area is asking for a loan from you. List the factors you might consider when deciding how much to lend to it.

Your list should have included various factors which determine how much money will be made available by financial institutions such as banks. They are:

GOVERNMENT MONETARY POLICY

This refers to how the government (and its bank, the Bank of England) attempts to change the total amount available in the economy to lend out to businesses and private individuals. In the second year of the Organisation in its Environment course, you will see how it does this.

THE ORGANISATION'S FINANCIAL POSITION

Before it lends out money, a bank or any other financial institution will make sure that the borrowing organisation is able to pay its interest and loan repayments. So it will examine its accounts to come to conclusions about:

1. **The amount of cash it has to pay off its debts** – as indicated by the level of its current assets in relation to its current liabilities (see Chapter 13).
2. **Security (or collateral), if required** – this is something which the lender can sell if the borrowing organisation fails to pay its loan or interest payments. So if the lender does require security, a firm wishing to borrow will have to own fixed assets suitable for this purpose.
3. **Its borrowing position** – an organisation should make sure that it does not over-borrow, because this will make it more difficult to find the cash to pay for loan repayments and interest. Laker Airways did just that, and it eventually went out of business (see Chapter 13).

   So it is important for an organisation to be aware of its borrowing position. It can do this by calculating its gearing ratio (see Chapter 13).

LEGAL FACTORS

Directors in a limited company must check that they have the power to borrow money on the company's behalf. This power is usually given to them by the company's Memorandum and Articles of Association. A bank must check that the purpose of the loan is not **ultra vires**, i.e. outside the scope of the company's objects, as laid down in its Memorandum. If it is, the loan may not be legally enforceable, and the bank could not successfully sue the borrower if loan repayments were not met. (See your Organisation in its Environment textbook on this.)

Sole traders, partnerships and private limited companies also cannot advertise to the public for money, but public limited companies can (see below). Raising finance for limited companies is made easier by the fact that their owners (shareholders) have **limited liability**, i.e. the amount they have to pay towards the debts of the company is limited to the amount they invested in the company. Limited partners in a limited partnership also have this advantage, but ordinary partners and sole traders do not.

Activity

List the advantages and disadvantages of giving limited liability to shareholders.

PURPOSE OF FINANCE

A financial institution will be less willing to lend money for an investment project which is highly risky. If it does decide to do so, it is likely to charge a higher rate of interest on the loan to compensate for the risk.

This is why small businesses often find it more difficult to raise finance than larger ones – a fact confirmed by the **1971 Bolton Committee on Small Firms**. This is why several government schemes have been introduced in recent years to help finance the smaller business, such as the **state-backed loan guarantee scheme** and the **Business Expansion Scheme**.

Activity

Write to your local Small Firms Centre and find out which government schemes are available to finance small businesses.

Organisational objectives

These will determine how much money an organisation needs to raise. An organisation which wants to expand very quickly (as is true of the Virgin Group, for example – see below) will require more money than a less ambitious one. Consequently an organisation's financial objectives are inevitably influenced by its expectations about the future – in particular, whether it is optimistic or pessimistic.

Activity

Choose an organisation with which you are familiar, e.g. church, social club, sports club. Try to find out whether its financial requirements are increasing or decreasing and the reasons for this.

Term of finance

Another important consideration is the repayment period of the finance. In this respect an organisation has a choice between long-, medium- and short-term finance (see below).

Sources of finance

Checklist: main sources of finance

An organisation's main sources of finance can be summarised as follows:

LONG–TERM

1. **Owners' capital**
   - Share capital (limited companies) – preference and/or ordinary shares.
   - Owners' savings (sole traders and partnerships).
   - Government grants and loans (local authorities and nationalised industries).
2. **Loan capital**
   - Debentures (limited companies only).
   - Bank loans.
   - Loans from other financial institutions:
     - Investors in Industry Group.
     - British Technology Group (incorporates National Resource Development Corporation and National Enterprise Board).
     - EEC's Social Fund and Regional Fund (particularly for nationalised industries).
3. **Reinvested profits** (for profit-making organisations).
4. **Subscriptions** (for clubs and other groups).

MEDIUM–TERM

1. **Bank loans.**
2. **Hire-purchase and credit sales.**
3. **Leasing** (including sale and lease-back).

SHORT–TERM

1. **Bank overdraft.**
2. **Trade credit.**
3. **Factoring.**
4. **Bills of exchange.**

Long-term finance

This is most suitable for the purchase of fixed assets, where the income from them is generated over a long period of time. Therefore, the finance can be repaid over a longer period of time. The normal repayment period for long-term finance is from five up to twenty-five years.

The main sources of long-term finance for a limited company are **shares**, **loans** and **reinvested profits** (see Fig. 11.3):

Fig. 11.3: Long-term sources of finance for all UK industrial and commercial companies

| | £000 million | | | |
	1977	1980	1981	1982
Share capital and reserves	70.6	112.8	126.7	137.3
Reinvested profits for the year	6.5	6.9	5.7	4.2
Long-term loans and debentures	15.1	17.8	19.3	18.1

Source: British Business, 30 May 1986.

SHARES

There are two types of share that can be sold by a limited company: **ordinary** and **preference**. If the company's profits are sufficient, all shareholders are entitled to receive a share of its profits, called a **dividend**.

Preference shareholders are paid a fixed rate of dividend, but as a source of long-term finance they have lost popularity in recent years, because loans have tax advantages. This fixed rate of dividend is quoted as a percentage of each preference share's nominal value (see also p. 66).

Example: 1,000 preference shares with fixed dividend of 5 per cent and nominal value of £1:

Dividend per share = 5 per cent of £1 = 5p (if profits are sufficient).

Total dividend paid = 5p × 1,000 = £50 (if profits are sufficient).

Most preference shareholders are **cumulative** in that, if they do not receive their full dividend, because the company is not making enough profit, these losses can be made up in future years when profits are higher. **Non-cumulative** preference shareholders cannot do this (see example below).

Ordinary shareholders are entitled to a dividend determined by the company's directors only after the preference shareholders have received theirs. So they carry the most risk – high dividends in good times, none at all in bad.

Example A – preference shares are cumulative. Assume:

1. All preference shareholders in a company are cumulative.
2. There are 100,000 preference shares (dividend 10 per cent, nominal value £1, i.e. they are entitled to a dividend of 10p per share, i.e. £10,000 in total every year).
3. The company's ordinary shareholders always receive the remainder of profits distributed to shareholders after the preference shareholders have been paid.
4. £5,000 profits are distributed to shareholders in 1985 and £75,000 in 1986.

The distribution of these profits to each type of shareholder would have been:

1985 – £5,000
Preference shareholders receive £5,000.
Ordinary shareholders receive *nothing*.
1986 – £75,000
Preference shareholders receive £15,000 (£10,000 + £5,000 'lost' in 1985).
Ordinary shareholders receive £60,000.

Example B – preference shares are non-cumulative. This has the same assumptions as Example A, except that all preference shareholders are non-cumulative (remember that £5,000 profits are distributed to shareholders in 1985 and £75,000 in 1986).

In this case, the distribution of profits to each type of shareholder would have been:

1985 – £5,000
Preference shareholders receive £5,000.
Ordinary shareholders receive *nothing*.
1986 – £75,000
Preference shareholders receive £10,000 (because they cannot make up the £5,000 which was 'lost' in 1985).
Ordinary shareholders receive £65,000.

Activity

A company has 250,000 5 per cent preference shares of £1 nominal value, and all dividends are distributed to ordinary shareholders after the preference shareholders have been paid theirs. Calculate the total dividend received for both types of shareholder, if the profits received by shareholders are:

Year 1: £10,000.
Year 2: £30,000.
Year 3: £100,000.

All preference shareholders are cumulative.

When offering its shares to the general public, a public limited company must publish a **prospectus** in periodicals and newspapers such as the *Financial Times*. This must give evidence of the company's past trading performance, including its profits and losses over the last ten years.

The shares are then sold either at a **fixed pre-determined price**, as with the British Telecom and TSB share issues, or **by tender**, where prospective shareholders state the price they are prepared to pay for the shares. They must offer at least the minimum price, as laid down in the prospectus, and the shares are sold to those people offering the highest price. This was the method used by the government in its issue of Britoil shares, and by the Virgin Group when it became a public limited company.

Activity

Make a list of the companies whose shares have been sold by the government since 1979.

Shares can also be offered to existing shareholders in the form of **rights issues** and **bonus** (or **scrip**) **issues**. In the former, shares are offered at a price below their market value (i.e. their present price on the Stock Exchange) in proportion to shares already held, e.g. one new share for every two existing shares.

Shares in a bonus issue are given away free to existing shareholders, e.g. one free share for every two shares owned. Such bonus issues are becoming an increasingly popular source of finance for limited companies.

LOANS

1. a) **Debentures** – these are loans to a company from a debenture holder who has bought debentures. In return (s)he receives a fixed rate of interest per year on the amount (s)he has lent, i.e. how much (s)he paid for the debenture. The loan is then normally repaid after a certain number of years.

   Example – debenture 10 per cent 1995. This means that the debenture holder reeives a 10 per cent rate of interest and is repaid in 1995.

   The debenture holder usually has some sort of security which the company has to sell if it fails to pay its interest or loan repayments. For **fixed debentures**, this security is a particular company asset such as a building. With **floating debentures**, however, the company can sell an asset of its choice.

The term **naked debenture** is given to debentures which do not have any security, i.e. debenture holders have no assets to sell if they are owed money.

2. **Bank loans** – these are repaid in regular instalments and are given by merchant banks and the commercial banks, e.g. Lloyds and National Westminster (see Chapter 3).

Activity

Using banking books in your library, make a list of merchant banks which operate in the UK today.

The rate of interest charged on these bank loans, as we have already seen, is determined by the lending bank's **base rate**. How much a borrower pays above this is dependent upon the level of risk involved for the bank. For example, big public limited companies pay a lower rate than riskier small businesses (e.g. Colin & Helen's partnership in Chapter 8).

Activity

Re-read the notes you made on bank lending services in Chapter 3.

3. **Loans from other financial institutions** – a limited company can also receive loans from:

   (a) The **Investors in Industry Group** (which includes the Industrial and Commercial Finance Corporation).

   (b) The **Agricultural Mortgage Corporation** (which finances the farming industry).

   (c) The **British Technology Group** (which oversees the operations of the National Research Development Corporation, which specialises in financing the development of new products, and the National Enterprise Board).

Activity

Find out the addresses of these organisations in the London telephone directory. Write to them to find out further details of their activities.

REINVESTED PROFITS

These are the profits left, after the payment of corporation tax and dividends to shareholders. They are an extremely important and cheap source of finance. However, you must not forget they have an opportunity cost, e.g. the interest the profits could have earned, if invested elsewhere (see Chapter 1).

SOURCES OF LONG-TERM FINANCE FOR OTHER TYPES OF ORGANISATION

1. **Sole traders** – savings of the sole trader, bank loans, loans from friends/relatives, reinvested profits.
2. **Partnerships** – savings of the partners, bank loans, loans from the partners, reinvested profits.
3. **Retail co-operative societies** – shares bought by customers, bank loans, reinvested profits.
4. **Workers' co-operatives** – bank loans, reinvested profits.
5. **Trade unions and other pressure groups** – subscriptions from members, bank loans.
6. **Clubs** – subscriptions from members, bank loans.
7. **Public corporations** (or **nationalised industries**) – grants and loans from the government, nationalised industry securities (loans from the public, which are similar to debentures in a limited company), bank loans, money from EEC institutions like the EEC Social Fund and EEC Regional Fund, reinvested profits.
8. **Insurance companies** – premiums from their policy holders, reinvested profits.
9. **Building societies** – money from investors, repayments from borrowers, money from financial institutions in the City of London.
10. **Banks** – money from depositors, shares, debentures, reinvested profits.
11. **Local authorities** – rates (a tax on property), grants from central government (called the rate support grant), local authority securities (loans from the public), income from local authority services (e.g. rent from council houses), and other sources of income, e.g. lotteries. Remember, we looked at West Sussex County Council's sources of income in Chapter 10.

Activity

Find out what the main sources of finance are for your college.

Medium-term finance

This refers to sources of finance whose repayment period is normally from one year up to five years. The following are the main types of medium-term finance for all types of organisation:

BANK LOANS

See above.

HIRE-PURCHASE AND CREDIT SALES

As we saw in Chapter 3, both of these allow an organisation to buy a fixed asset over a long period and so avoid the need to buy it immediately with a large cash payment – money it may not have. Hire-purchase and credit sales are similar in that monthly instalments (including interest) are paid to a finance house.

However, they differ in that ownership of the asset passes to the user once the last instalment has been paid with hire purchase, and once the first instalment has been paid with credit sales.

LEASING

Leasing, or renting, a piece of equipment from a leasing company has several advantages:

1. Like hire-purchase and credit sales, it avoids buying the equipment with a large initial cash payment.
2. The leasing company is usually responsible for the repair and maintenance of the equipment.
3. If the equipment is likely to become obsolete within a short period of time, e.g. a computer, it can be replaced without great cost.

Sale and lease-back is also becoming an important source of finance. This involves organisations selling fixed assets which they own to a leasing company and then leasing them back.

Short-term finance

The main sources of short-term finance (repayment period up to one year) are:

BANK OVERDRAFT

This gives an organisation the right to overdraw its current account at the bank by a certain amount. Interest is charged on a day-to-day basis on the amount overdrawn (see Chapter 3).

TRADE CREDIT

This refers to credit given by an organisation's suppliers in the normal course of business. They normally allow a firm a few days to pay for goods or services supplied.

FACTORING

Sometimes called **debt factoring**, this occurs when a firm sells its debts to a factoring company for less than its face value, e.g. a £100 debt is sold for £95. The factoring company then becomes responsible for collecting the debt and, if the debt is repaid in full, will make a profit (in our example £5 less expenses).

This service is particularly useful to companies with a large number of customers who buy on credit. It is also useful for small businesses for whom unpaid debts could be financially disastrous (see Chapter 13).

BILLS OF EXCHANGE

Under a bill of exchange the buyer of goods (called the **drawee** of the bill) agrees to pay the seller (the **drawer**) in a certain period of time, usually three months. In other words, it is a form of credit for the buyer.

Most of you will examine these in detail in other areas of the course (particularly Business Law and Banking I and II).

Case study: Virgin Group plc

In recent years Virgin has become one of Britain's fastest growing limited companies. For example, its net profit before tax in the first half of 1984 totalled £5 million, as compared with £1.8 million in the first half of 1983. Indeed this success enabled it to become a public limited company in 1986 after several years as a private limited company.

The group is run by its chairman, the flamboyant Richard Branson, who has a natural eye for publicity. For example, he was seen in 1930s-style flying gear to launch the company's transatlantic cheap-fares airline. Branson was also involved in the successful attempt by the *Virgin Atlantic Challenger* to cross the Atlantic in record time.

Branson also has a shrewd financial brain. He originally set up the business as a mail-order record firm in 1970. He has always believed in tight control over costs and in taking advantage of any profitable activities within the leisure industry.

VIRGIN'S ACTIVITIES

The company, and its subsidiary, Voyager Ltd, carry out the following activities:

MUSIC

Virgin publishes and records popular music which contributes around 70 per cent of the company's profits, from sales within the UK and overseas. It artists include Culture Club, UB40, Genesis, Phi Collins, Human League and Julian Lennon.

RETAILING

Virgin owns sixty-five record shops throughou the country, of which the biggest is its Megastore in Oxford Street.

PUBLISHING AND BROADCASTING

Virgin owns 15 per cent of Radio Mercury, a radic station, and 45 per cent of Music Channel, a television channel that broadcasts sixteen hours a day of pop music and videos via cable and satellite to Britain and Europe.

It also makes computer games, with about 5 per cent of the UK market, publishes books or pop music and computers, and produces video cassettes. Virgin also makes and distributes films – *1984*, starring Richard Burton and John Hurt, wa one of its first major film projects.

OTHER ACTIVITIES

Virgin has interests in construction, heating systems, pubs, nightclubs and Synthaxe, a music synthesiser that can be played like a guitar. It also runs Virgin Atlantic, Virgin's cut-price transatlantic airline.

How does Virgin finance these activities?

Virgin has financed them in a number of different ways:

SHARES

As a private limited company, Virgin issued 100,000 ordinary shares. Of these, 85,000 were owned by Richard Branson and 15,000 by J. S. Draper, co-founder of the business. Towards the end of 1985, Virgin also sold £25 million of preference shares to twenty-four financial institutions in the City of London.

However, becoming a public limited company has given Virgin the ability to raise more cash through selling shares to the general public. For example, when Virgin Group plc was formed, it was able to raise £70 million through the sale of 50 million shares.

BANK LOANS AND OVERDRAFTS

These totalled £2,345,000 on 31 January 1984, of which £1,192,000 was to be repaid during 1984.

REINVESTED PROFITS

The company reinvested £4,485,000 of its profits for the year ended 31 January 1984.

DEBENTURES

These totalled £2,480,000 on 31 January 1984, of which £1,861,000 was to be repaid during 1984.

Summary

Up until 1985 reinvested profits, bank borrowing and debentures were the most important sources of finance for the company. However, shares are becoming increasingly important and will become even more so now that Virgin has become a public limited company.

Activity

Read the above section on Virgin Group plc again and answer the following questions:

1. How would you advise the company to finance its future expansion plans?
2. Where would you invest the money? Would you expand its existing activities and/or diversify into new areas?
3. What do you think are the strengths and weaknesses of the company?

Conclusion

You should now be familiar with how different types of organisation raise money to finance their activities. They buy assets with this money, of course, and in Chapter 12 we shall look at how accountants value such assets and choose which ones to buy.

Assignment (intramodular assignment with Organisation in its Environment I)

Imagine you are setting up a sandwich bar in your college, giving snacks to people at lunchtime. You are required to carry out the following tasks:

1. Estimate your capital and revenue expenditures in your first year's trading. For example, you will need to estimate any rent to be paid and the amount of bread and materials used, based upon the number of customers.
2. Predict what your profit and loss account and balance sheet would look like at the end of the first year's trading.
3. Describe how you would finance the business.
4. Describe how you would make the business a success.

Skills tested:
- Numeracy.
- Learning and studying.
- Information gathering.
- Communicating.

PART FIVE
Management Accounting

12
Valuation and Purchase of Assets

We have already seen that an organisation can own two types of asset: fixed and current. Chapter 11 showed how it can get the money to buy them. The second half of this chapter will discuss the techniques used by accountants to decide whether or not to buy a particular fixed asset such as a shop or a piece of machinery. These are called **investment appraisal techniques**.

First of all, however, we must look at how accountants value assets and how their valuation is affected by inflation, i.e. a rise in prices.

Valuation of assets and the effects of inflation

Activity

Think of one fixed asset which you own, such as a stereo, motor bike or car. How would you value it?

You should have found out from this problem that there are a number of possible ways to value an asset. Three possibilities are valuing it according to

- its **purchase price** (i.e. **cost**);
- its **sale price**;
- its **replacement cost** (i.e. how much it would cost to replace it with a new one).

Question

Can you remember which method of valuation is favoured by accountants?

Answer: Valuation based upon the asset's cost or purchase price (sometimes called its **historical cost**). There is one slight exception to this general rule: **the valuation of stocks**.

Valuation of stocks

Stocks are usually valued according to their cost or market value, whichever is lower. For example, if all or part of an organisation's stocks are worth less than they originally cost, i.e. their market value is less than their cost price, then the stocks must be valued according to their market value.

If the market value is higher than the cost price, the stocks are always valued according to their cost price (this is most frequently the case).

Example – Colin Smith, Greengrocer (mentioned in Chapters 6 and 7):

(a) If Colin had stocks of fruit and vegetables in his shop wich cost £2,000 but would sell for only £1,500, they would be valued at £1,500 in his accounts.
(b) If Colin had stocks which cost £2,000 and their market value was £2,500, they would be valued at £2,000 in his accounts.

There are two further things you should know about with respect to the valuation of stocks:

1. LIFO and FIFO.
2. How to find out the cost price of stocks if you know only their selling price.

LIFO AND FIFO

These are two alternative ways of finding out which stocks are sold first. As we shall see in the example below, they have an important effect on he valuation of stocks. First of all, though, we must explain what the terms mean:

- **LIFO** means **'last in, first out'**, i.e. the stocks bought last are the first ones to be sold, and so the stocks bought first are the last ones to be sold.
- **FIFO** means **'first in, first out'**, i.e. the stocks bought first are the first ones to be sold, and so the stocks bought last are the last ones to be sold.

Example – Colin Smith, Greengrocer (note: stocks are valued according to their cost price because their market value, i.e. selling price, is higher):

Apples Colin bought in his first month's trading (June 1985)
  1 June: 100 lb @ 15p = £15
  8 June: 100 lb @ 20p = £20
15 June: 100 lb @ 25p = £25
22 June: 100 lb @ 30p = £30

If Colin had 100 lb of apples left at the end of the month these stocks would be valued at:

(a) *15p per lb under the LIFO principle.* Why? These are the ones which were bought first and so have to be sold last.
(b) *30p per lb under the FIFO principle.* Why? These are the ones which were bought last and so have to be sold last.

Activity

If Colin had 200 lb of apples left at the end of the month, what would be the value of these stocks under:

1. The LIFO principle?
2. The FIFO principle?

FINDING OUT THE COST PRICE OF STOCKS

Colin Smith, Greengrocer, like many other organisations, makes a profit on the stocks that it sells. So we have the following relationship:

Cost price of stocks + profit = selling price of stocks.

The profit when expressed as a percentage, or fraction, of the cost price is known as the **mark-up**. The profit when expressed as a percentage, or fraction, of the selling price is known as the **margin**.

Knowing all of this can help us find out the cost price of stocks (assuming we do not know this) if we know their selling price and the mark-up (expressed as a percentage of their cost price). We can do this using the formula:

$$C = \frac{S}{1 + P}$$

where C = cost price of the stocks, S = selling price of the stocks, P = mark-up as a percentage of the cost price (expressed as a fraction, e.g. 8 per cent = $8/100$).

Example. The selling price of stocks is £6,000 and the mark-up is 20 per cent of the cost price. What would be the value of these stocks based upon their cost price?

$$\text{Cost price } (C) = \frac{6,000}{1 + \left(\frac{20}{100}\right)}$$

$$= \frac{6,000}{1 + \frac{1}{5}}$$

$$= \frac{6,000}{(6 \div 5)}$$

$$= 6,000 \times \frac{5}{6} = £5,000.$$

Activity

What would the cost price of stocks in the following examples be?

1. Mark-up 10 per cent of cost, Selling price £11,000.
2. Mark-up 33⅓ per cent of cost, Selling price £1,000.
3. Mark-up 50 per cent of cost, Selling price £2,000.
4. Mark-up 25 per cent of cost, Selling price £20,000.

Problems with historical costing in times of high inflation

In times of fairly stable prices the system of historical costing works well, because an asset's cost is easy to find out and rarely in dispute. However, in times of high inflation (when prices are rising very quickly), serious problems begin to emerge with historical costing.

STOCKS

Because prices are rising, the cost of replacing stocks increases in times of inflation. This means that an organisation's profit based upon historical costing is higher than indicated by the real financial state of the business.

Example – Colin Smith, Greengrocer. Colin buys some fruit and vegetables for £25. Because of very high inflation, he then sells them a week later for £40 and replaces them for £35. His profit and loss account, based upon historical costing (just like all the profit and loss accounts in the previous chapters), will say that the business has made a profit of £15, ignoring all other expenses (i.e. £40 less £25).

However, to maintain the original level of stocks Colin has to use £10 of this £15 'profit'. This is because it cost £10 more – £35 less £25 – to replace the stocks. So Colin's 'true' profit is only £5.

Activity

Karen, a newsagent, buys some sweets for £50. A month later she sells them for £100. However, since she bought them, their cost price has increased by 50 per cent.

1. What is Karen's profit based upon historical costing?
2. What is her 'true' level of profit?

DEPRECIATION

Activity

What is the main problem with calculating depreciation on the basis of a fixed asset's historical cost in times of inflation?

You might have remembered from earlier chapters that the main problem is that not enough cash will be set aside to replace the fixed asset at the end of its useful life.

Example – Colin Smith's motor van. If you remember from Chapter 6, the van's cost was £2,000, its expected useful life was six years, and its expected scrap or resale value was £200. Therefore, using the straight-line method, the annual depreciation was £300.

So £1,800 of depreciation (6 × £300) would be set aside in total over the van's lifetime; and, including the scrap or resale value, £2,000 would be available to replace the van. However, inflation will mean that it will cost much more than £2,000 to replace the van.

Activity

Calculate how much money would have to be set aside in depreciation over the six years to replace a van *if*

(a) the price of such a van was increasing 10 per cent every year;
(b) the expected scrap or resale value of the van was £200;
(c) its cost price was £5,000.

WORKING CAPITAL (i.e. CURRENT ASSETS LESS CURRENT LIABILITIES)

In times of inflation the amount owed by an organisation's customers, i.e. its debtors, will increase faster than the amount owed to its suppliers, i.e. its creditors. The reason for this is that the general price level will be lower when the business is buying supplies. In other words, working capital (the value of debtors, a current asset, less creditors, a current liability) is artificially increased in times of inflation.

Example – Colin Smith buys £2,000 worth of fruit and vegetables on credit on 1 June 1985. We can look at two possible situations for Colin here, assuming that he sells all of his fruit and vegetables on credit:

1. **No inflation**, i.e. prices are not rising – by the end of the week (i.e. by 7 June) he has sold these fruit and vegetables on credit for £2,200, i.e.

   Debtors = £2,200
   Creditors = £2,000 (the amount he owes his supplier)
   Working capital = £200 (assuming no other current assets or current liabilities)

2. **Very high inflation** (price of fruit and vegetables doubles in the week ending 7 June) – by 7 June he has sold the fruit and vegetables on credit for £4,400, twice the price he would have sold them at without inflation, i.e.

   Debtors = £4,400
   Creditors = £2,000
   Working capital = £2,400

   You can now see why high inflation artificially increases the amount of working capital.

SALES AND PROFITS

The accounts of a business may show that sales (or turnover) and profits have both increased by say 5 per cent p.a. in money terms. However, this will not indicate an improvement in its financial position if the value of money has fallen by more than 5 per cent, i.e. inflation is more than 5 per cent. So inflation makes it difficult to compare one year's sales or profit performance with another.

FIXED ASSETS

In times of inflation, an organisation's fixed assets are often likely to be undervalued in accounts based upon historical costing. For example, Colin and Helen's first shop was valued at its original cost of £80,000 in Fruit & Veg Ltd's balance sheet on 31 May 1989 (see Chapter 9). However, because it had been bought more than two years earlier, its market value would have been much higher, because of rising property prices.

BORROWING

Under historical costing, only the amount originally borrowed is shown in the balance sheet. However, inflation means that the real value of a loan falls in terms of what it can buy.

Example: The £10,000 bank loan in Fruit & Veg Ltd's balance sheet on 31 May 1989 (see Chapter 9) will be able to buy fewer goods than the £10,000 bank loan in Smith & Baptiste's balance sheet on 31 May 1987, if prices are rising.

How then have accountants tried to overcome these problems? The answer is that they have proposed in recent years two methods of accounting for inflation: **current purchasing power (CPP) accounting**, and **current cost accounting (CCA)**.

Methods of inflation accounting

CURRENT PURCHASING POWER (CPP) ACCOUNTING

CPP Accounting adjusts the value of assets in the balance sheet according to changes in the general price level, as measured by the government's Retail Prices Index (RPI). The only assets not adjusted in this way are an organisation's cash and bank balance.

Example: If the RPI increased by 10 per cent in the year up to 31 May 1989, then the value of its assets in Fruit & Veg Ltd's balance sheet would have all been increased by 10 per cent with the exception of its cash and bank balance (refer again to Chapter 9).

CURRENT COST ACCOUNTING (CCA)

CCA values fixed assets and stocks according to their **current replacement cost**, i.e. how much it will cost to replace them. This method of inflation accounting was preferred to CPP Accounting by the **Sandilands Committee** in 1975, which was appointed by the government to investigate how accounting methods should change in times of rising prices.

So CCA is currently used by accountants under SSAP 16 (see Chapter 9 if you have forgotten what SSAPs are). This requires that certain organisations must publish accounts based upon CCA in addition to the ones based upon historical costing (which have been shown in previous chapters). These organisations are:

1. Public limited companies which are quoted on the Stock Exchange.
2. Any other business that can satisfy at least two of the following criteria:
   (a) a turnover of £5 million or more;
   (b) total assets worth more than £2.5 million in the historical cost accounts;
   (c) an average number of employees in the UK of 250 or more.

For example, H. P. Bulmer Holdings plc is quoted on the Stock Exchange and consequently had to publish current cost accounts for the year ended 26 April 1985 in addition to the historical cost ones, shown in Chapter 9.

Purchase of fixed assets: investment appraisal techniques

Whether to buy a fixed asset or not is an important decision. Various investment appraisal techniques are used by accountants to help an organisation make such a decision.

Investment appraisal in non-profit-making organisations

An organisation's objectives will determine which fixed assets it will choose to buy. As we shall see in Chapter 15, these objectives are likely to vary from one type of organisation to another. In most of this chapter we shall assume that **making a profit** is an important objective when decisions about investment in fixed assets are made. This applies to sole traders, partnerships and limited companies, which have already been mentioned in this book.

However, as we saw in Chapter 10, many organisations are not in business to make a profit

Activity

List ten organisations whose main objective is not to make a profit.

You should have come up with organisations like schools, colleges, universities, local authorities, charities, libraries and sports clubs. For these non-profit-making organisations, the sole purpose of investment in a fixed asset is not to make money but to achieve other objectives, whilst making sure that the money invested is used as efficiently as possible and so not wasted.

Example – a technical college. This college has a choice between building a new computer centre and a new sports hall. How the college specifies its objectives will determine which one is chosen. For example, if it places greater emphasis on academic achievement by its students, it will probably choose to build the computer centre. On the other hand, if greater emphasis is placed upon the students' extra-curricular activities, it will probably go for the sports hall.

However, once the decision is made one way or the other, the college must ensure that a builder is chosen who can offer the best deal in terms of price charged and the quality and speed of workmanship.

You should be able to see from this example the importance of the economist's concept of **opportunity cost** in investment appraisal. If you remember from Chapter 1, this is the cost of something in terms of the benefits given up to obtain it. In other words, from the college's point of view, the opportunity cost of building the computer centre is the benefits it could have reaped from building the sports hall, and vice versa.

For profit-making organisations, which we shall turn to next, the opportunity cost of investing in a particular fixed asset is *either*

- the profits which could have been earned from investing in another fixed asset; *or*
- (if it is decided not to invest in a fixed asset at all) the interest which could have been earned by investing the money elsewhere, e.g. in a building society.

Activity

Imagine that you are the principal of your college and you have three alternative building projects to choose from:

1. A new swimming-pool.
2. An extension and improved facilities for the library.
3. A new refectory.

Explain the one you would choose and the reasons for your decision. What is the opportunity cost of your decision?

Investment appraisal techniques in profit-making organisations

For such organisations there are two major considerations when deciding whether or not to invest in a fixed asset:

1. The total profits earned by the fixed asset over its useful life.
2. How quickly the asset will pay off its cost.

The one that is given greater emphasis will again be dependent upon the organisation's objectives.

For example, a business that is short of cash is more likely to favour an investment which earns profits more quickly. On the other hand, another business in a better financial position may be willing to accept lower profits, or even losses early on, in the hope that profits in the long-term will be high.

We shall now discuss the main investment appraisal techniques which are used to help businesses make decisions about investing in fixed assets. To do this we shall make the following assumptions:

1. On 1 January 1990 Fruit & Veg Ltd is faced with a choice between buying a shop in Carlisle or one in Newcastle-upon-Tyne.
2. The company's objective is to make as much profit as possible from the new shop.
3. The expected useful life of each shop is four years (because they each have a lease with only four years to run).
4. The expected scrap or resale value of each shop is nil (they will be worth nothing when the lease runs out).
5. The cost of each shop is £10,000.
6. The expected net profits before tax and the annual depreciation for each shop are:

Carlisle shop

Year	Net profits before tax	Depreciation	Total earnings
	£	£	£
1990	27,500	2,500	30,000
1991	27,500	2,500	30,000
1992	37,500	2,500	40,000
1993	37,500	2,500	40,000
	130,000		

Newcastle shop

Year	Net profits before tax	Depreciation	Total earnings
	£	£	£
1990	7,000	2,500	9,500
1991	27,500	2,500	30,000
1992	47,500	2,500	50,000
1993	57,500	2,500	60,000
	139,500		

Activity

Using the straight-line method, check why annual depreciation is £2,500 for each shop.

On the basis of these figures, there are three main investment appraisal techniques that can be used to decide which shop should be bought. They are:

1. Payback method.
2. Rate-of-return method.
3. Net present value method.

PAYBACK METHOD

This finds out the number of years it takes to recover the cost of the investment (in our example £10,000 for each shop) from its earnings. Earnings here are usually defined as the expected net profits before tax from the asset *plus* its depreciation. This is how we calculated the 'total earnings' column in the table on p. 94.

The Carlisle shop 'pays for itself' in this way in 1990, but the Newcastle shop 'pays for itself' only during 1991. So the Carlisle shop would be chosen using this method.

Organisations will expect a particularly short payback period from fixed assets whose useful lives will be short, e.g. computers which can become obsolete very quickly.

The main problem, though, with the payback method as an investment appraisal technique is that it does not take into account the profits an asset earns after its cost has been paid for. This problem is overcome by the rate-of-return method.

RATE-OF-RETURN METHOD

This calculates the percentage rate of return on each asset as follows:

average profit ÷ asset's cost × 100%

where average profit = total net profit before tax over asset's lifetime ÷ useful life of the asset in years

For example:

Carlisle shop
Average profit = 130,000 ÷ 4 = £32,500
Percentage rate of return = (32,500 ÷ 10,000) × 100% = 325%

Newcastle shop
Average profit = 139,500 ÷ 4 = £34,875
Percentage rate of return = (34,875 ÷ 10,000) × 100% = 348.75%

Therefore, using this method, the Newcastle shop would be chosen – which immediately shows you some of the problems that can occur in real life. This conclusion directly contradicts the result of the payback method!

The answer to this dilemma is likely to depend upon Fruit & Veg Ltd's financial position at the time it buys the shop. If it needs cash as quickly as possible, it is likely to prefer the Carlisle shop (because of its quicker payback period). If it can afford to wait a bit longer before it recovers the shop's costs, it is likely to go for the Newcastle shop.

NET PRESENT VALUE (NPV) METHOD AND DISCOUNTED CASH FLOW (DCF)

Another problem with the two methods above is that money received today, e.g. profits from a fixed asset, is worth more than money received at a future date. This is because the money can be invested to earn interest. This problem is overcome by using discounted cash flow (DCF) techniques, and such techniques are widely used by accountants for investment appraisal.

Example. If £100 can be invested at 10 per cent p.a., then the value today (i.e. the **present value**) of £110 received in one year's time will be £100. In other words, if £100 was invested today, it would have become £110 in a year's time (£100 + £10 interest).

The rate of interest (in our example 10 per cent, remember) is called the **discount rate**.

The **net present value (NPV) method** is the most important method of investment appraisal which uses DCF techniques. It converts the earnings, i.e. net profits before tax plus depreciation, from a fixed asset into their present values. This is done by using appropriate tables (see Appendix: Present Value of 1 on p. 139) or by using the formula (again for the more mathematically minded):

Present value of £1's earnings (i.e. the value of earnings when the asset was bought =

$$\frac{1}{(1 + r)^n}$$

where r = discount rate, n = the number of years after the purchase of the fixed asset that the earnings take place.

The present values of the earnings are then added up, and the cost of the investment is deducted from the total. This gives the asset's **net present value**, and the fixed asset with the highest net present value will be chosen.

Before we see how this can be done to help Fruit & Veg Ltd choose between the shops in Carlisle and

Newcastle, we must make a further comment about the discount rate. Businesses often take this to be the cost (i.e. the rate of interest) on money borrowed to buy the fixed asset. This is because, if the money is borrowed at, say, 20 per cent p.a. any profits from the fixed asset can be used to repay some of the money borrowed and so 'earn' 20 per cent interest.

Example – Fruit & Veg Ltd. We shall assume that the discount rate is 10 per cent, and so the net present value of each shop will be:

Carlisle shop

Year	Earnings	Present value of £1's earnings	Present value of earnings
	£		£
1990	30,000	0.909 $\left(\dfrac{1}{1 + 10\%}\right)$	27,270
1991	30,000	0.826 $\left(\dfrac{1}{(1 + 10\%)^2}\right)$	24,780
1992	40,000	0.751 $\left(\dfrac{1}{(1 + 10\%)^3}\right)$	30,040
1993	40,000	0.683 $\left(\dfrac{1}{(1 + 10\%)^4}\right)$	27,320
			109,410
		deduct cost of shop	10,000
		Total net present value	99,410

Mathematical notes:
1. 10 per cent for calculation purposes needs to be converted into a fraction, i.e. $10 \div 100$ or $\frac{1}{10}$.
2. $\dfrac{1}{(1 + 10\%)^2} = \dfrac{1}{(1 + 10\%)} \times \dfrac{1}{(1 + 10\%)}$

$\dfrac{1}{(1 + 10\%)^3} = \dfrac{1}{(1 + 10\%)} \times \dfrac{1}{(1 + 10\%)} \times \dfrac{1}{(1 + 10\%)}$ etc.

Activity

Calculate the net present value of the Newcastle shop.

You should have got something like this:

Newcastle shop

Year	Earnings	Present value of £1's earnings	Present value of earnings
	£		£
1990	9,500	0.909 $\left(\dfrac{1}{1 + 10\%}\right)$	8,636
1991	30,000	0.826 $\left(\dfrac{1}{(1 + 10\%)^2}\right)$	24,780
1992	50,000	0.751 $\left(\dfrac{1}{(1 + 10\%)^3}\right)$	37,550
1993	60,000	0.683 $\left(\dfrac{1}{(1 + 10\%)^4}\right)$	40,980
			111,946
		deduct cost of shop	10,000
		Total net present value	101,946

Therefore, using the net present value method Fruit & Veg Ltd should choose the Newcastle shop because it has a higher net present value.

You should be able to see from the example above that, if we increase the discount rate, the present value of the earnings will fall, and so the net present value of the asset will also fall. In other words, as the discount rate gets higher and higher the net present value gets smaller and smaller. So eventually the discount rate can be increased to the point where the net present value is zero.

This discount rate is called the **internal rate of return** and is sometimes used as another method of investment appraisal. The fixed asset with the highest internal rate of return will normally be chosen.

Activity

Calculate the net present value of each shop with a discount rate of 15 per cent and then 20 per cent.

Activity

You are given the following information:

1. XYZ Ltd is faced with a choice between two machines, A and B on 1 January 1991.
2. It wants to make as much profit as possible.
3. Each machine costs £150,000.
4. The scrap or resale values of both machines will be zero at the end of their useful lives.
5. Each machine has an expected useful life of five years.
6. The expected net profits before tax from each machine are:

	A £	B £
1991	10,000	30,000
1992	20,000	40,000
1993	30,000	30,000
1994	60,000	30,000
1995	70,000	40,000

7. The company always uses the straight-line method to calculate depreciation.
8. The cost of borrowing money is 15 per cent p.a.

Make recommendations to the company on which machine it should choose, using the following methods of investment appraisal:

(a) Payback method.
(b) Rate-of-return method.
(c) Net present value method.

Accuracy of forecasts and availability of resources

When using investment appraisal techniques, there are two final things that an organisation's management must always bear in mind:

ACCURACY OF FORECASTS

The forecasts of profits (and so its sales and costs) from a fixed asset during its life must be as accurate as possible. The usefulness of investment appraisal techniques and the correctness of the decisions resulting from them will obviously decrease if these forecasts are inaccurate.

The importance of such forecasting is mentioned again in Chapter 14.

AVAILABILITY OF RESOURCES

Investment appraisal techniques may indicate that a particular investment is highly profitable, but it may be impossible to undertake it through a lack of resources. For example, building a new factory may be impossible through a lack of:

1. **Land**, i.e. no space to build the factory, or refusal by the local authority to give planning permission to build it.
2. **Labour**, i.e. not enough employees to run the factory.
3. **Machinery**, i.e. not enough machinery to equip it.
4. **Raw materials**, i.e. not enough materials to make the product which is to be made in the factory.
5. **Capital**, i.e. not enough cash to finance the purchase of the factory.

Activity

What resources do Fruit & Veg Ltd need for their shops in Carlisle and Newcastle?

Conclusion

Cash (or lack of it) is obviously an important factor in an investment decision. In Chapter 11 we discussed how an organisation can raise more cash. In Chapter 13 we look at how an organisation can improve its financial position still further through interpretation of its accounts.

Assignment (intramodular assignment with People in Organisations I)

A small travel agent in your local town has to spend £600 on new computerised equipment. It has the choice of buying either a word processor or a microcomputer at this price.

The objective is to improve administrative efficiency, reduce costs and so increase profits. In fact, the net profits before tax expected for each machine during their useful lives are:

	Word processor £	Microcomputer £
Year 1	200	100
Year 2	300	100
Year 3	400	300
Year 4	500	700
Year 5	500	700
Year 6	500	700

The scrap or resale value is expected to be zero for both machines. The discount rate is 10 per cent.

You are required to make recommendations to the manager of the travel agency about which item of equipment it should choose and their possible uses within the business. (See also Chapter 16 for this assignment.)

Skills tested:
- Numeracy.
- Identifying and tackling problems.
- Communicating.

13
Interpretation of Accounts

Activity

Imagine that you were comparing your balance sheet and income and expenditure statement for this year ending 31 December with those of Paul McCartney.

Think what differences there would be.

You should have concluded that Paul McCartney had:

1. More income and so less need to borrow.
2. More fixed assets, such as recording studios, which enable him to earn even more money in the future.
3. More current assets, e.g. his bank balance, which should enable him to pay off any debts more easily.

Such interpretation of accounts has relevance to organisations as well. Compare, for example, the financial position of H. P. Bulmer's in Chapter 9 with that of British Rail in Chapter 10.

As we saw in Chapter 5, one of the main concerns of management accounting is to interpret the accounts prepared by the financial accountant. Therefore, three broad indicators of an organisation's financial performance are examined in this chapter (see Fig. 13.1):

- **Liquidity** – can it pay off its debts when they become due?
- **Profitability** – is it making enough money?
- **Capital structure** – is it borrowing too much?

To answer these questions, the management accountant calculates **financial ratios** on the basis of figures from the balance sheet and profit and loss account, such as net profit, sales and current assets. An organisation's financial performance can be assessed by comparing such ratios with the same ratios of previous years and with those of similar organisations in the same industry (what is sometimes called **inter-firm comparison**).

We shall now examine how these ratios and other methods are used to assess an organisation's liquidity, profitability and capital structure. A case study on the collapse of Laker Airways (remember Freddie Laker?) will then illustrate how they can be applied in practice.

Liquidity and profitability – an introduction

An organisation's liquidity (or **solvency**, as it is sometimes called) refers to its **ability to pay its debts with cash when they become due**.

Activity

Read through Fruit & Veg Ltd's balance sheet in Chapter 8. Which parts of it are relevant to the company's liquidity?

Fig. 13.1: Indicators of financial performance

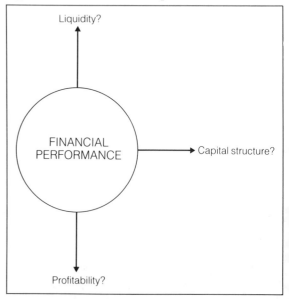

You should have come up with:

1. Its **current assets**, which are either cash or assets that can be converted into cash during the year immediately after the date of the balance sheet.
2. Its **current liabilities** (i.e. creditors: amounts falling due within one year), which are debts due to be paid during the year immediately after the date of the balance sheet.

In other words, it is spending on **working capital** (the same thing as **net current assets**, i.e. current assets less current liabilities) which improves an organisation's liquidity position (see Fig. 13.2).

Fig. 13.2: Liquidity v. profitability

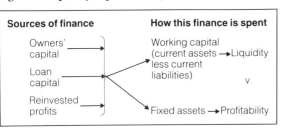

Activity

Compare the working capital figures for H. P. Bulmer's (Chapter 9), West Sussex County Council (Chapter 10) and British Rail (Chapter 10).

However, as we saw in Chapter 12, an organisation can also spend money on **fixed assets**. This is important because it enables the organisation to increase production, sales and therefore profits. For example, Colin and Helen's profits rose when they bought another shop.

So an important overall objective for management accountants is to ensure that an organisation maintains an appropriate balance between:

- **spending on fixed assets** (which increases profitability), and
- **spending on working capital** (which improves liquidity).

Too much spending on fixed assets will leave it short of working capital and so cause problems in paying off its debts. Overspending on working capital will mean that not enough is being spent on fixed assets to boost profitability (Fig. 13.2).

EXAMPLE – YOUR OWN FINANCIAL POSITION

You know only too well that buying a fixed asset (like a stereo or a car) can leave you short of cash (i.e. short of working capital) to spend on nights out, clothes, etc.

PROFITS ARE NOT THE SAME THING AS CASH

Activity

Can you think why this is sometimes true?

The reason is that sales (and therefore profits) can be recorded in the accounts, but, because customers buy on credit, an organisation does not receive cash from them straight away. So delayed payment by these customers (the firm's debtors) can create a cash shortage. We can see this by looking at the organisation's **working capital cycle**, which shows how cash circulates around it (see Fig. 13.3).

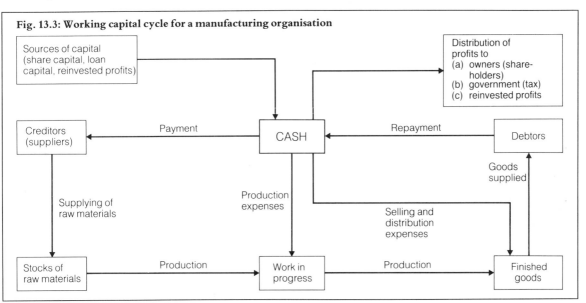

Fig. 13.3: Working capital cycle for a manufacturing organisation

The importance of liquidity

Activity

Put yourself in the shoes of Colin and Helen at Fruit & Veg Ltd. You find yourself unable to pay off your debts to the fruit and vegetable wholesaler.

What will the consequences of this be for the company? What can you do about it?

These are important questions. We shall deal with the first question here and the second question in the next section.

The inability to pay off debts, or **insolvency** as it is sometimes called, has the following undesirable consequences for an organisation:

1. Difficulty of obtaining credit from suppliers, because of the bad feeling caused by delayed payment.
2. Inability to take advantage of cash discounts.
3. Damage to a firm's standing in the eyes of potential investors and lenders, which will make it more difficult to raise finance in the future.
4. Inability to pay for future financial commitments which could be highly profitable and possibly vital to an organisation's survival, e.g. the introduction of a new product, or the purchase of raw materials and new equipment.
5. The possible necessity of having either to borrow money at high interest rates, or to sell fixed assets as a means of improving the organisation's cash position.
6. The possibility of going out of business, if sources of additional cash cannot be found (resulting in bankruptcy for sole traders and partnerships, and liquidation for limited companies).

Management of cash flow: methods of avoiding a cash shortage

Methods of avoiding a cash shortage can be summarised as:

1. **Increasing capital.**
2. **Delaying payment for assets.**
3. **Selling fixed assets.**
4. **Factoring.**
5. **Using a cash flow forecast.**
6. **Credit (or debtor) control.**
7. **Stock control.**
8. **Creditor control.**
9. **Ratio analysis.**

Fruit & Veg Ltd should have considered one or more of these methods.

INCREASING CAPITAL

As we saw in Chapter 11, extra money can be raised from an issue of shares and/or debentures, borrowing from financial institutions such as banks and reinvesting more profits (which for a limited company may mean reducing its dividends to shareholders).

DELAYING PAYMENTS FOR ASSETS

This may occur through bills of exchange, trade credit, leasing, hire-purchase, and credit sales (see pp. 87–8).

SELLING FIXED ASSETS

This may be considered as a last-resort measure, although **sale and lease-back** has become increasingly common in recent years. This occurs when an organisation sells one of its fixed assets to a leasing company and then leases it back (see p. 87).

FACTORING

Selling debts to a factoring company (see pp. 87–8).

USING A CASH FLOW FORECAST

This illustrates a firm's cash incomes and expenditures for a period of time and so should emphasise any potential cash shortages (see p. 115).

CREDIT (OR DEBTOR) CONTROL

This is the process by which a firm tries to ensure that its debtors pay up on time. This can be achieved by:

(a) Ensuring that invoices are sent out at the same time that the goods are delivered to customers.
(b) Preparing a debtor analysis at the end of each month, showing those debts which are overdue for payment. Reminders can then be sent to these people, threatening legal action if necessary.
(c) Checking on the creditworthiness of customers by, for example, examining their published accounts (if a limited company) and asking for credit references from banks or credit reference agencies.
(d) Stopping supplies to customers who look unlikely to pay.
(e) Calculating the debt collection period (see below in the section on ratio analysis).

STOCK CONTROL

Activity

What would be the disadvantages to Fruit & Veg Ltd of having too many stocks?

The objective of stock control is to strike a balance between having too low a level and too high a level of stocks, because both have their disadvantages.

Disadvantages of too few stocks:

- Stocks of finished goods will be inadequate to meet unexpected rises in demand and to keep customers supplied while production is disrupted. For example, such disruption could be caused by industrial action or by shortages of raw materials.
- Advantage is not being taken of discounts from bulk purchases of raw materials.
- Lost production due to a shortage of raw materials.
- A firm is more vulnerable to large increases in the price of raw materials. (Try to think of the reason for this.)

Disadvantages of too many stocks:

- Too much working capital is being spent on stocks which could otherwise be more usefully employed buying fixed assets to increase future profits.
- Increased expenses of handling, storage and insurance required for stocks.
- It becomes more likely that the large amounts of unused stocks will either deteriorate or become damaged or obsolete (i.e. out of date).
- The interest to pay on any money borrowed to buy the stocks.

Stock control will normally require the calculation of the **rate of stock turnover** (see below) and the preparation of **stock record cards**. These record the number of items the organisation has in stock. Goods are reordered when they reach their **reorder level**, thus maintaining a reasonable level of stocks.

Today many organisations use computers to carry out stock control. This will be discussed further in Chapter 16.

CREDITOR CONTROL

This is concerned with delaying payments to suppliers (creditors) as long as possible and so can obviously help an organisation with a cash shortage. However, delaying payment has the following disadvantages:

- Loss of discounts for prompt payment from suppliers.
- Suppliers may refuse to deliver goods in the future and may eventually sue for the money owed.

So consequently it is advisable for a firm to prepare a **creditor analysis** at the end of each month, which lists creditors who are due to be paid. This will serve as a reminder to pay up, when necessary.

RATIO ANALYSIS (SEE FIG. 13.4 ON P. 102)

Accountants calculate four main financial ratios to assess an organisation's liquidity position: the current ratio, quick ratio, debt collection period and rate of stock turnover.

1. **Current ratio** (sometimes called the **working capital ratio**) and **quick ratio** (sometimes called the acid-test ratio).

The **current ratio** is:

$$\frac{\text{current assets}}{\text{current liabilities (or creditors: amounts falling due within one year)}}$$

The **quick ratio** is:

$$\frac{\text{current assets} - \text{closing stock}}{\text{current liabilities}}$$

(Remember, closing stock is the value of stocks in the balance sheet.)

Example – Smith & Baptiste, Greengrocers, year ended 31 May 1987 (refer to the balance sheet on p. 58):

$$\text{Current ratio} = \frac{5{,}300}{600} = 8.8.$$

$$\text{Quick ratio} = \frac{5{,}300 - 3{,}600}{600} = \frac{1{,}700}{600} = 2.8.$$

Typically the current ratio should be about **1.5 to 2** and the quick ratio should be about **1**.

If both the quick ratio and current ratio are very low (e.g. less than 1), it indicates that an organisation cannot pay off its current liabilities (i.e. short-term debts) from assets which can be easily converted into cash (current assets). The result is all the undesirable consequences of the inability to pay off debts, which have already been described.

Fig. 13.4: Summary of the main ratios

Liquidity

(a) *Current ratio*: $\dfrac{\text{current assets}}{\text{current liabilities}}$

(b) *Quick ratio*: $\dfrac{\text{current assets} - \text{stocks}}{\text{current liabilities}}$

(c) *Debt collection period*: $\dfrac{\text{debtors}}{\text{sales}} \times 52$ (weeks)

(d) *Rate of stock turnover*: $\dfrac{\text{cost of sales}}{\text{average stock}}$

Profitability

(a) *Return on capital employed*:

$$\frac{\text{net profit before tax (excluding extraordinary items)} + \text{interest on loans}}{\text{fixed assets} + (\text{current assets} - \text{current liabilities})} \times 100\%$$

(b) *Gross profit/sales*:

$$\frac{\text{gross profit}}{\text{sales}} \times 100\%$$

(c) *Net profit/sales*:

$$\frac{\text{net profit before tax (excluding extraordinary items)} + \text{interest on loans}}{\text{sales}} \times 100\%$$

(d) *Earnings per share*:

$$\frac{\text{net profit after tax} - \text{preference dividends}}{\text{Number of ordinary shares issued}} \times 100 \text{ (pence)}$$

(e) *Dividend yield*:

$$\frac{\text{dividend per ordinary share (in pence)}}{\text{market price per ordinary share (in pence)}} \times 100\%$$

(f) *Price earnings ratio*:

$$\frac{\text{market price per share (in pence)}}{\text{dividend per ordinary share (in pence)}}$$

Capital structure

(a) *Gearing ratio*:

$$\frac{\text{long-term loans} + \text{short-term loans and overdrafts} + \text{preference shares}}{\text{ordinary shares} + \text{reserves}}$$

or

$$\frac{\text{long-term loans} + \text{short-term loans and overdrafts}}{\text{fixed assets} + (\text{current assets} - \text{current liabilities})} \times 100\%$$

(b) *Interest cover*:

$$\frac{\text{net profit before tax} + \text{interest payable on loans}}{\text{interest payable on loans}}$$

Note: net profit before tax is the equivalent of net profit for a sole trader or partnership (see Chapters 7 and 8).

If both ratios are very high (e.g. more than 3), it would indicate that the organisation is **over-liquid**, i.e. it is spending too much on working capital and not enough on fixed assets to increase future profits.

Comment on Smith & Baptiste's position. Both the current and quick ratios are very high (particularly the current ratio). This indicates that the partnership is over-liquid and has spent too much on working capital.

Activity

Calculate the current and quick ratios for each year shown in the accounts of:

(a) Colin Smith, Greengrocer (only for the week ended 7 June; see Chapter 7).
(b) H. P. Bulmer Holdings plc (Chapter 9).
(c) West Sussex County Council (Chapter 10; note that stocks = works in progress + stocks in hand).
(d) British Rail (Chapter 10).

Make some comments on these ratios.

2. **Debt collection period** – this shows how long debtors take to pay the money that they owe. It is calculated as:

$$\frac{\text{debtors}}{\text{sales}} \times 52 \text{ (in weeks)}.$$

A debt collection period of **six to seven weeks** is normal. If this is rising rapidly, it indicates that an organisation is waiting longer to be paid by its debtors and so could find itself short of cash.

However, the debt collection period can be too short – demanding cash payments or a shorter debt collection period could drive a firm's customers into the hands of its competitors.

Example – Smith & Baptiste, Greengrocers, year ended 31 May 1987 (refer to the balance sheet (p. 58) and profit and loss account (p. 55)):

Debt collection period =

$$\frac{1{,}000}{200{,}000} \times 52 \text{ weeks} = 0.26 \text{ weeks (nearly 2 days)}.$$

Comment. This would indicate that Smith & Baptiste's debtors are paying very quickly, and there is no need to worry.

Activity

Calculate the debt collection period for each year shown in the accounts of:

(a) Colin Smith, Greengrocer (only for week ended 7 June; see Chapter 7).
(b) H. P. Bulmer Holdings plc (Chapter 9).
(c) British Rail (Chapter 10).

Comment on your results.

3. **Rate of stock turnover** – this is calculated as:

$$\frac{\text{cost of sales}}{\text{average stock}}$$

where average stock = opening stock + closing stock ÷ 2.

Calculating this ratio helps an organisation to assess how successful it has been in having the right balance between too many and too few stocks – the main objective, remember, of stock control.

A stock turnover figure of about **3 or 4** is often normal for an average manufacturing business and would indicate that such a balance is being achieved. A much higher figure would indicate that it has too few stocks, and a much lower figure might well indicate there are too many stocks:

- low figure – too many stocks;
- high figure – too few stocks.

However, this guideline of 3 or 4 should not be applied to all types of organisation. For example, organisations like supermarkets with a low profit margin would normally expect a much higher stock turnover figure.

Example – Smith & Baptiste, Greengrocers – year ended 31 May 1987:

$$\text{Rate of stock turnover} = \frac{130,000}{(5,000 + 3,600) \div 2}$$

$$= \frac{130,000}{4,300} = 30.23.$$

Comment. This is extremely high and indicates that Smith & Baptiste has too few stocks and should probably buy some more.

Activity

1. Calculate the rate of stock turnover for each year shown in the accounts of:

   (a) Colin Smith, Greengrocer (only for the week ended 7 June, see Chapter 7).
   (b) H. P. Bulmer Holdings plc (Chapter 9).
   (c) British Rail (Chapter 10).

Note: for Bulmer's and British Rail, assume that the closing stock figure is also the average stock figure.

2. Make a list of organisations you would expect to have a high rate of stock turnover.

Activity

List the methods of avoiding a cash shortage which would be most appropriate for Fruit & Veg Ltd.

Profitability

We saw in earlier chapters that an organisation's profit and loss account calculated its net profit for the year as follows:

total sales revenue (i.e. number of units sold × their selling price) *less* **total costs.**

As we saw in Chapter 1, such costs can be either **fixed** or **variable**. These will be discussed further in Chapter 14.

Accountant's v. economist's definition of profit

It should be explained again here that an accountant's definition of cost differs from that of an economist. As we saw in Chapter 12, an accountant traditionally bases an asset's cost upon its purchase price (or its historical cost). Only costs relating to the purchase of goods and services by an organisation are included.

An economist, though, defines cost in terms of something's **opportunity cost**, i.e. its cost in terms of the benefits given up to obtain it (discussed in Chapter 1). So, for a sole trader like Colin Smith, an economist would include not only costs relating to the purchase of goods and services but also:

1. the wages (s)he could have obtained in alternative employment, and
2. the interest (s)he could have earned on the money that (s)he has invested in the business.

Activity

Re-read the section on opportunity cost in Chapter 1. Compare Colin Smith's net profit/loss for the week ended 7 June 1985 before tax from:

(a) an accountant's point of view;
(b) an economist's point of view.

Assume Colin could have earned 10 per cent p.a. on the money he has invested in the business (be careful: this is the rate of interest *per year*). He could also have earned £10,000 p.a. in another job.

Ways of increasing profit

Whatever definition of cost we use, it should be obvious from our definition of profit that there are two ways of increasing an organisation's profitability:

- **increasing sales revenue** and/or
- **reducing costs**.

An organisation can increase its sales revenue by increasing the demand for its product(s) through improved marketing (e.g. the introduction of a new product and increased advertising), and then increasing production to meet this extra demand. Therefore, the number of products sold will rise. Alternatively it will be able to increase its revenue by increasing the price of its product(s), if customers are prepared to pay this higher price.

Activity

Look up the term **elasticity of demand** in your Organisation in its Environment textbook. What is the relevance of this concept to our discussion here?

Reductions in costs can be achieved by:

- closing down any loss-making parts of the organisation;
- greater automation (so reducing the number of employees required);
- budgetary control, which we shall look at in Chapter 14.

Financial ratios used to assess profitability

It is no good comparing absolute levels of profit between different businesses. £10,000 profit for a small business like Smith & Baptiste, Greengrocers, would be a much better performance than the same profit for a much bigger firm like H. P. Bulmer's.

To solve this problem, management accountants compare the level of profit with either capital employed or sales (see Fig. 13.4). Note that net profit before tax is the equivalent of net profit for a sole trader or partnership (see Chapters 7 and 8).

1. **Return on capital employed (ROCE)** –

$$\frac{\text{net profit before tax (excluding extraordinary items)} + \text{interest on loans}}{\text{fixed assets} + (\text{current assets} - \text{current liabilities})} \times 100\%.$$

2. **Profit/sales ratios** –

either $\dfrac{\text{gross profit}}{\text{sales}} \times 100\%$

or

$$\frac{\text{net profit before tax (excluding extraordinary items) plus interest on loans}}{\text{sales}} \times 100\%$$

Example – Smith & Baptiste, Greengrocers, year ended 31 May 1987 (refer again to the balance sheet (p. 58) and profit and loss account (p. 55)):

$$\text{Return on capital employed} = \frac{52,500 + 1,000}{86,100} \times 100\%$$

$$= \frac{53,500}{86,100} \times 100\% = 62\%$$

(Note the interest on partners' loans is always excluded.)

$$\text{Gross profit/sales ratio} = \frac{70,000}{200,000} \times 100\% = 35\%.$$

$$\text{Net profit/sales ratio} = \frac{52,500 + 1,000}{200,000} \times 100\%$$

$$= \frac{53,500}{200,000} \times 100\% = 26.75\%.$$

ROCE should be at least **the rate of inflation plus 2% or 3%** for a typical firm, and a usual figure for the gross profit/sales ratio is about **8% to 10%**.

However, the level of profitability we would expect from a particular organisation is likely to vary from year to year and from industry to industry, for the following reasons.

1. **How business is carried out in the industry** – for example, we would expect a much lower gross profit/sales ratio in supermarkets than in a local corner shop. This is because they have much higher sales and a lower profit margin (i.e. price less costs per unit).
2. **General economic conditions** – the following economic factors can all change an organisation's expected profitability:
   - Changes in the rate of inflation (which obviously affect the organisation's costs).
   - Changes in customers' real disposable incomes (look up this term in your Organisation in its Environment textbook).
   - The introduction of controls on price increases by government.
   - Other factors leading to a change in the demand for the organisation's product(s).

Activity

Read the section in your Organisation in its Environment textbook on factors affecting demand.

Comments on Smith & Baptiste's profitability. The return on capital employed and profit/sales ratios all look very healthy. This partly reflects the fact that small retailers like Smith & Baptiste usually have a relatively high profit margin.

However, it is particularly encouraging that the return on capital employed is so high.

Activity

Calculate the return on capital employed and profit/sales ratios for each year shown in the accounts of:

(a) Colin Smith, Greengrocer (only for the week ended 7 June; see Chapter 7).
(b) H. P. Bulmer Holdings plc (Chapter 9).
(c) British Rail (ignore the effects of the coal strike and remember that its profit is called a surplus; see Chapter 10).

Multi-product firms

These are firms, like Bulmer's, which make or sell more than one product. In such circumstances it will be more useful for their management to know and assess the profitability of every individual product.

Other profitability ratios for investment analysis

Some ratios analyse a company's profit performance in terms of dividend received and are used primarily by potential investors in companies and by financial institutions, such as stockbrokers, advising them.

The principal types of this kind of ratio are (see Fig. 13.4):

1. **Earnings per share** –

$$\frac{\text{Maximum amount of money available to ordinary shareholders as dividends (i.e. net profits after tax – preference dividends)}}{\text{number of ordinary shares issued by the company at the end of the accounting year}} \times 100 \text{ pence.}$$

2. **Dividend yield** –

$$\frac{\text{dividend per ordinary share (in pence)}}{\text{market price per ordinary share (in pence)}} \times 100\%.$$

3. **Price earnings ratio** –

$$\frac{\text{market price per ordinary share (in pence)}}{\text{dividend per ordinary share (in pence)}}.$$

Example – H. P. Bulmer Holdings plc, year ended 26 April 1985 (refer to H. P. Bulmer's balance sheet (p. 72) and profit and loss account (p. 70)):

1. **Earnings per share** – net profit after tax less preference dividends = £6,945,000 – £1,945,000 = £5,000,000. Number of ordinary shares issued at the end of the year = 51,865,000.

$$\text{Earnings per share} = \frac{5,000,000}{51,865,000} \times 100 \text{ pence}$$

$$= 9.64 \text{ pence (as stated in the balance sheet).}$$

2. **Dividend yield** (based upon market price of the share on 28 June 1986) –

$$\frac{\text{Dividend}}{\text{per share}} = \frac{\text{ordinary dividends}}{\text{number of ordinary shares}} \times 100 \text{ (pence)}$$

$$= \frac{2,541,000}{51,865,000} \times 100 \text{ pence} = 4.90 \text{ pence.}$$

Market price per ordinary share on 28 June 1986 = 160 pence.

$$\text{Dividend yield} = \frac{4.9}{160} \times 100\% = 3.06\%.$$

3. **Price earnings ratio** (based upon market price of the share on 28 June 1986) –
Market price = 160 pence.
Dividend per ordinary share = 4.90 pence.

$$\text{Price earnings ratio} = \frac{160}{4.9} = 32.65.$$

Activity

Calculate the earnings per share for Fruit & Veg Ltd for the year ended 31 May 1989.

Capital structure

This is concerned with how an organisation decides upon its long-term sources of finance.

Activity

Read through Chapter 11 again.

You should have noticed that the main problem here is to choose between two alternative ways of raising money:

1. **Borrowing or debt** (loans and debentures in a limited company), and
2. **equity** (the term normally given to the total of issued share capital and reinvested profits in a limited company).

Borrowing

In particular, an organisation must make sure that it does not over-borrow, as Laker Airways did (see pp. 109–10). If it does, it may not be able to pay the interest and loan repayments. This is more likely when interest rates are high and sales of the organisation's product(s) are low.

Activity

What would be the consequences of this for:

1. A limited company like Fruit & Veg Ltd?
2. A sole trader like Colin Smith, Greengrocer?

On the other hand, if an organisation under-borrows (i.e. its borrowing is very low), it is failing to benefit from the advantages that borrowing can give it.

ADVANTAGES OF BORROWING

1. *Borrowing enables an organisation to raise money without affecting the degree of control which existing owners have over it.* On the other hand, selling shares in a limited company results in more shareholders and so reduces the amount of power which the existing shareholders have over the company.

Example. XYZ Ltd has 1,000 shares. Susan owns 510 of these (i.e. 51 per cent of the shares). So she has 51 per cent of the votes and thus a majority at the annual general meeting. If 1,000 new shares are sold to other people, can you calculate what percentage of the shares Susan now owns?

You should have noticed that she has lost her majority.

2. *Interest on loans is tax deductible.* It is deducted from an organisation's profit and so reduces its tax liability.

3. *Lenders might expect a lower return than shareholders.* This is because they receive certain benefits that shareholders do not. In particular, they receive a guaranteed return and the option of selling their security (or collateral) if necessary. Shareholders carry more risk, because their return (i.e. dividends), particularly for ordinary shareholders, can vary from one year to the next (see Chapter 11).

So it is important for an organisation to know what its borrowing position is. The two ratios used by management accountants to do this are the organisation's **gearing ratio** and its **interest cover** (see Fig. 13.4).

GEARING RATIO

There are several ways of calculating this but the most commonly used is:

$$\frac{\substack{\text{long-term loans}^\star \text{ (debentures + other long-term} \\ \text{loans) + short-term loans and overdrafts}^{\star\star} + \\ \text{preference shares}}}{\text{ordinary shares + reserves}}$$

★ In a limited company this figure is taken from the section headed 'creditors: amounts falling due after more than one year'.
★★ In a limited company this figure is taken from the section headed 'creditors: amounts falling due within one year'.

If this ratio is greater than 2, an organisation is likely to be over-borrowing, and so it may have difficulty in meeting its interest and loan repayments. This will be particularly true for firms whose profits fluctuate greatly from one year to another, because they will struggle to meet their loan commitments when their profits are very low.

Example – Fruit & Veg Ltd on 31 May 1989 (refer again to Fruit & Veg Ltd's balance sheet on p. 65):

$$\text{Gearing ratio} = \frac{12,000 + 2,000 + 10,000}{84,000 + 4,700}$$

$$= \frac{24,000}{88,700} = 0.27.$$

Note:

Long-term loans = £2,000 (debenture loan) + £10,000 (bank loans and overdrafts) = £12,000.
Short-term loans and overdrafts = £2,000 (bank loans and overdrafts).
Preference shares = £10,000 (10,000 at £1).
Ordinary shares = £84,000 (84,000 at £1).
Reserves = £4,700.

Comment. This would indicate that Fruit & Veg Ltd has not over-borrowed.

Another way of calculating the gearing ratio is:

$$\frac{\text{long-term loans + short-term loans and overdrafts}}{\text{fixed assets + (current assets – current liabilities)}} \times 100\%.$$

If this goes above 50 per cent, it might well indicate that the organisation is over-borrowing.

Example – Fruit & Veg Ltd on 31 May 1989: Using the method of calculation above, the gearing ratio would be:

$$\frac{12,000 + 2,000}{90,800 + (11,043 - 5,343)} \times 100\%$$

$$= \frac{14,000}{196,500} \times 100\% = 7.12\%.$$

Comment. This again indicates that Fruit & Veg Ltd has not over-borrowed.

INTEREST COVER

This is calculated as follows:

$$\frac{\text{net profit before tax (excluding extraordinary items) + interest payable on loans}}{\text{total interest payable}}$$

A low interest cover (e.g. less than 2) indicates that an organisation is over-borrowing. A high interest cover (e.g. over 6) indicates that an organisation is under-borrowing and so is more likely to receive a loan from a bank, if it wants one.

Example – Fruit & Veg Ltd, year ended 31 May 1989 (refer to p. 63):

$$\text{Interest cover} = \frac{7,400 + 1,400}{1,400} = \frac{8,800}{1,400} = 6.29.$$

Comment. This is high, and so the company should have no difficulty getting a loan from the bank. This interest cover confirms the fact that the company has certainly not over-borrowed.

Activity

Calculate the gearing ratio and interest cover of H. P. Bulmer's for the years shown in the accounts (see Chapter 9).

Limitations of financial ratios

Financial ratios are an important way of assessing an organisation's financial problems. However, there are problems which result from using them.

Historical costing

Activity

Read through Chapter 12 again.

We saw in Chapter 12 that the use of historical costing in times of high inflation makes comparison between the ratios of different years more difficult. Assets bought recently will be overvalued in comparison with those bought at an earlier date, simply because prices are rising so quickly.

Large organisations

Calculating the ratios for the whole of a very large organisation (such as British Petroleum) is often not very informative. What is more useful in such circumstances is to calculate the ratios of different parts of the organisation such as its subsidiaries and/or its individual divisions.

Inter-firm comparison

Comparison between firms is made more difficult because firms can use different accounting methods, for example, to value stocks and calculate depreciation.

Out-of-date information

Ratios are based upon financial transactions that have already taken place, and so they can assess only an organisation's **past performance**. They are not so useful in predicting what will happen in the future and what is happening now.

Who wants to interpret accounts?

An organisation's management is not the only group of people who will want to look at its accounts and so obtain information about its financial performance.

Fig. 13.5: Who wants to interpret accounts?

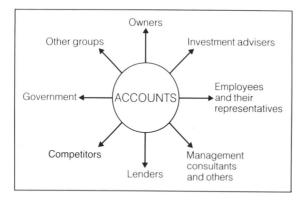

Activity

Make a list of the other groups of people who will want to interpret an organisation's accounts. You should have come up with the following (see Fig. 13.5):

Owners (e.g. shareholders)

Shareholders may want to see a company's accounts before investing in it. They will, of course, be interested in the dividend that they are paid.

Investment advisers

Financial institutions like stockbrokers will need information about a company before they decide to invest their clients' money in it.

Employees and their representatives (e.g. trade unions)

Individual employees may be interested in the performance of their organisation and in the proportion of the value added (see Chapter 9) which is given to them as wages and salaries. For this reason many large public limited companies issue glossy leaflets, and sometimes videos, summarising the information in their annual report and accounts.

Trade unions need financial information about the employers of their members. This enables them to negotiate more effectively on behalf of their members.

Activity

Think what information would be particularly useful to a trade union.

Lenders

As we saw in Chapter 11, potential lenders of money to an organisation, such as banks, will want to analyse its accounts in depth. Their main concern is making sure that, if they do give a loan, the borrower can meet the interest and loan repayments.

Competitors

An organisation's competitors will be able to pick up some useful information about its financial performance.

Government (i.e. the Inland Revenue)

The government wants to know an organisation's profit or loss, so that it can calculate the amount of tax it has to pay.

Other groups

Pressure groups, such as consumer and environmental groups, may gather information about organisations which they are campaigning against. **Management consultants** will want financial information about the organisations which they are advising. **Teachers** of accounting are also interested, as are writers of textbooks!

Activity

1. Look up pressure groups in your Organisation in its Environment textbook.
2. Find out from books in your library what management consultants do.

Interpreting accounts: summary

Whoever is looking at an organisation's accounts ought to look at the following from the last **five** years' accounts:

1. Sales (i.e. turnover)

Are sales rising steadily?

Yes – good.
No – the organisation is probably in decline.

Net profit/sales ratio

Is it rising?

Yes – good.

No – the organisation could well be in trouble; profits are not rising as fast as sales. So in the future it may not have cash to pay for more stocks, plant and machinery which the higher sales will require.

Reinvested profits

Are they sufficient to finance net asset growth, i.e. any increase in fixed assets plus current assets less current liabilities?

Yes – good.

No – the organisation could well be in trouble; again, not enough cash is being generated by it to finance its expansion.

Example – XYZ plc:

	1982	1983	1984	1985	1986
Fixed assets (£ million)	1	2	4	8	15
Current assets *less* current liabilities (£ million)	2	2	3	5	6
Net asset growth (£ million)		1*	3	6	8
Reinvested profits (£ million)	5	6	7	5	4
		Good		Danger	

* The 1983 total (£4 million) less the 1982 total (£3 million).

This company could have financial problems in 1985 and 1986, because its reinvested profits are less than its net asset growth.

Activity

Comment upon a limited company's financial position on the basis of the following information:

	1982	1983	1984	1985	1986
Fixed assets (£ million)	5	6	8	9	12
Current liabilities (£ million)	1	2	1	1.5	0.5
Reinvested profits (£ million)	6	8	4	0.5	2
Current assets (£ million)	2	3	2	2.5	2

4. Liquidity

Are the current and quick ratios relatively stable?

Yes – good; this indicates a sound liquidity position.

No – dramatic changes in the ratios might indicate problems. Big increases indicate that it is becoming over-liquid. Big decreases (particularly when they fall well below one) may indicate that it does not have enough cash.

5. Borrowing

Is the gearing ratio rising and is the interest cover falling?

Yes – danger; this could indicate that the organisation is over-borrowing.

No – the present borrowing position is more sound, and banks will be more likely to lend it money.

We shall now use the example of Laker Airways to see how this analysis can work out in practice. Then, in Chapter 14, we shall examine the importance of financial planning and control.

Case study: Laker Airways

Introduction

Laker Airways was set up as a private limited company by Sir Freddie Laker in 1966 with £211,500 of his own money. He owned 90 per cent of the ordinary shares, and his first wife owned the other 10 per cent.

In its early years the company earned high profits, largely because of the growth in the package-holiday trade during the 1960s and 1970s. Laker's dream, though, was to introduce a low-price transatlantic service with instant booking – what he called the 'Skytrain'. After a ten-year legal battle with the government and the major airlines, the first Skytrain flight from Gatwick to New York took off on 26 September 1977.

The Skytrain service was subsequently extended to Los Angeles, Miami and Hong Kong. However, by 1982 the bubble had burst. In that year the company went into liquidation. The reasons for this can be seen from an analysis of Laker Airways' accounts in the years leading up to its collapse.

Laker Airways' accounts

EXTRACTS FROM ITS PROFIT AND LOSS ACCOUNTS

	1976	1977	1978	1979	1980
Sales (£ million)	43	52	76	92	111
Net profit before tax (£000s)	564	776	1,525	2,538	191
Reinvested profits (£000s)	535	763	1,525	2,529	182

EXTRACTS FROM ITS BALANCE SHEETS

	1976	1977	1978	1979	1980
Share capital *plus*					
Reserves (£ million)	3	4	6	14	23
Loans (£ million)	25	22	37	61	111
Current liabilities					
(£ million)	10	12	18	22	31
Fixed assets (£ million)	29	27	45	83	145
Current assets (£ million)	9	11	16	14	20

Reasons for Laker Airways' collapse

Activity

On the basis of Laker Airways' accounts, calculate the following for each year:

1. Net profit/sales ratio.
2. Net asset growth.
3. Current ratio.
4. Gearing ratio (use loans as a percentage of fixed assets plus (current assets less current liabilities)).

Analysing these figures, we can identify the following points.

1. SALES

Good – they are rising.

2. NET PROFIT/SALES

Rising until 1980, but problems indicated by a sharp fall in that year.

3. REINVESTED PROFITS

All right in 1977 (net asset growth fell in that year). However, from 1978 to 1980 there was a massive gap between reinvested profits and net asset growth which would indicate that the company was expanding far too quickly.

4. LIQUIDITY

Current ratio was fairly stable up to 1978 but was lower in 1979 and 1980. This would indicate that the liquidity position was getting worse.

5. BORROWING

The company had borrowed heavily since 1976, in particular since 1979 (loans increased from £37 million in 1978 to £111 million in 1980).

Conclusions

1. The company was expanding too quickly.
2. It was borrowing too much to finance this expansion.
3. Its liquidity position was poor, despite rising profits and sales up to 1979.

Activity

On the basis of the financial information given about Fruit & Veg Ltd in Chapter 9, and about Tottenham Hotspur plc in Fig. 13.6, you are required to prepare a written report which:

1. Comments upon the liquidity, profitability and capital structure of each organisation.
2. Compares their financial performance.
3. Makes recommendations about how each organisation may be able to increase its future profitability.

Skills tested:
- Numeracy.
- Identifying and tackling problems.
- Communicating.

Fig. 13.6: Tottenham Hotspur plc – summary of financial results 1983–5

	Year ending		
	31 May	31 May	31 May
(£000)	1983	1984	1985
Fixed assets	7,946	8,227	8,654
Current assets	477	872	610
(Including stocks	114	92	50)
Creditors due within one year	2,883	1,838	1,910
(Including short-term			
loans and overdrafts	1,190	1,027	248)
Creditors due after one year	3,149	139	169
Share capital (ordinary shares			
25p)	5	2,295	2,295
Total reserves	2,386	4,827	4,890
Turnover	3,566	4,759	4,867
Net profit (loss) before tax	(449)	410	653
Net profit (loss) after tax	(430)	410	430
Ordinary dividends	—	117	367
Retained profit (or loss)	(430)	293	63

Source: Annual Report and Accounts.

14
Financial Planning and Control

Activity

List what you think are the functions of Bobby Robson, England's football team manager – in other words, what does he do?

A Frenchman, Henri Fayol (1841–1925), suggested that the functions of any manager, such as Bobby Robson, are:

1. **Planning** – deciding the objectives and policies of the organisation and preparing how to carry them out.
   (In Robson's case, the objectives are to win matches and promote the name of English football.)
2. **Controlling** – checking performance against the objectives and policies laid down in the planning stage.
   (Are England winning their football matches? If not, what can be done to improve their performance?)
3. **Organising** – determining what activities are necessary to achieve the objectives, and designing an appropriate organisational structure to carry out these activities.
   (Robson must pick the right players and choose the most effective formation – does he need a sweeper, or does he need an extra player in attack? He must also make sure his 'back-up' team is as well organised as possible – the coaches, doctor, physiotherapist, and so on.)
4. **Commanding** – supervising and helping employees to make the maximum contribution to the objectives of the organisation.
   (Robson must encourage or criticise his players, where appropriate. He must also protect them, if possible, from attacks from the media. He must inspire his players and have their respect, so that he can motivate them to do well on the pitch.)
5. **Co-ordinating** – making sure that an organisation's resources are combined in the most effective manner.

(With his captain, Robson must make sure that England work together as a team, and are all 'working for each other', as the commentators say.)

The last three of these functions will be dealt with in other areas of the course. What needs to be emphasised here is that finance is one of the resources (along with people, raw materials and buildings) which must be effectively combined by managers. This chapter concentrates on the importance of **planning** and **control**.

Functions of planning and control

Planning

Any organisation must plan for the future, so that it can, to some extent, anticipate events and so improve its performance. For example, if tobacco companies had not planned for the long-term fall in demand for cigarettes by buying businesses in other areas, they would be in a far worse financial state than they are now.

EXAMPLE – BRITISH AMERICAN TOBACCO (BAT) PLC

Up until the early 1960s tobacco sales accounted for most of BAT's profits. However, in 1962 a medical report was published which firmly linked cigarette smoking with various diseases, including lung cancer. So, faced with the probability that demand for cigarettes would be in long-term decline, BAT started to buy a range of non-tobacco businesses, including Lentheric (makers of Tweed and Charlie perfume), Argos stores and Eagle Star Insurance.

The result is that the company has become less dependent upon the profits of its tobacco products, which include Benson and Hedges, Lambert and Butler, and State Express.

Planning involves two main activities:

- **Determining the organisation's objectives.**
- **Deciding upon the policies to carry them out.**

An organisation will usually prepare plans for the year ahead (**short-term plans**), and sometimes it may also prepare **medium-term** (up to five years ahead) and **long-term plans** (up to ten or fifteen years ahead).

As we saw in Chapter 5, an organisation is likely to have primary objective(s) and secondary objectives, which are set for each section of the business, e.g. sales, production, and so on. We shall return to the subject of objectives in Chapter 15.

Controlling

This again involves two main activities:

- **Comparison between what was planned and what actually happened.**
- **Analysing the reasons for any differences and taking corrective measures, wherever possible** – e.g. to cut costs, if the organisation is spending more than was planned.

Planning and control affect all the major activities of an organisation:

MARKETING PLANNING AND CONTROL

This identifies customers' future needs and wants and how they can be best satisfied.

MANPOWER PLANNING AND CONTROL

This identifies an organisation's future manpower requirements and how they can be satisfied through recruitment, selection and training.

PRODUCTION PLANNING AND CONTROL

This identifies an organisation's future production requirements and how they can be met.

FINANCIAL PLANNING AND CONTROL

This looks at an organisation's future financial requirements and how they can be met. They are important because they help to ensure that

(a) the organisation has enough cash, and
(b) reduces its costs to a minimum, so that its profits can be as high as possible.

This is the aspect of planning and control that we shall concentrate on in this book.

Financial planning and control

How should you plan your finances, so that you can minimise your expenses and save as much as possible? If you remember, we answered this question in Chapter 2. The answer was preparing a budget (a process called **budgeting**) and then comparing what you actually spent with what you planned to spend.

This last process is, therefore, a method of controlling your spending, and for this reason it is called **budgetary control**.

This is very similar to what happens in an organisation. Financial planning within it involves a system of budgeting. Financial control involves a system of budgetary control and adequate control over debtors, creditors and stocks.

We shall deal with financial planning first and then look at financial control.

Financial planning – budgeting

Effective budgeting

An effective budgeting system needs the following (see Fig. 14.1):

Fig. 14.1: How budgeting should work

- Sales budget
- Production budget
- Capital expenditure budget
- Revenue expenditure budgets (including manufacturing overheads budget)
- Debtors and creditors budgets
- Cash budget
- Profit and loss account budget ⎫
- Budgeted balance sheet   ⎬ Master budget
                                       ⎭

CORPORATE OBJECTIVES

The objectives of the organisation must be set. This will normally include some sort of profit target, e.g. to increase profits as a percentage of sales by 5 per cent during the budget period (i.e. the period of time covered by the budgets – usually a month or a year; see below).

SALES FORECAST/PRODUCTION FORECAST

The next step is to calculate sales and production forecasts based upon the corporate objectives, e.g. it may be planned to increase them both by 10 per cent, so that profits can be increased by 5 per cent.

Any sales forecast must take into account any future changes in:

(a) The price of the organisation's product(s) (the subject of pricing is dealt with in more detail later in the chapter).

(b) The demand for its product(s).

(c) Production capacity, if a manufacturing organisation – there is no point planning to increase sales by 10 per cent if production capacity is not increased accordingly. So the production forecast is linked very closely to the sales forecast.

POLICIES

Policies for managers in each department must be worked out and adequately co-ordinated, so that the sales and production forecasts can be achieved.

BUDGETS

On the basis of these policies, budgets will be drawn up for each department and the organisation as a whole. These show the department's and the organisation's planned (or budgeted) production levels, earnings and expenditures during the budget period. This is the period of time for which a budget is prepared and used. Usually at least monthly budgets will be prepared.

Managers should be heavily involved in the preparation of these budgets because they are the people who have to carry them out. Many organisations therefore give a team of managers the job of preparing budgets. This is usually called the **budget committee**.

Main types of budget

SALES BUDGET

This outlines planned sales for the budget period, usually month by month. There will often be a column in the budget for actual sales (see Fig. 14.2), so that planned and actual sales figures can be easily compared.

Fig. 14.2: Fruit & Veg Ltd – sales budget for the year ended 31 May 1990

Month	Planned sales (£000s)	Actual sales (£000s)
June 1989	20	
July	25	
August	20	
September	20	
October	25	
November	20	
December	30	
January 1990	35	
February	30	
March	35	
April	25	
May	30	
Total	315	

Note: These planned sales figures are also in the profit and loss budget for the year (Fig. 14.4, p. 114).

PRODUCTION BUDGET

This outlines planned production levels (in units) for the budget period, usually month by month. Again there will often be a column in the budget for actual production levels, so that planned and actual production figures can easily be compared.

This budget is very important to manufacturing organisations and is closely linked to the sales budget. Planned production levels are, of course, heavily dependent upon planned sales figures.

CAPITAL EXPENDITURE BUDGET

This outlines planned expenditure on fixed assets for the budget period, usually month by month. Again there will often be a column in the budget for actual levels of capital expenditure, so that the planned and actual figures can easily be compared.

In a manufacturing organisation, the budget is arrived at after comparing planned production levels in the production budget with existing production facilities. If these facilities are inadequate, planned expenditure on fixed assets (i.e. new plant and equipment) will very probably have to increase over the budget period.

REVENUE EXPENDITURE BUDGETS

These outline planned revenue expenditures for the budget period. Again there will often be a column for actual expenditure in each expenditure budget (see the administrative expenses budget as an example in Fig. 14.3).

Fig. 14.3: Fruit & Veg Ltd – administrative expenses budget for June 1989

Administrative expenses	Planned £	Actual £
Directors' salaries	2,850	
Auditor's fees	50	
Light and heat	50	
Other administrative expenses	50	
Total	3,000	

Note: The total of planned administrative expenses is shown in the profit and loss budget for June (Fig. 14.4).

The main revenue expenditure budgets are likely to be:

1. **Administrative expenses budget** – which outlines planned administrative expenses (see Fig. 14.3).
2. **Direct materials budget** – which outlines planned expenditure on direct materials, i.e. materials used directly in the production of an organisation's product(s).
3. **Direct labour budget** – which outlines planned expenditure on direct labour, i.e. the wages and other costs of employees directly involved in the production process.
4. **Manufacturing overheads budget** – which outlines the planned level of production overheads for the budget period. Overheads are often defined as those expenditures not associated with either labour or materials (see p. 116).
5. **Increase/decrease in stock budget** – which outlines planned changes in stocks over the budget period, i.e. level of stocks at the end of the period less their level at the start of it.
6. **Distribution costs budget** – which outlines planned distribution costs. These include advertising, for which organisations may prepare a separate budget.

With information from all the budgets above, an organisation is then able to prepare a **profit and loss account budget**.

PROFIT AND LOSS ACCOUNT BUDGET

This shows a summary of the organisation's planned incomes and expenditures and its net profit before tax over the budget period (see Fig. 14.4 – compare this with Fruit & Veg Ltd's profit and loss account in Chapter 9).

DEBTORS AND CREDITORS BUDGETS

These outline the planned level of debtors and creditors at the end of the budget period.

Fig. 14.4: Fruit & Veg Ltd – profit and loss budget for the year ended 31 May 1990

£000s	June 1989	July	Aug.	Sep.	Oct.	Nov.	Dec.	Jan. 1990	Feb.	Mar.	Apr.	May	Total
Sales	20	25	20	20	25	20	30	35	30	35	25	30	315
Direct materials	11	11	11	11	11	11	11	11	11	11	11	11	132
Direct labour	2	2	2	2	2	2	2	2	2	2	2	2	24
Increase (or decrease in stock)	0	0	1	2	(1)	2	3	1	2	(2)	2	2	12
Cost of sales	13	13	14	15	12	15	16	14	15	11	15	15	168
Gross profit	7	12	6	5	13	5	14	21	15	24	10	15	147
Distribution costs	2	2	2	2	2	2	2	2	2	2	2	2	24
Administrative expenses	3	3	3	2	2	2	2	3	3	3	3	3	32
Net profit before tax	2	7	1	1	9	1	10	16	10	19	5	10	91

Note: Any decrease in stock (in brackets) is deducted from direct materials and direct labour to obtain cost of sales.

BUDGETED BALANCE SHEET

This shows a summary of the organisation's planned capital assets and liabilities at the end of the budget period (in our example, 31 May 1990). Together with the profit and loss accounts budget, it is sometimes referred to as the **master budget**. The layout of the budgeted balance sheet would look very similar to Fruit & Veg Ltd's balance sheet in Chapter 9.

CASH BUDGET

Often called a **cash flow forecast**, this outlines an organisation's planned **cash payments** and **cash receipts**, usually month by month (as in the example in Fig. 14.5).

The amount of cash held by the organisation at the beginning of each month is the 'opening balance'. The closing cash balance at the end of each month is then found by adding cash receipts to the opening balance and deducting cash payments from it, i.e.

opening balance *plus* cash receipts *less* cash payments = closing balance (see Fig. 4.5).

Such a cash flow forecast is essential, because it will indicate when an organisation might be short

of cash, and therefore when it might have to raise further finance. As we saw in Chapter 13, even a highly profitable organisation can find itself short of cash, and a cash flow forecast helps it to avoid such a shortage.

Activity

Prepare XYZ Ltd's cash flow forecast for the year ended 31 December 1987 on the basis of the following information:

(a) Cash sales – £10,000 per month.
(b) Cash from debtors – £2,000 per month.
(c) Payments to creditors – £4,000 per month.
(d) Capital expenditure – £1,000 per month.
(e) Other expenses – £1,000 per month.
(f) Opening balance on 1 January 1987 – £10,000.

Financial control

This requires four main methods of control: **budgetary control**, **debtor control**, **creditor control** and **stock control**.

Fig. 14.5: Fruit & Veg Ltd – cash flow forecast for the year ended 31 May 1990

£000s	June 1989	July	Aug.	Sep.	Oct.	Nov.	Dec.	Jan. 1990	Feb.	Mar.	Apr.	May	Total
Opening balance	6.4	7.4	8.4	6.4	4.4	5.4	0.4	5.4	10.4	9.4	11.4	10.4	85.8
Receipts													
From debtors	—	1	—	1	—	1	1	—	—	—	1	—	5
Cash sales	20	24	20	19	25	19	29	35	30	35	24	30	310
Total (A)	20	25	20	20	25	20	30	35	30	35	25	30	315
Payments													
To creditors	14	19	17	17	19	20	20	25	26	28	21	24	250
Capital expenditure	—	—	—	—	—	—	—	—	—	—	—	—	—
Other expenses	5	5	5	5	5	5	5	5	5	5	5	5	60
Total (B)	19	24	22	22	24	25	25	30	31	33	26	29	310
Add Net inflow (A−B) (*Deduct* Net outflow (B−A)	1	1	(2)	(2)	1	(5)	5	5	(1)	2	(1)	1	5
Closing balance	7.4	8.4	6.4	4.4	5.4	0.4	5.4	10.4	9.4	11.4	10.4	11.4	90.8

Notes:
1. The opening balance in June 1989 is the 'cash at bank and in hand' in the balance sheet on 31 May 1989 (i.e. £64,000 – see p. 65).
2. The closing balance in May 1990 would be shown as the 'cash at bank and in hand' figure in the budgeted balance sheet as at 31 May 1990.
3. Capital expenditure is spending on fixed assets – no such expenditure is planned by Fruit & Veg Ltd as you can see.

Budgetary control

This compares an organisation's actual incomes and expenditures with the planned incomes and expenditures in its budgets. The **budget committee** (mentioned earlier in the chapter) usually carries out this process.

Any differences between planned and actual incomes and expenditures are called **variances**, so the term **variance analysis** is often used to describe the analysis of such differences. The variance is called **favourable** when actual performance is better than what was planned in the budget. It is **adverse** where actual performance is worse.

For example, if actual expenditures are greater than planned expenditures (i.e. there is an adverse variance), this could indicate:

- *either* overspending has taken place due to inefficiency or waste;
- *or* the budget is unrealistic, i.e. planned expenditures have been set too low.

Consequently, if budgets are realistically set, budgetary control can have the following advantages:

1. **Efficiency standards** – efficiency can be measured by whether planned expenditures or incomes have been exceeded or not.
2. **Motivation** – trying to beat the standards laid down in the budgets can encourage greater efficiency and effort amongst employees.
3. **Cost control** – it discourages overspending by encouraging managers to keep within their planned expenditures.

Debtor control

Sometimes called **credit control**, this attempts to ensure that an organisation's debtors pay up on time (see p. 100).

Creditor control

This attempts to ensure that an organisation pays its creditors on time (see p. 101).

Stock control

The aim of stock control is to ensure that an organisation maintains the right balance between having too many and too few stocks (see p. 101).

Costing

This is the process of working out an organisation's costs or expenditures and is worth a special mention for a number of reasons. As we have just seen, costing is very important in the process of budgeting and budgetary control. It is also necessary for the calculation of an organisation's profits (see below) and for the calculation of its prices (as we shall also see later in the chapter).

First of all, though, it is necessary to look in some detail at what an organisation's costs are.

Types of cost

An organisation's costs can be divided up into three groups:

1. **Materials** – goods required to run the organisation, e.g. fruit and vegetables for Fruit & Veg Ltd.
2. **Labour** – all costs associated with the organisation's employees, including wages, salaries, National Insurance, and pension contributions.
3. **Overheads** – all other costs, such as rent, rates, depreciation, gas and electricity.

As we saw in Chapter 1, these costs can be either fixed or variable:

- **Fixed costs** – these do not change with the level of an organisation's sales or production in the short term, i.e. they are the same whatever the level of production/sales.

    Examples are rent and rates, insurance, auditor's fees, advertising, interest on loans and managers' salaries.

Activity

Make a list of Smith & Baptiste's fixed costs in Chapter 8.

- **Variable costs** – these do vary with the level of production/sales, i.e. they increase (decrease), when production/sales increase (decrease).

    Examples are electricity, raw materials, overtime payments and maintenance costs of machinery.

Activity

Make a list of Smith & Baptiste's variable costs in Chapter 8.

Break-even analysis

Production/sales – (a) (units)	Fixed costs – (b)	Variable costs – (c) (variable costs per unit × (a))	Total costs ((b) + (c))	Sales revenue (price × (a))
0	10,000	0	10,000	0
1,000	10,000	1,000	11,000	2,000
2,000	10,000	2,000	12,000	4,000
3,000	10,000	3,000	13,000	6,000
4,000	10,000	4,000	14,000	8,000

MARGINAL COST

Another type of cost you may come across is **marginal cost**. This is defined as the increase in total costs (i.e. fixed costs plus variable costs) which results from increasing production by one unit. Usually this is the same as variable costs per unit, which the following example should help to illustrate.

Example:

Fixed costs – £10,000
Variable costs per unit – £1
Production increase by one unit from 100 to 101 units

Total cost of 100 units = fixed costs + total
variable costs
= £10,000 + (100 × £1)
= £10,100

Total cost of 101 units = fixed costs + total
variable costs
= £10,000 + (101 × £1)
= £10,101.

Increase in total costs of increasing production by one unit (i.e. marginal cost)
= £10,101 − £10,000
= £1, which is the variable
costs per unit.

Costs and the calculation of profits

As we saw in earlier chapters, an organisation's net profit is calculated by deducting its costs (or expenditures) from its income (its sales revenue).

Information about the organisation's costs and income can also enable us to find out its **break-even point**. This refers to how many units or products the organisation has to produce or sell to make **zero profit**, i.e. where

sales revenue (selling price × units sold) = total costs (fixed costs + variable costs)

Break-even analysis

The break-even point can be calculated in two ways:

1. **By formula** –
   i.e. break-even point (in units produced or sold)

$$= \frac{\text{fixed costs (£)}}{\text{selling price (£)} - \text{variable costs per unit (£)}}$$

2. **By drawing a graph** (called a **break-even chart**) – an example will show how this is done.

EXAMPLE – MANUFACTURER OF TOY CARS

Let us assume that:

(a) Fixed costs are £10,000.
(b) The selling price of each car is £2.
(c) Variable costs per unit (i.e. per car produced) are £1.
(d) The manufacturer sells all the cars it produces.

By the formula, its break-even point is

$$\frac{10{,}000 \text{ units}}{2-1} = 10{,}000 \text{ units}.$$

To draw the break-even chart, we need to find out the total costs and sales revenue at each level of production (see break-even analysis table at top of page).

Activity

Complete the above table up to 15,000 units produced and sold. Calculate the profit or loss at each level of production/sales.

The break-even chart would look like Fig. 14.6. Notice from this that, if the manufacturer produces less than the break–even point, it will make a loss. (Why? Total costs are greater than sales revenue.) If the manufacturer produces more than the break-even point, it makes a profit. (Sales revenue is greater than total costs.)

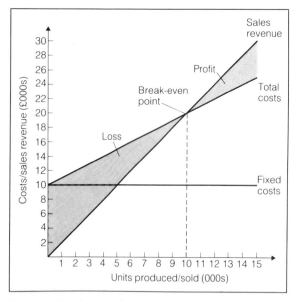

Fig. 14.6: Break-even chart

Activity

One of Fruit & Veg Ltd's shops is operating with the following revenue and cost information:

(a) Fixed costs are £50,000.
(b) Average selling price per unit = £3 (one unit = 10 lb of fruit and vegetables).
(c) Variable costs per unit are £2.

Calculate the shop's break-even point by the formula and then by drawing a break-even chart.

ADVANTAGES OF BREAK-EVEN CHARTS TO MANAGEMENT

1. They indicate how much profit or loss an organisation's product(s) make at different levels of production.
2. When assessing the introduction of a new product, its expected break-even chart can be drawn. This shows managers how much of the product will have to be produced before it makes a profit. This in turn will indicate how much investment is required in, for example, factories and equipment to make the product.
3. A product's **contribution** can be calculated (contribution per unit is defined as **selling price less variable costs per unit**). Therefore, in our example, contribution per unit is £1, and so total contribution (sales revenue *less* total variable costs) is £10,000 at the break-even point.
   The concept of contribution is useful because it indicates how much money is being earned to pay for an organisation's fixed costs.

Therefore, if its total contribution is positive i.e. sales revenue is greater than total variable costs, a firm should still continue to produce in the short term even if it is making a loss (when total costs are greater than sales revenue). The reason is that continuing to produce will help to pay off the fixed costs.

Activity

Calculate Fruit & Veg Ltd's contribution per unit in the activity above. What is its total contribution at its break-even point?

4. A break-even chart illustrates the important effect that fixed costs have on profits:
   (a) *A high level of fixed costs means that the break even profit is high* (for example, calculate Fruit & Veg Ltd's break-even point, if its fixed costs went up to £200,000). So in these circumstances a firm would have to produce and sell a lot to make a profit. Therefore, it would be more likely to make a loss if it was hit by production breakdowns, strikes or falling demand for its product.
   (b) *Low fixed costs means that a firm has a lower break-even point* (for example, calculate Fruit & Veg Ltd's break-even point if its fixed costs were £10,000). So a firm would not have to produce and sell so much to make a profit. This makes it less vulnerable to production stoppages and falls in demand.
5. A break-even chart can be used in the process of budgetary control. In other words, a budget chart can be prepared (based upon planned sales, costs and profits/losses) and then later compared with the actual break-even chart.
6. The break-even chart indicates possible ways of reducing the break-even point – increasing the selling price, reducing fixed costs and reducing variable costs per unit. This re-emphasises the importance of cost control in reducing the level of production and sales at which a firm starts to make a profit.

Activity

Calculate Fruit & Veg Ltd's break-even point in each of the following instances:

1. Its selling price increases to £4.
2. Its fixed costs are reduced to £5,000.
3. Its variable costs per unit fall to £1.

Compare these results with the original break-even point that you calculated earlier in the chapter.

PROBLEMS WITH BREAK-EVEN CHARTS

Some costs are difficult to identify as either fixed or variable and are sometimes referred to as **semi-variable costs**. The costs of a telephone are one example – telephone rental charges are fixed, but the cost of calls is variable.

Activity

Can you think of any other examples of semi-variable costs?

In a break-even chart variable costs are assumed to be the same for each unit produced. When the level of production increases, however, this may be inaccurate, because organisational difficulties may arise and managerial costs increase.

You may also have heard of something called the **law of diminishing returns** in Organisation in its Environment. This states that, with a fixed amount of land and equipment, more and more variable costs per unit (e.g. labour) will be required to increase production.

Activity

Look up the term **law of diminishing returns** in your Organisation in its Environment textbook or in an economics book in your library.

3. The chart refers only to one moment in time and so must be continually updated to reflect any changes in costs.

Costs and pricing

Pricing factors

You will find out from Organisation in its Environment that the following factors must be considered by a firm when it is setting the price of its product(s):

1. DEGREE OF COMPETITION FOR THE FIRM

The greater the competition, the lower the price.

2. PRODUCT'S PRICE ELASTICITY OF DEMAND

This measures how demand for a product is affected by changes in its price.

Activity

Look up the terms **elastic demand** and **inelastic demand** in your Organisation in its Environment textbook. Why are they relevant here?

3. GOVERNMENT POLICY

Government policies can also directly affect the prices which an organisation will charge. You will examine these in Organisation in its Environment.

Activity

Find out, from your Organisation in its Environment textbook and other books in your library, what effects the following have on the prices that a firm can charge:

1. Resale Prices Act 1964.
2. Trade Descriptions Act 1968.
3. Fair Trading Act 1973.
4. Prices and incomes policies.

4. FINDINGS OF MARKETING RESEARCH

The aim of marketing research is to find out what customers want – for example, by asking them to complete a questionnaire. One important question they can be asked is whether changes in a product's price affect whether or not they will buy that product.

The other major factor, affecting the price of a firm's product, is more the concern of this book, i.e. **the firm's costs**. Indeed, a very popular method of pricing used by organisations today is **cost-plus pricing**. The costs of producing each product are calculated and then a percentage profit (i.e. the profit margin) is added, i.e.

costs per product + profit = price

Other pricing methods

Other methods of pricing used today are:

COMPETITIVE PRICING

This means that firms fix prices in relation to the price charged by their major competitors. Competitive pricing methods include:

1. **'Going rate' pricing** – where a firm keeps its price at the average for the industry. This is

often done when the costs of producing a product are difficult to calculate, and the firm does not wish to trigger off a price war.

2. **Sealed bid pricing** (or **pricing by tender**) – here the firm makes an offer price (a tender) to gain a contract based upon its estimate of the cost involved. The tenders are kept secret until the contract is awarded to the firm offering the lowest price. This type of pricing is particularly common for building contracts, e.g. for the construction of motorways.

TRANSFER PRICING

This refers to the pricing of products produced by one subsidiary of an organisation and sold to another part of the same organisation, e.g. Cadbury's cocoa plantations selling cocoa to its British chocolate factories.

As you will see in Organisation in its Environment, multinational enterprises may use this method of pricing to minimise their tax bill.

VARIABLE PRICING

Different prices can be charged by a firm for the same product to maximise its sales and profits. Examples are cheap day returns on the railways, off-peak rates for electricity and cheaper telephone calls after 6 p.m.

Activity

Think of two other examples of variable pricing.

PSYCHOLOGICAL PRICING

Prices are set to make products look cheap, e.g. £1.99 instead of £2.

Activity

Think of three examples of psychological pricing that you have seen recently.

PRESTIGE PRICING

A firm can give prestige to its product(s) by charging prices well in excess of its competitors and its costs. Many cosmetics and clothing companies (e.g. Estée Lauder and Yves St Laurent) do this.

Activity

Think of four other products which do this.

PRODUCT-LINE PRICING

This refers to the use of **'loss leaders'** by retailers i.e. products sold at a loss. This is done to attract people into the shop so that they buy other products with higher profit margins.

Activity

When you are next in your local supermarket make a note of items which could be possible loss leaders.

Conclusion

You should now be aware of the importance to an organisation of financial planning and control, and of costing and pricing. They should be borne in mind when we look in Chapter 15 at the role of finance in organisational decision-making.

Assignment (intramodular assignment with Organisation in its Environment I and People in Organisations I)

You are working in the finance department of a small fountain-pen manufacturer which is a private limited company. It produces only one type of pen, and its sales and profits have been falling rapidly in recent years.

The firm's costs have also been rising, as you can see from the following information:

	1982	1983	1984	1985	1986
Number of pens produced and sold	150,000	120,000	100,000	90,000	70,000
Selling price of each pen	£2	£2	£2	£3	£3
Total variable costs	£150,000	£120,000	£100,000	£180,000	£140,000
Total fixed costs	£100,000	£110,000	£105,000	£95,000	£90,000
Current assets	£20,000	£40,000	£50,000	£60,000	£90,000
Stock	£2,000	£3,000	£4,000	£4,000	£4,000
Current liabilities	£3,000	£4,000	£5,000	£4,000	£3,000
Loans	—	—	—	—	—
Fixed assets + (current assets − current liabilities)	£120,000	£160,000	£150,000	£150,000	£160,000

The organisation has no system of budgetary ntrol, and as far as you can see the marketing of product leaves a lot to be desired. Indeed, many iployees describe it as 'unattractive and inelent'.

The company's production equipment is out date, and new computerised equipment would quire six fewer people in the production partment. The introduction of two new word ocessors would require two fewer employees in e administrative departments.

The age profile of the employees is:

oduction	Number
–25	5
–40	6
–55	6
er 55	7
tal	24

dministrative departments	Number
–25	3
–40	2
–55	2
er 55	2
tal	9

Faced with the company's worsening financial situation, your boss, the financial manager, has asked you to prepare:

1. A report on:

   (a) The company's profitability and liquidity position (using financial ratios and charts, where appropriate).

   (b) Recommendations to improve the company's profitability.

   (c) The implications of your recommendations for its employees.

2. An oral presentation for the board on your report, lasting fifteen minutes.

Skills tested:
- Numeracy.
- Learning and studying.
- Design and visual discrimination.
- Information gathering.
- Communicating.

15
Finance and Organisational Decision-Making

Objectives and decision-making

Activity

Re-read the case study on the Virgin Group at the end of Chapter 11. Then, on the basis of what we have discussed in the previous chapters, try to answer the following questions:

1. What is the main purpose of financial and management accounting to the Virgin company?
2. What information does financial and management accounting give to Richard Branson and his management team to enable them to make better decisions?

You should have remembered that the main purpose of both financial and management accounting is to help to achieve an organisation's objectives (in Virgin's case, making as much profit as possible).

Financial accounting also has another important objective of disclosing information about the organisation's financial position to people who are interested in its activities. These include, of course, its owners (in Virgin's case, the shareholders), its creditors, its employees, the government and people from the local community in which it operates (see p. 108).

The second question is just as important. Managers need to have as much information as possible when making decisions. They need to know how well their organisation has done in the past, so that they can learn from their mistakes and build upon their successes. They need to be informed when dealing with employee representatives within the workplace and with outside bodies such as trade unions and banks.

For example, as we saw in Chapter 11, a bank will want certain information when considering a loan application. Financial information will also be necessary to decide what pay increase, if any, the organisation can afford to pay its employees.

In this respect both financial and management accounting are particularly useful to managers.

They provide them with accurate information about their organisation in the following areas:

1. Its income and expenditure, and profit or loss.
2. Its assets and liabilities (and consequently, as we saw in Chapter 13, how much cash it has to pay off its debts).
3. Its possible sources of finance and the right one to use in a particular situation.
4. Which new products it should invest in (by estimating the costs and profitability of each alternative).
5. Which fixed assets it should buy (using investment appraisal techniques).
6. Its financial performance compared with that of its competitors.
7. How to forecast and plan its future profit and cash requirements (through, for example, the use of cash flow forecasts).
8. How to price its product(s).
9. How to control its expenditure – for example, Virgin has always acknowledged the importance of tight budgetary control.

In particular, accounting tells us that two things are essential: **profits** (or, in the case of non-profit-making organisations, **efficiency**, i.e. carrying out their activities at the lowest possible cost) and **cash**.

Profits are necessary to reward the owners of the organisation and to finance future investment. Cash is needed to pay off its debts as they become due. As we saw with Laker Airways in Chapter 13, profits are not necessarily the same thing as cash.

Activity

Re-read Chapter 13, particularly the case study on Laker Airways. Why are profits not necessarily the same thing as cash?

How accounting overlaps with other managerial activities

As we saw in Chapter 5, the role of accounting should not be seen in isolation. To use a well-worn phrase, it is a piece (although an important one) in the 'managerial jigsaw'. In other words, its activities inevitably overlap with those of specialist employees from other areas like marketing, personnel and production. So it is essential that the efforts of different employees are fully integrated and co-ordinated.

EXAMPLE – THE DEVELOPMENT OF A NEW PRODUCT

In this case accountants can provide the money necessary to finance the project and can work out appropriate budgets, so that the costs of developing the new product are kept under control. They can also make predictions about the product's costs, its future profitability and its effect upon the organisation's cash position.

Marketing specialists must identify the potential customers for the product and how their needs or wants can be best satisfied. The research-and-development and production teams must make sure that the product is as simple and cheap to produce as possible. Personnel specialists, on the other hand, must ensure that there are sufficient numbers of employees who are trained and motivated enough to produce the new product.

Activity

Think of a suitable idea for setting up a business on your college premises. Working in groups of four, identify the financial, marketing, production and personnel implications for your new business.

Every group should then give a brief talk to the other students about their findings (a different person should deal with each of the four categories).

How is co-operation between employees achieved?

To achieve co-operation between employees, a company may appoint **product** (or **brand**) **managers**, who are responsible for co-ordinating the activities of different employees – so that, for example, a new product can be developed and successfully sold to the public. As you will see in People and Organisations next year, the co-operation of employees can also be achieved through the formation of **project teams**, based upon a matrix type of organisation.

However, how difficult is it to achieve such co-operation?

Activity

Imagine that your group has been given £5,000. In groups of five briefly discuss (for about twenty minutes) what you would do with this money. Then elect a spokesperson who will report your conclusions to the rest of the course group.

Then the whole group should decide which group's conclusions to support.

You should have found out from this activity that conflicts and disagreements between individuals are inevitable when decisions have to be made.

The same thing happens in organisations. Conflicts can occur between individual employees, and these obviously make co-operation between them more difficult to achieve. You will look at this in greater detail in other parts of the course.

However, it is the job of an organisation's **top management** (e.g. the board of directors in a limited company) to make sure that co-operation is made easier by:

- taking action to reduce the amount of conflict between employees (how could this be done, do you think?); and
- ensuring that the interests of one particular department or individual(s) do not predominate to the disadvantage of everybody else (i.e. ensuring their actions do not stop the organisation's objectives being achieved).

EXAMPLE 1. – ENGLAND'S FOOTBALL TEAM

England's football manager, Bobby Robson, must make sure that his players do not argue amongst themselves on the pitch. He must also avoid one individual player playing selfishly and so damaging the team's overall performance.

EXAMPLE 2. – INDUSTRY AND COMMERCE

An organisation's accountants may wish that the development of a new product be abandoned because of its rising cost. On the other hand, the research-and-development team are likely to support its continuation enthusiastically, bearing in mind the amount of time they will have already spent on the project. These arguments – of cost v. research – were very much evident in the development of Concorde during the 1960s and early 1970s.

It is up to the top managers to resolve such conflicts. The policy they choose will be heavily dependent upon their organisation's objectives. Is policy *A* (continuing to develop a new product) more likely to achieve these objectives than policy *B* (dropping the new product)?

An organisation's objectives are such an important factor in decision-making that we shall have to look at the subject in greater detail now.

Organisational objectives

Activity

Define the objectives of your college. Who do you think determines these objectives? How do they differ from those of a large public company like H. P. Bulmer's?

When thinking about these questions you should have come up with two general conclusions:

1. An organisation's objectives are determined to a large extent by the values and attitudes of those people who run it (shareholders and management for Bulmer's, and the local authority and the college management for your college).
2. Objectives can differ from one type of organisation to another, for reasons which we shall now discuss.

Factors affecting an organisation's objectives

The factors affecting an organisation's objectives can be summarised as:

1. **Ownership**
   (a) *Private sector* – profit objectives important.
   (b) *Public sector* – non-financial objectives more important.
2. **Size of the organisation**
   (a) *Small businesses* – owners control them, and so profit objectives are important.
   (b) *Large businesses* – managers are not owners, and so non-financial objectives may be more important.
3. **Social considerations**
   Social responsibilities – an organisation's responsibilities towards its stakeholders (customers, employees, local community, owners and creditors):
   (a) They have certain advantages, e.g. avoiding government legislation.
   (b) They may decrease short-term profits but increase long-term profits.

We now look at these factors in turn.

OWNERSHIP

Organisations in the private sector, which are owned and controlled by private groups and individuals, are likely to have different objectives to firms in the public sector, which are owned and controlled by the government.

Activity

Have a look at your Organisation in its Environment notes on nationalised industries. Then explain how Fruit & Veg Ltd's objectives are likely to differ from those of British Rail.

With some exceptions, such as charities and building societies, organisations in the private sector place a great emphasis upon financial objectives, i.e. making as much profit as possible.

In the public sector, non-financial objectives become more important, although financial considerations, such as keeping costs to a minimum, are still taken into account.

Example. A college or hospital has to be efficiently run, but its main objective is to provide either education to children, or health care to the public in a particular area.

We shall examine the objectives of public-sector organisations in greater detail later in the chapter.

SIZE OF THE ORGANISATION

Small organisations in the private sector (sole traders, partnerships and private limited companies) are controlled by their owners, so that making a profit will be particularly important to them. Profits are needed for reinvestment and to give the owners a return on the money they have put into the business. Non-financial objectives, such as personal independence ('being your own boss') and doing something enjoyable, are also likely to be important.

Activity

List five reasons why you might set up your own business. How many of them are financial?

However, some people, such as the Canadian economist, J. K. Galbraith, have argued that in large public limited companies, non-profit objectives may be even more important than in smaller businesses. They say that the people who control such companies, their managers and directors, do not have a major stake in the ownership of their com-

...anies, i.e. they are not major shareholders. Therefore, they may be prepared to sacrifice profits in pursuit of their own personal objectives, such as:

- Maximising their perks, e.g. company cars.
- Increasing their power and status.
- Taking into account social considerations – the topic we turn to next.

SOCIAL CONSIDERATIONS

When determining their organisation's objectives, managers may well take into account its **social responsibilities**. These can be defined as an organisation's responsibilities towards its customers, its employees, the community in general, its owners and its creditors (e.g. banks). These are sometimes called its **stakeholders**, and it is the job of management to strike a balance between their different interests.

Example. A decision to voluntarily reduce the pollution from a firm's factories may be made to further the interests of its employees and the local community, even though it costs money, reduces profits and so appears to harm the interests of its owners.

Activity

Identify the stakeholders of your college and list what their different interests are.

Some people believe that 'socially responsible' policies should be voluntarily pursued by organisations, even at the expense of profits, and that **social audits** should be carried out to monitor and record them. Arguments normally put forward for such policies are:

1. They improve the public image of business and discourage the need for government intervention and legislation (e.g. to reduce pollution), which may be expensive to regulate and difficult to enforce.
2. They take into account the morals and ethics of managers.
3. Without such policies, managers would be subject to action from pressure groups, e.g. environmental groups like Friends of the Earth, and possibly the government (through more legislation and regulation). The consequences of such action may be even more undesirable than those of voluntary action.

The relevance of social responsibilities towards your course is that they may result in managers making decisions where financial (i.e. profit and cost) considerations are of only secondary importance.

Before we discuss in detail the areas of policy where this is most likely to happen, one important point must be made: *socially responsible policies may be expensive and so reduce an organisation's profits in the short term, but in the long term they may actually increase profits.*

For example:

- Measures, such as job enrichment (look this term up in your library), make employees' jobs more interesting and satisfying. So they are likely to improve the quality of their work, increase their productivity (the amount produced per employee) and thus increase their organisation's profits. They may also reduce the number of employees leaving (i.e. reduce labour turnover – look this up as well) and so decrease the costs of recruiting, selecting and training new staff.
- Strict product quality standards obviously protect customers' interests but also encourage them and others to buy the product again – creating what marketing experts call **brand loyalty**.

Activity

Make a list of ten products which you consider to have brand loyalty. Then find out which companies make them and how profitable each of them is (use a copy of *The Times 1,000* for this from your college or local library).

Is there any relationship between the profitability of a company and brand loyalty for its product(s)?

We shall see at the end of this chapter how one company, Marks & Spencer plc, puts these ideas about social responsibilities into practice. First of all, though, we must discuss the policy areas where financial factors (i.e. those concerned with profit and costs) may become secondary.

Where financial factors are secondary in decision-making

Policy areas where financial factors are secondary in decision-making can be identified under the following headings and summarised as:

1. **Customers – marketing policies** (see pp. 126–7)
   (a) *Public relations.*
   (b) *Consumer protection legislation.*
   (c) *Social marketing* (marketing for non-profit-making organisations).

2. **Employees – personnel policies** (see p. 127)
   (a) *Motivation* (non-financial factors important such as the interesting nature of the job).
   (b) *Employee relations* (managements have to take trade unions into account).
   (c) *Employment legislation* (forces managements to spend money on things which help employees).
3. **The community in general** (see p. 128)
   (a) *Sponsorship of sport and the arts.*
   (b) *Measures to reduce pollution.*
4. **Owners and creditors** (see p. 128)
   Disclosure of financial information which is expensive to prepare.
5. **The state** (see p. 128)
   (a) *As a legislator.*
   (b) *As a buyer* (preference for 'buying British').
   (c) *As an employer* (non-financial reasons for government-run organisations).

These areas will now be considered in turn.

Customers – marketing policies

Activity

Read up about marketing in your Organisation in its Environment textbook. Then write *in one sentence* what it is concerned with.

You should have said that marketing is concerned with **satisfying customers' needs and wants**. It is all about putting the organisation's customers first. Their needs and wants must be identified, and then products must be produced and sold which can satisfy those needs and wants.

Activity

Think of which of your needs and wants the following products satisfy:

1. Your toothpaste.
2. Your aftershave/perfume.
3. A pop record.
4. A car.

Various marketing techniques are used by managements to achieve this objective of satisfying customers, including market research and advertising. You will examine these in more detail in other areas of the course like Organisation in its Environment and People in Organisations.

Financial considerations are obviously uppermost in management's mind when carrying out this marketing philosophy of satisfying the customer. This will generate more business and more profit. However, there are three areas of marketing where such financial considerations are likely to be secondary:

1. PUBLIC RELATIONS

Activity

Look this term up in your library.

You should have found out that public relations is concerned with improving an organisation's public image (or **corporate image**, as marketing experts call it) through, for example, sponsoring sports events and helping charities. An organisation may be willing to spend money in this way even though the immediate financial benefit from it in terms of increasing profits is likely to be small.

A good recent example of this is the money that has been provided by the cigarette companies through their representative body, the Tobacco Advisory Council, to discourage smoking by the under-sixteens.

Activity

List five ways through which your college might be able to improve its public image.

2. CONSUMER PROTECTION LEGISLATION

Activity

Using your Organisation in its Environment textbook, complete the following tasks:

1. Identify the main objectives of consumer protection legislation.
2. List five Acts of Parliament related to consumer protection and briefly outline their provisions.

The main objective of consumer protection legislation is to protect consumers (i.e. customers) from defective and dangerous products. It is necessary because some organisations may be tempted to produce and sell defective and perhaps dangerous products in an attempt to cut their costs and so increase their short-term profits. Their profits in the long term may well fall, though, because of the bad name their products have earned.

Any organisation must take account of these laws in its decision-making, and this is why you study them in some detail in other areas of your course. In addition, an organisation must take into account the actions of consumer pressure groups like the Consumers' Association, which publishes *Which?* magazine.

3. SOCIAL MARKETING

This is the term given to marketing as applied to non-profit-making organisations like charities and hospitals. All of these organisations have customers' needs and wants to satisfy, and so effective marketing policies are still essential, even though profit is not a major consideration for them.

Activity

Identify the customers of the following organisations:

1. Your college.
2. Oxfam.
3. Your local hospital.

What are their needs and wants?

Employees – personnel policies

The Institute of Personnel Management (the professional body representing personnel managers) defines personnel management as '**that part of management which is concerned with people at work and with their responsibilities within an enterprise**'. Its purpose is to ensure that an organisation has enough employees to carry out its activities. It must also make sure they combine together effectively when at work. Therefore, it is the concern of *every* manager within an organisation and not just of a few specialists who work in the personnel department.

Personnel management helps to increase an organisation's profits by improving employees' performance and effectiveness. This is particularly true of three subjects that it is concerned with:

- **Manpower planning**.
- **Job evaluation**.
- **Performance appraisal**.

Activity

Look these terms up in your library and make a note of what they are. List some reasons why you think they might be able to increase an organisation's profits.

However, there are three other areas covered by personnel management where non-financial considerations become more important. They are motivation, employee relations and employment legislation:

1. MOTIVATION

Activity

Look up the term **motivation** in your library. Then read and make brief notes on the work of F. Herzberg in any management textbook.

Motivation is the study of what makes employees work harder. Present evidence, based upon the work of people like Herzberg, suggests that non-financial factors like job content are just as important as money in this respect. So schemes like job enrichment (you looked this up earlier, remember!) have been introduced which give people greater responsibility and interest in their work.

Activity

On the basis of a job you have done recently (paid or unpaid – you could choose your 'job' as a student), rate each of the following factors according to how important they were in making you work harder (10 points for extremely important, through to 0 for not important at all):

1. Pay.
2. Relations with superiors.
3. Relations with colleagues.
4. Working conditions.
5. Responsibility involved in the job.
6. How worthwhile the job was.

Your findings should then be discussed amongst the whole group.

2. EMPLOYEE RELATIONS

This is concerned with matters arising from employer–employee relations, such as dismissals, redundancies, health and safety, and negotiations with trade unions over pay and working conditions.

Employees and trade unions must be considered by managements in their decision-making. The threat or use of industrial action, such as strikes, may force them to pay higher wages and to delay the introduction of new technology and more efficient working practices. Profits are consequently sacrificed for industrial peace.

The classic example of this is the newspaper industry, where print unions have been able to negotiate high wages and, until recently, delay the introduction of new computer technology. This technology makes the printing process easier and cheaper.

Activity

Using books from your library, make a list of the possible types of action that trade unions can take against management.

3. EMPLOYMENT LEGISLATION

Personnel management is directly concerned with legislation which gives rights to trade unions and to individual employees. This can force management to spend money on things which help their employees – for example, paying compensation to an employee who has been unfairly dismissed.

Activity

Using your Organisation in its Environment textbook, find out five rights which have been given to individual employees and/or trade unions by legislation.

The community in general

This refers to policies which directly attempt to benefit the community within which the organisation operates. Apart from providing employment and wealth, this may include **sponsorship of sport and the arts** and, in particular, measures to **protect the environment** from pollution created by the organisation. Some firms may do this voluntarily, but they must also abide by anti-pollution laws like the Clean Air Acts.

Activity

List the advantages and disadvantages of cigarette companies sponsoring sport. Then have a debate about it in your group.

Owners and creditors

Profits are crucial to satisfying the interests of a profit-making organisation's owners (shareholders in a company) and creditors. Profits enable it to pay owners a return on their investment (dividends for shareholders) and also to repay debts to creditors.

In addition, as we have seen throughout this book, the various Companies Acts make sure that limited companies disclose adequate and accurate information to both owners and creditors, so that they can invest in a company with their eyes wide open. Without these Acts, such disclosure of information might not take place, because of the expense involved.

The state

Businesses often give advice to governments on the formulation of economic policy, through bodies like the Confederation of British Industry (CBI). In addition, the state (i.e. the government) has the following influence upon an organisation's decision-making:

1. AS A LEGISLATOR

As we have seen, organisations must obey laws concerning, for example, consumer protection, employment protection, the environment and companies.

2. AS A BUYER

Governments are more likely to buy from British firms, even though they might be able to get a better deal from overseas ones. The reason is to protect jobs in this country. For example, the police force, wherever possible, buys British cars.

3. AS AN EMPLOYER

There are reasons why governments prefer to own and control certain organisations, like nationalised industries and hospitals. Some of them are financial; e.g. it may be more efficient to have one big government-run organisation in an industry than several smaller ones which are privately owned. However, there are also some important non-financial reasons:

(a) **Social** – government enterprises can provide social necessities such as education and health care to everyone free or at a low price. They can also provide services which make a loss but are considered worthwhile, such as postal and railway services in rural areas. Loss-making services may also be kept open to prevent redundancies in areas of already high unemployment. If you remember, this was one of the major issues of the 1984–5 coal strike.

(b) **Political** – the Labour Party has always traditionally been in favour of greater government control over the economy.

:) **Security** – for security reasons it is best to have atomic energy, the police and the armed forces run by the government.

Activity

Discuss in your group the view that 'all state intervention in business is a waste of time and money'.

Case studies: Marks & Spencer and BL

Marks & Spencer plc: a case study in social responsibilities

Marks & Spencer, possibly more than any other company, acknowledges the fact that it has responsibilities not only to its shareholders but also to its customers, employees, suppliers and the local community.

Ever since Michael Marks started the business as a stall in Leeds Market in 1884, the company's primary concern has always been to satisfy the needs and wants of its customers. It does this by offering them a fairly narrow range of high-quality and well-designed goods at reasonable prices, all of them sold under the St Michael brand name. Marks & Spencer achieves this aim through a high level of administrative efficiency and cost control and, as we shall see, through its special relationship with its suppliers. The company's employee relations policy also ensures that its employees are well trained and motivated to serve customers in the most effective way.

Marks & Spencer's top management has always attached great importance to personnel management. The company is renowned for the benefits it gives to its employees: excellent canteen facilities, above-average wages, free dental and medical treatment, a company pension plan and a profit-sharing scheme. It even provides hairdressing and chiropodist services. It also spends much time and money on staff training and consulting employees over decisions which directly affect them.

The company's commitment to the community is unquestionable. In 1981 it gave more money to charities (£1,205,000) than any other company, over half of which went to medicine, education, welfare and the arts. Employees are encouraged to participate in fund-raising activities and are given secondment for community projects aimed at job creation and training for unemployed young people. Marks & Spencer also participates in the government's Youth Training Scheme and has devised schemes to help small businesses in the inner cities.

However, it is the company's special relationship with its suppliers which makes it unique. Ever since 1924 Marks & Spencer has bought its goods direct from manufacturers, and has built up a very close relationship with them. It encourages them to adopt the Marks & Spencer style of management and helps them to increase efficiency by assisting them with modernisation of their plant and machinery and providing advice over factory administration, layout and production problems. This helps the manufacturers to meet the strict guidelines, laid down by Marks & Spencer for the quality and production of their goods.

Despite these guidelines, Marks & Spencer's suppliers benefit from the fact that they are given guaranteed orders. It is no coincidence that major St Michael suppliers like Coral (makers of knitwear) and Dewhirst (makers of suits, jackets and skirts) have consistently earned better profits than the rest of the UK textile industry. Marks & Spencer's policy of buying British, wherever possible, means that these benefits are largely reaped by British companies, which helps the UK economy. More than 90 per cent of the goods it sells are made in Britain.

Marks & Spencer is living proof that a socially responsible organisation can be highly successful. It is one of the most profitable companies in the UK, and over recent years its growth rate has been astonishing. Indeed, you could say that its socially responsible policies have directly contributed to its success.

This success has also enabled the company to be generous. For example, its employees have not had to be made redundant, unlike in BL in recent years where many thousands have been put out of work in an attempt to reduce costs and return the company to profitability. We shall now look at the BL case in more detail, particularly when Sir Michael Edwardes was its chairman, appointed by the government to get the company back into shape in the 1970s.

Activity

What are the advantages and disadvantages (if any) of Marks & Spencer's policies for:

1. Its shareholders.
2. Its employees.
3. Its creditors.
4. The local community.
5. The government.

BL under Michael Edwardes

BL (or British Leyland, as it used to be called) came into existence in 1968 through the merger of British Motor Holdings and the Leyland Motor Corporation. The former company owned Austin, Morris and Jaguar, and Leyland manufactured trucks and buses and also owned Standard-Triumph and Rover.

As the one remaining British-owned mass producer of motor vehicles, BL's success was (and still is) considered essential to the UK economy. For example, the *Guardian* newspaper estimated in October 1981 that the effects of BL's closure would be:

	1982	1983
National output	−0.62%	−0.77%
Unemployment	+204,000	+230,000
Balance of payments (£ billion)	−0.7	−0.5
Public sector borrowing requirement: (PSBR) (£ billion)	+0.9	+1.4
Public spending (£ billion)	+0.2	+0.37
Investment	−0.5%	−1.0%

Source: *Guardian*, October 1981.

Activity

1. Look up all the terms in the table above in your library. (Be careful – investment is *not* savings but the economist's definition of the word.)
2. Using the *Annual Abstract of Statistics*, find out what the changes in national output and investment would have been in money terms.

The higher PSBR would be the result of the costs of higher unemployment in terms of higher unemployment benefit and losses in tax revenue. This higher unemployment would occur not only within BL but also amongst its component suppliers such as Lucas Industries (providers of electrical fittings) and Chloride (suppliers of batteries).

The lower national output would result from fewer goods being made and sold by UK firms, so reducing the country's wealth. This would also hit the balance of payments – BL's exports would be lost, and car imports would be likely to rise.

You will look at these issues in greater depth in the second year of your Organisation in its Environment course. However, you should be able to see why both Labour and Conservative governments have been committed to BL's survival and have been prepared to give it money since the mid-1970s. Without it, the company would have certainly gone out of business. For example, in the year 1974–5 alone the company made a net loss of £300 million.

However, governments wanted some assurance that the company would be more efficiently run and would eventually eliminate its losses, and so return to profitability again. This was the job given to Michael Edwardes in 1977 as BL's new chairman.

WHAT EDWARDES INHERITED

A report on the British motor vehicle industry in 1975 concluded that the problems of the industry and the companies within it, including BL, were caused by:

1. **Too much production capacity** – i.e. too many manufacturers and plants.
2. **Too many models** – BL was the worst offender in this respect. In 1975 it had twelve different models. This meant that no single model could be produced in sufficiently large quantities to benefit from **economies of scale** (look this term up in your Organisation in its Environment textbook).
3. **Poor quality and unreliable products.**
4. **Poor delivery records** – to some extent caused by strikes.
5. **Poor relations between management and employees** – resulting in poor quality workmanship, and strikes, which reduced production levels.
6. **Low productivity** – caused by inefficient working practices (e.g. more people doing a job than is required) and lack of investment in new plant and machinery.

These problems had become so serious at BL in 1975 that the government called in some experts to make proposals for the company's future. However, the result, the **Ryder Plan**, was not a great success. In particular, the organisation structure it recommended was inefficient.

Michael Edwardes was then called in to pick up the pieces.

WHAT EDWARDES DID

In an attempt to achieve long-term profitability for the company, Edwardes carried out the following policies:

1. **Management reorganisation** – his principal objective was to decentralise management, i.e. split the company up into different sections and

let them work more or less independently. For example, the Cars Division was split up into:

(a) Austin–Morris.
(b) Specialist Cars (Jaguar–Rover–Triumph).
(c) BL Components (manufacturer of car bodies and components).

It was hoped that this would increase the identification of workers and management with their particular factory and so make them work harder.

2. **Rationalisation of model range** – the number of car models was reduced, and a completely new model range was gradually introduced: the Metro (in 1980), the Maestro (1983), the Montego (1984) and the Rover 800 (1986). The Rover was developed in collaboration with Honda of Japan. Such collaboration was considered vital to enable BL to compete more successfully with its much bigger competitors in the USA, Japan and Europe. In particular, it provided extra cash to develop new models.

3. **Reduced costs** – this was achieved by the closure of car, bus and truck factories (ten major plants were closed by Edwardes), the introduction of strict cost controls, and large-scale redundancies. In fact, BL's work-force was more than halved from 1978 to 1984; it had 198,000 employees in 1978 and 96,001 in 1984.

   Through these measures BL claims to have reduced its fixed costs by at least £250 million p.a. from their 1978 level. The advantage of this to the company is that this reduces its break-even point (as we found out in Chapter 14).

4. **Investment in new plant and machinery** – BL's remaining factories were completely modernised, using new microelectronic technology. Robots are used for welding, paint spraying and fitting windscreens. Computer-aided engineering has also been introduced, which allows design details of a new car to be drawn on a VDU using a light-pen.

5. **Purchasing policy** – after 1977 BL became more conscious of the price and quality of products from its UK suppliers. Raw materials and components account for about 60 per cent of the cost of a car. However, a survey carried out by BL in 1980 found that only 30 per cent of its UK suppliers were as competitive as their overseas rivals. So BL changed some suppliers to ensure that it got the best possible deal from them in terms of price and quality.

6. **Employee relations** – Edwardes adopted a tough approach to BL's trade unions from the start. Derek Robinson (called 'Red Robbo' by the popular newspapers), one of the most powerful union figures in the company, was sacked. The Transport and General Workers' Union (TGWU) was also defeated during the 1979 pay dispute.

Helped by these successes and by the fear of redundancies amongst the employees, Edwardes managed to keep wage increases down, reduce the number of strikes to virtually zero and introduce more efficient working practices.

CONCLUSION: WHAT DID EDWARDES ACHIEVE?

Edwardes's reign at BL did produce some substantial benefits. He managed to increase productivity (production per employee) significantly and to introduce a new model range which has been generally well received. The decentralised management structure works well, and he put paid to the myth that BL's work-force was unmanageable.

However, BL is not out of the woods yet. It is still heavily dependent upon government finance. In 1985 its share of the UK car market was only 17.9 per cent (19 per cent is required for the company to break even); and there is no guarantee that the improvement in employee relations is permanent. There is evidence that many employees deeply resented Edwardes's 'bully-boy' tactics, and the still relatively poor quality of BL's cars indicates that employees may not be as committed to the organisation as they could be.

From our point of view, Edwardes's policies provide an interesting case study of the role that finance can play in organisational decision-making. We have seen that cost control and the need for cash were of paramount importance, but just as important was getting the marketing, personnel and production policies right, so that profits could be increased and the need for government finance removed. Efficient production techniques, satisfying customers' requirements through good models and the co-operation of the work-force were just as necessary as effective accounting policies.

Activity

1. Compare the approaches of Marks & Spencer and BL to employee relations. Would Marks & Spencer's approach have worked at BL?
2. List the possible ways in which BL could improve its financial performance still further.
3. List BL's main competitors in the truck and car markets. Are their models better or worse than BL's? Give reasons for your answer.

Conclusion

You might have gathered from this chapter that a manager's lot is not necessarily an easy or a happy one! Top management must ensure that all the different functions within the organisation – finance, production, marketing and personnel – are properly co-ordinated, so that organisational objectives can be achieved. To do this it must obtain the co-operation of the work-force, which is not always easy, as BL's history shows.

Managers must also cope with the fact that there are factors outside their organisation which are beyond their control but still have an important influence upon decision-making. These factors are:

1. **Changes in the economic environment** – e.g. changes in customers' incomes, inflation, unemployment, interest rates, exchange rates and competitors' products.
2. **Changes in the social environment** – e.g. changes in people's values and attitudes, and the actions of pressure groups.
3. **Changes in the political/legal environment** – e.g. changes in legislation and new governments.
4. **Changes in the technological environment** – e.g. new scientific discoveries and advances in computer technology.

Computers are having an increasingly important impact upon organisational decision-making, as the robots at BL clearly show. They and their effects upon accounting are the subject of Chapter 16.

Assignment (intramodular assignment with Organisation in its Environment I)

Archangel is a beautiful Welsh town in the middle of some of the loveliest countryside in the United Kingdom. Tourists from home and abroad come to see its beauty. It is also a popular place to live.

Property prices in the town have gone up considerably in recent years – much quicker, in fact, than the national average.

New properties and businesses are being built all the time, but in small numbers. The local authority (Cymru County Council) is keen to control development, so that the beauty of the town can be preserved and local amenities are not over stretched. In fact, with the town's present population (4,000), the schools are full and its doctor cannot take many more patients.

Local-authority policy in this respect has been supported by people owning houses in the town (mostly retired people and people who commute to work in a city twenty-five miles away). However the policy has met with some opposition from young people in the area, who want to see new jobs created. Unemployment in the area is above the national average.

Against this background, a local building company (Bricks & Mortar Ltd) has proposed a plan to build some houses and a small industrial estate in a beautiful spot on the outskirts of the town.

You are required to:

1. Carry out a debate in your group about whether the development should take place. One-half of the group should present the arguments of the local ratepayers' association. The other half should represent the views of Bricks & Mortar Ltd.
2. Prepare a report on behalf of Cymru County Council's planning department, recommending whether or not planning permission should be given to the development. The report must include a detailed analysis of the arguments for and against the proposal.

Skills tested:
- Identifying and tackling problems.
- Information gathering.
- Communicating.
- Working with others.

PART SIX
The Future Role of Computers

16
Computers and Accounting

Introducing computers

IT – is this another Steven Spielberg movie? No, it certainly is not! As you probably know already, it refers to **information technology**, which in turn is concerned with the computerisation of activities carried out at work and at home.

The reason why IT has become such a topical issue in recent years is that computer technology has advanced very fast since the first electronic computer was invented in 1946. The most important changes are that computers have become:

- much smaller;
- much cheaper and so more widely available to both individuals and businesses;
- much more powerful, i.e. they can be applied to a large number of jobs;
- easier to operate.

The reason for these developments is the invention of the first **microprocessor** in 1975. This allows a computer (called a **microcomputer** – see below) to carry out many complex tasks. However, the processor can be printed upon a piece of silicon, called a **micro chip**, which is smaller than a postage stamp.

The microcomputer has made information technology available to even the smallest of organisations, such as sole traders, and also to the vast majority of people in Britain.

Activity

Think of how many products have a microprocessor in them.

You may have come up with things like electronic games (Space Invaders, Pac Man, etc.), digital clocks and watches, electronic calculators, and microcomputers such as the Sinclair ZX80 and the Acorn BBC.

What you probably did not mention, however, is the impact that computers are having upon organisations in both the private and public sectors. We mentioned in Chapter 15, for example, the use that BL has made of robots to produce its cars.

Computers are also having a major impact upon accounting, and this is what we shall be concentrating on in this chapter. First of all, we must introduce you to the computer jargon in use today, even though some or all of it may be familiar to you already.

The different types of computer

MAINFRAME COMPUTERS

These are large (although getting smaller) and very powerful. Because they are so expensive, they are used only by larger organisations. The mainframe computer market is dominated by IBM, the United States company.

The usefulness of mainframe computers is increased by the fact that terminals (with a keyboard and a screen) can be linked to the computer and distributed throughout an organisation. This allows its employees to use the computer for such things as electronic mail, viewdata and word processing (see later in the chapter).

MINICOMPUTERS

A minicomputer is about the size of a small filing-cabinet and can have terminals linked to it, like a mainframe computer.

MICROCOMPUTERS (SOMETIMES CALLED 'PERSONAL COMPUTERS')

As we have already said, these now probably have the greatest impact upon businesses, particularly upon smaller ones. Two of the leading manufacturers of business microcomputers are Apple and IBM.

How does a computer operate?

A computer has two major components: its **hardware** and its **software**.

HARDWARE

This is the name given to the computer's physical pieces of equipment, which can be seen and touched. These are:

1. **Input devices** – used to enter data (i.e. words or figures) or instructions into the computer. The most common input device is a **keyboard**, which makes keyboarding skills so useful when operating a computer. Information can also be put into the computer by floppy or hard disks (see below).
2. **Central processing unit (CPU)** – commonly known as the **microprocessor** (which we mentioned earlier) or the **central processor**. It makes sure that the computer carries out the tasks it has been asked to do.
   The CPU has a **memory unit** which allows it to store data, so that it can make many calculations at the same time. These calculations are carried out by the CPU's **arithmetic unit**.
3. **Storage devices** – used to store data put into the computer, so that it can be retrieved at a later date and perhaps modified, e.g. making alterations to a report which has been stored in the computer. They are also used to store programs (see below in the 'Software' section). Notice, the spelling is **program** not 'programme'.
   The most commonly used storage devices in business microcomputers are:

(a) **Floppy disks** (yes, spelt like this, not 'disc'!) – light and flexible, made of vinyl and a bit similar to pop records. They are also portable and so susceptible to accidental damage.
(b) **Hard disks** (sometimes called Winchester disks) – sealed units and actually built into the computer. They are not portable and so not liable to accidental damage. Most microcomputers with hard-disk storage also have the facility to insert additional information (e.g. a software programme) with a floppy disk.

4. **Output devices** – used to display and record information obtained from the computer. The two main output devices are:

(a) The **printer** – which automatically types out material from the computer.
(b) The **visual display unit (VDU)** – a television-type screen, which can display graphs, tables, documents, etc.

SOFTWARE

This refers to instructions fed into the computer which control it and enable it to carry out certain tasks. These instructions are contained in **computer programs**, sometimes called **software packages** (or packages, for short).

An organisation can write its own programs (or hire a software company to do the job for it), so that its specific requirements are met exactly. This is mostly likely to occur only in the largest accountancy firms, because of the high cost involved.

Alternatively an organisation can buy a software package which has already been prepared by a computer software company. A wide variety of these packages are now available (see later in the chapter). They are also relatively cheap, so that most organisations with computers use them, particularly the smaller ones.

Summary

We can now summarise how a computer operates

Fig. 16.1: How a computer operates

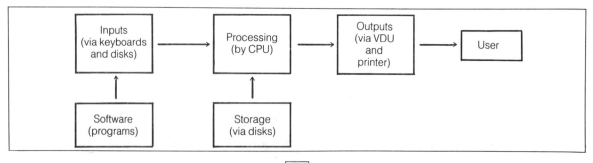

(see Fig. 16.1) and then illustrate this with a simple example.

EXAMPLE – AN ELECTRONIC CALCULATOR

Inputs: press 2, '+', 2, and '='.
Processing: calculation made by the microprocessor in the calculator, almost instantaneously.
Output: the answer, 4, on the screen of your calculator.

Computer applications in accounting

The use of computers in accounting can be summarised under the following headings:

1. **Spreadsheet**.
2. **Database**.
3. **Sales ledger**.
4. **Purchases ledger**.
5. **Nominal ledger**.
6. **Stock control**.
7. **Payroll**.
8. **Electronic mail**.
9. **Digital PABX**.
10. **Teletext and viewdata**.
11. **Word processing**.
12. **Graphics**.

We will now look at each application in turn.

Spreadsheet

Spreadsheets provide the user with a large 'electronic' sheet on the VDU which is ideal for preparing cash flow forecasts and helping with budgets. **Visicalc** is probably the most widely used spreadsheet package, although others on the market include Supercalc, Multiplan and Lotus 123.

More sophisticated packages are also available for financial planning purposes, sometimes called **financial modelling** packages.

VISICALC – AN EXAMPLE

The Visicalc spreadsheet is arranged as 254 rows (numbered 1 to 254) and columns labelled A, B, C, etc. Column A is used to identify what is in the other columns, e.g. sales or payments. Each column is nine characters (or letters) wide.

For example, a display like Fig. 16.2 can be shown on a VDU screen.

The figures in Column B would have been entered in by the user, but the other columns would have been calculated by the computer. These calculations were based upon the following assumptions which had been fed into it:

Fig. 16.2: Spreadsheet display

	A	B	C	D	E
1.	CASH FLOW	1987	1988	1989	
2.					
3.	BAL. BF	2,000	2,500	3,100	
4.					
5.	RECEIPTS				
6.	SALES	4,000	4,400	4,840	
7.					
8.	TOTAL	4,000	4,400	4,840	
9.					
10.	PAYMENTS				
11.	TO. CRED.	2,000	2,200	2,420	
12.	CAP. EXPEN.	500	500	500	
13.	OTHER EXP.	1,000	1,100	1,210	
14.					
15.	TOTAL	3,500	3,800	4,130	
16.					
17.	BAL. CF	2,500	3,100	3,810	
18.					
19.					
20.					

Note:
BAL. BF = balance brought forward, i.e. opening balance.
TO. CRED = to creditors.
CAP. EXPEN. = capital expenditure.
OTHER EXP. = other expenses.
BAL. CF. = balance carried forward, i.e. closing balance.

1. Sales and other expenses both increase by 10 per cent per year.
2. Payments to creditors are 50 per cent of sales revenue.
3. Capital expenditure does not change.

The package could also automatically work out the cash flow situation in each year, if one or more of these assumptions changed; e.g. payments to creditors are 70 per cent of sales revenue, not 50 per cent as previously.

Database packages

These can be used to file information in the computer about, for example, sales by product. The computer can then pick out from these files specific pieces of information for the user, e.g. the best selling product during the past year.

Sales ledger

The details of each of an organisation's customers are stored on a disk, e.g. account number, name and address, balance outstanding.

This means that a computer with a sales ledger package can produce:

1. A particular customer's details, which can be displayed on the VDU at any time by quoting the appropriate account number.

2. Statements of customers' accounts each month.
3. A list of debtors who still owe the organisation money.
4. Printed invoices to send out to customers.

Purchases ledger

Such a package allows the computer to produce details about suppliers (their names and addresses, amount owed, etc.), a list of invoices received from suppliers and a list of the ones that remain unpaid.

Nominal ledger

Such a package can produce:

1. A summary of an organisation's assets, liabilities and sources of income.
2. Monthly, quarterly or annual statements showing expenditure by type (e.g. wages or materials) and, when required, variances from budget.
3. A trial balance on a particular day and the balances in each of an organisation's ledger accounts.
4. A record of each day's transactions as recorded in the ledger accounts.

Stock control

Stock control packages can produce:

1. A complete list of an organisation's items of stock at any time. This finds out the availability of stocks instead of people having to physically check them.
2. Orders to suppliers when stocks reach their reorder level.
3. An analysis of stock movements; i.e. the computer can tell the organisation how quickly particular items of stock are being sold or used.

Payroll

A payroll package can calculate each individual employee's pay, tax and National Insurance contributions. Then the computer can automatically print out his/her pay-slip.

Electronic mail

Terminals linked to either a mainframe computer or a minicomputer can communicate directly with one another. This allows an employee on one terminal to give a message immediately to another employee on another terminal. This other terminal could be in the same building, or in another part of the country, or even in another part of the world (because computers can communicate via satellites).

If the employee wants the message circulated to several employees, all (s)he has to do is to put his/her address on the message fed into the computer, and the computer will automatically 'post' them. The receivers of the message can read it on their terminals.

The advantage of this to an accountant is that detailed information from the computer (e.g. reports and information from spreadsheets) can be sent quickly, cheaply and efficiently. Another advantage of such a private electronic mail system is that of **diary management**. Employees at each terminal feed into the computer the times of their future planned appointments. This enables the computer to choose a time for a meeting when all its participants are free. This saves a lot of time trying to phone them all up!

Documents sent out by each employee can also be filed very conveniently on disk. Of course, this occupies much less space than a paper filing system using filing-cabinets.

Public electronic mailing systems are also available for organisations which do not have their own mainframe or minicomputer. An example is British Telecom's **Telecom Gold**. This allows computers of subscribers to communicate with one another via a telephone link with British Telecom's mainframe computer.

You will look at electronic mailing systems in more detail in People in Organisations.

Activity

Using books from your library and your People in Organisations textbook, find out two other public electronic mailing systems operating in the United Kingdom today.

Digital PABX

This refers to computer-controlled telephone exchanges.

Activity

Using books from your library and your People in Organisations textbook, find out the following:

1. What PABX stands for.
2. The name of two digital PABXs in use in the UK today.

Teletext and Viewdata

These allow subscribers to obtain pages of information about various topics on a television screen.

Activity

Using your People in Organisations textbook and other books in your library, find out the following:

1. Two examples of teletext systems in the UK today.
2. The name of the viewdata system run by the Post Office, how many pages of information it offers, and the types of information that are available.

Word processing

A word processor is either of the 'stand-alone' type, which does nothing else apart from word processing, or a microcomputer with a word-processing package, which can do other things as well with different packages. One of the most popular word-processing packages is called **Word Star**.

A word processor's job is to type documents, but it has several advantages over an ordinary typewriter.

Activity

If you have used a word processor before, think of at least three advantages it has over an ordinary typewriter.

You should have come up with the following:

1. Words can be easily corrected, inserted into, and deleted from, the text (e.g. a report, letter or document), whilst the text is shown on the VDU.
2. The text can be reorganised, e.g. paragraphs and sentences rearranged.
3. Reports, letters and documents can be stored in the word processor and easily reprinted.
4. Typing the text is quicker.

Graphics

A graphics package can print pie charts, bar charts and graphs, in colour if required. These are used in business reports and to understand the trends in any set of figures (e.g. are an organisation's profits and sales rising or falling?).

Activity

If you have one available in your college, practise using one of the above packages.

The accountant and computers: the evidence

This section is based upon the findings of two research studies:

- **Information Technology and the Accountant**, by J. G. Carr (published in 1985 by Gower for the Association of Certified Accountants).
- **The Impact of Information Technology on the Management Accountant**, by P. A. Collier (published in 1984 by the Institute of Cost and Management Accountants).

Collier's main conclusions were:

1. Fifty per cent of the management accountants in his survey used a microcomputer actively and frequently.
2. Thirty-two per cent were actively involved with some form of computer. If their companies had computer facilities, 43 per cent of such accountants had some involvement with a word processor.
3. Financial planning packages, e.g. spreadsheets, were the most popular application of computers amongst management accountants.
4. Management accountants made little use of viewdata or of electronic mailing systems.

Carr's main conclusions were:

1. Computers are used more by certified accountants in industry and commerce than by those in private practice.
2. Word processing and financial planning were considered by certified accountants to be the most useful and were therefore the most popular applications of computers. Less well used were electronic mailing, local area network (where computers are linked to one another in the same building or department), digital PABX and viewdata (see Fig. 16.3 on p. 138).

However, Carr predicts that by 1988 information technology will be used more widely in all areas. This is particularly true for accountants in private practice (see Fig. 16.4 on p. 138).

Conclusion

It is inevitable that accounting will become increasingly computerised over the next few years, as computers become even cheaper and more sophisticated. For example, it is predicted that

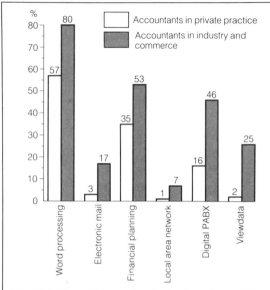

Fig. 16.3: **Use of information technology by certified accountants, 1984**

Source: J. G. Carr, *Information Technology and the Accountant* (Gower, 1985).

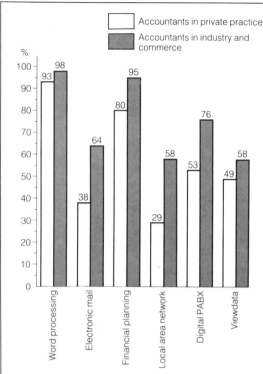

Fig. 16.4: **Estimated use of information technology by certified accountants, 1988**

Source: J. G. Carr, *Information Technology and the Accountant* (Gower, 1985).

voice-recognition computers will be on the market by 1990. A computer will be able to understand spoken instructions and type documents dictated to it.

However, whether or not you become an accountant, you will still find useful the basic techniques of financial and management accounting, as outlined in this book.

It is often said that money is the root of all evil. But I hope that you have not found this book too evil and that you have enjoyed reading it – at least some of the time!

Activity

You are working as an accounts clerk in a small accountancy practice in your local area. It is an ordinary partnership, with four partners. Two of them work in the main office, where you work. The other two partners run the practice's two other offices. All three offices are within a twenty-mile radius of your college.

The practice has twenty employees who are either secretarial staff or accounts clerks. In comparison with its competitors, its wage costs as a proportion of its income are high. So its fees are not as competitive as they might be.

This has prompted the partners to think long and hard about how they might be able to cut costs. In fact, one of the partners, John Morris, has just seen a television programme on computer applications in business, and he thinks that information technology could be the answer to the firm's problems.

The other partners are not so enthusiastic, and John has not enough knowledge of computers to make recommendations about whether or not the introduction of information technology would be desirable.

However, John has heard that you have just completed a business studies course. He has therefore given you the job of preparing a report for him on whether or not information technology should be introduced into the business.

(*Note*: Use a word processor, if possible, to type the report.) Skills tested:

- Identifying and tackling problems.
- Learning and studying.
- Information gathering.
- Communicating.
- Information processing.

Appendix: Present Value of 1

(see Chapter 12)

Years	1%	2%	3%	4%	5%	6%	7%	8%	9%	10%	12%	14%	15%
1	0.990	0.980	0.971	0.961	0.952	0.943	0.935	0.926	0.917	0.909	0.893	0.877	0.870
2	0.980	0.961	0.943	0.925	0.907	0.890	0.873	0.857	0.842	0.826	0.797	0.769	0.756
3	0.971	0.942	0.915	0.889	0.864	0.840	0.816	0.794	0.772	0.751	0.712	0.675	0.658
4	0.961	0.924	0.889	0.855	0.823	0.792	0.763	0.735	0.708	0.683	0.636	0.592	0.572
5	0.951	0.906	0.863	0.822	0.784	0.747	0.713	0.681	0.650	0.621	0.567	0.519	0.497
6	0.942	0.888	0.838	0.790	0.746	0.705	0.666	0.630	0.596	0.564	0.507	0.456	0.432
7	0.933	0.871	0.813	0.760	0.711	0.665	0.623	0.583	0.547	0.513	0.452	0.400	0.376
8	0.923	0.853	0.789	0.731	0.677	0.627	0.582	0.540	0.502	0.467	0.404	0.351	0.327
9	0.914	0.837	0.766	0.703	0.645	0.592	0.544	0.500	0.460	0.424	0.361	0.308	0.284
10	0.905	0.820	0.744	0.676	0.614	0.558	0.508	0.463	0.422	0.386	0.322	0.270	0.247
11	0.896	0.804	0.722	0.650	0.585	0.527	0.475	0.429	0.388	0.350	0.287	0.237	0.215
12	0.887	0.788	0.701	0.625	0.557	0.497	0.444	0.397	0.356	0.319	0.257	0.208	0.187
13	0.879	0.773	0.681	0.601	0.530	0.469	0.415	0.368	0.326	0.290	0.229	0.182	0.163
14	0.870	0.758	0.661	0.577	0.505	0.442	0.388	0.340	0.299	0.263	0.205	0.160	0.141
15	0.861	0.743	0.642	0.555	0.481	0.417	0.362	0.315	0.275	0.239	0.183	0.140	0.123
16	0.853	0.728	0.623	0.534	0.458	0.394	0.339	0.292	0.252	0.218	0.163	0.123	0.107
17	0.844	0.714	0.605	0.513	0.436	0.371	0.317	0.270	0.231	0.198	0.146	0.108	0.093
18	0.836	0.700	0.587	0.494	0.416	0.350	0.296	0.250	0.212	0.180	0.130	0.095	0.081
19	0.828	0.686	0.570	0.475	0.396	0.331	0.276	0.232	0.194	0.164	0.116	0.083	0.070
20	0.820	0.673	0.554	0.456	0.377	0.319	0.258	0.215	0.178	0.149	0.104	0.073	0.061
25	0.780	0.610	0.478	0.375	0.295	0.233	0.184	0.146	0.116	0.092	0.059	0.038	0.030
30	0.742	0.552	0.412	0.308	0.231	0.174	0.131	0.099	0.075	0.057	0.033	0.020	0.015

Years	16%	18%	20%	24%	28%	32%	36%	40%	50%	60%	70%	80%	90%
1	0.862	0.847	0.833	0.806	0.781	0.758	0.735	0.714	0.667	0.625	0.588	0.556	0.526
2	0.743	0.718	0.694	0.650	0.610	0.574	0.541	0.510	0.444	0.391	0.346	0.309	0.277
3	0.641	0.609	0.579	0.524	0.477	0.435	0.398	0.364	0.296	0.244	0.204	0.171	0.146
4	0.552	0.516	0.482	0.423	0.373	0.329	0.292	0.260	0.198	0.153	0.120	0.095	0.077
5	0.476	0.437	0.402	0.341	0.291	0.250	0.215	0.186	0.132	0.095	0.070	0.053	0.040
6	0.410	0.370	0.335	0.275	0.227	0.189	0.158	0.133	0.088	0.060	0.041	0.029	0.021
7	0.354	0.314	0.279	0.222	0.178	0.143	0.116	0.095	0.059	0.037	0.024	0.016	0.011
8	0.305	0.266	0.233	0.179	0.139	0.108	0.085	0.068	0.039	0.023	0.014	0.009	0.006
9	0.263	0.226	0.194	0.144	0.108	0.082	0.063	0.048	0.026	0.015	0.008	0.005	0.003
10	0.227	0.191	0.162	0.116	0.085	0.062	0.046	0.035	0.017	0.009	0.005	0.003	0.002
11	0.195	0.162	0.135	0.094	0.066	0.047	0.034	0.025	0.012	0.006	0.003	0.002	0.001
12	0.168	0.137	0.112	0.076	0.052	0.036	0.025	0.018	0.008	0.004	0.002	0.001	0.001
13	0.145	0.116	0.093	0.061	0.040	0.027	0.018	0.013	0.005	0.002	0.001	0.001	0.000
14	0.125	0.099	0.078	0.049	0.032	0.021	0.014	0.009	0.003	0.001	0.001	0.000	0.000
15	0.108	0.084	0.065	0.040	0.025	0.016	0.010	0.006	0.002	0.001	0.000	0.000	0.000
16	0.093	0.071	0.054	0.032	0.019	0.012	0.007	0.005	0.002	0.001	0.000	0.000	
17	0.080	0.060	0.045	0.026	0.015	0.009	0.005	0.003	0.001	0.000	0.000		
18	0.069	0.051	0.038	0.021	0.012	0.007	0.004	0.002	0.001	0.000	0.000		
19	0.060	0.043	0.031	0.017	0.009	0.005	0.003	0.002	0.000	0.000			
20	0.051	0.037	0.026	0.014	0.007	0.004	0.002	0.001	0.000	0.000			
25	0.024	0.016	0.010	0.005	0.002	0.001	0.000	0.000					
30	0.012	0.007	0.004	0.002	0.001	0.000	0.000						

Appendix for Lecturers: an Integrated Teaching Strategy

Course objectives and structure

As you probably already know, BTEC's new National level course specifications emphasise the importance of the following:

1. Specification of course objectives

All BTEC courses have the following general objectives:

- Meeting the changing needs of industry, commerce and the public services.
- Providing students with an intellectual challenge.
- Developing in students skills and personal qualities of general importance and applicability to all aspects of working life.
- Enabling students to be more effective in their present or future employment.

2. Development of appropriate course structure to achieve these objectives

In this context BTEC recommends the following:

- Activity-based learning, i.e. 'learning by doing'.
- Progressive development of business-related skills, i.e.
  - learning and studying;
  - working with others;
  - communicating;
  - numeracy;
  - information gathering;
  - information processing;
  - identifying and tackling problems;
  - design and visual discrimination.
- Integrated assignments and interdisciplinary themes (where realistic scenarios or situations are employed as a basis for using the skills and knowledge obtained from the different units in the course). BTEC particularly recommends joint assignments for Finance and Organisation in its Environment I in the first year.
- Encouragement of involvement by local employers.

3. Review and development

That is, checking whether the course objective have been achieved, and constantly trying to improve and update the course structure in line wit BTEC's philosophy.

An integrated teaching strategy

With these recommendations in mind, I have proposed an integrated teaching strategy for the cor units of the first-year BTEC National Certificate Diploma in Business and Finance. It can also be used as a basis for the Public Administration and Distribution Studies courses.

I would not suggest that it is perfect, and I know that colleges like to 'do their own thing'. However you might get some useful ideas from it. The teaching strategy has been split up into three sections:

1. **Foundation course** – the aim here is to draw upon and relate to the experiences of the students as much as possible. It is meant to act as a bridge between the individual and the world of business.
2. **Setting up a business** – this section is based upon each group of students setting up an imaginary business. The various stages in the growth of the business are looked at from being a sole trader to finally becoming a public limited company.
3. **Policy-making** – this gives a broad overview of organisational policy-making and should serve as an introduction to what will be developed further in the second year of the course.

Topics in boxes (e.g. 'buying your own home') are included occasionally into the strategy so that they can form the basis of further integrated teaching between the core units.

Intramodular assignments are also included in the strategy and they are written out in detail later on in this appendix. Other assignments are written at the end of each chapter in the book.

Organisation in its Environment I	objective	Finance	objective	People in Organisations I	objective	book	(IMAS)
1. Introduction to assignment on your college Emphasise that organisations have common characteristics, e.g. objectives, sources of finance, organisational structure (see People in Organisations).	A	*Personal finance* **1. Personal income and expenditure** Including the concept of opportunity cost.	A	**1. Introduction to organisational structure** (using the college as a case study) (a) Presentation of organisation charts in diagrammatic form. (b) Introduction to the main functional areas. (c) Levels of responsibility and authority in specific organisations. (d) Relationship between organisational structure and communication systems.	A E	1	1. Your college (p. 148)
2. Different types of organisation, an individual's role in them, and how an individual benefits from them (a) Discussion of organisations with which students are familiar. (b) List the products from each student's household and name the manufacturer. • Building societies only to be looked at briefly. They will be looked at in detail later under 'buying your own home'.	A	**2. Saving** (a) How budgets can help an individual save. (b) Methods of saving (excluding building societies; these will be looked at later). *Note:* This should complement what is done in the option unit, Banking I.	A	**2. Finding out and storing information** (a) Study skills – importance of planning study time and note-making. (b) Use of library. (c) Sources of information from local areas and place of work. (d) Information storage – manual, electronic and photographic cataloguing systems.	A A A	2	2. Newspaper (p. 148)
3. Reasons for different types of organisation E.g. limited liability, reasons for public enterprises – nationalisation or privatisation?	C	**3. Borrowing** (Excluding mortgages.) **4. Personal accounts** • Receipts and payments statement. • Income and expenditure statement. • Balance sheet. • Sources and application of funds statement.	A A	**3. Introduction to the giving and exchanging of information** (a) Outline of methods of oral and written communication. (b) Barriers to effective communication. (c) Awareness of recipient's needs.	A, B, F	3 4	
Buying your own home (a) Building societies as a type of organisation – their legal status, how they are formed, etc. (b) Conveyancing – legal consequences of buying property (freehold v. leasehold). (c) Types of insurance relevant to house purchase.	A	*Buying your own home* (a) Expenses of buying a home. (b) Building-society investment accounts. (c) Mortgages. *Note:* This should complement what is done in the option unit, Banking I.	A	*Buying your own home* (a) The organisational structure of a building society. (b) Design, structure and use of application forms (using mortgage application forms as an example).	A C	2, 3	3. Buying a new home (p. 148)

Setting up a business

Content/learning activities: Organisation in its Environment I	General objective	Content/learning activities: Finance	General objective	Content/learning activities: People in Organisations I	General objective	Relevant chapters in book	Intramodular assignments (IMAs)
1. Introduction to framework of business		**1. Recording financial information**		*Giving and exchanging information – written communications*		6, 7	
(a) Choice between business units – the imaginary business will be a sole trader first of all.	C	• Introduction to double-entry book-keeping.	C	**Introduction**			
(b) Sole trader as a business organisation.	A, B	• Accounting concepts and conventions.	D	1. Grammatical conventions and sentence structure.	C		
(c) What area of business? Students to draw up a list of possible products for the business, of which each group will choose one (i.e. one business for each group).		• Trial balance and final accounts of a sole trader.	E	2. How to use a word processor – an introductory course.	D		
(d) Legal liability of business – civil and criminal.	I	• Other documents for recording financial information, e.g. cash book, sales book.	C	(a) Business documents:	B, C		
(e) Resources required by the business:		• Depreciation.	D	• Types, design and format.			
• Capital (each sole trader has invested £10,000 and has £500 savings).	I	*Note:* Business documents dealt with in People in Organisations.		• Computer applications in equipment associated with document production and transmission.			
• People.				• Documentation systems and procedures.	E		
• Information.	I			(b) Letters	E		
• Land and premises (see point 2 below).	K			• Format and uses.	B, C		
2. Introduction to factors affecting location				(c) Reports:	B, C		
• Business to be in the county in which your college is situated.	I			• Format and uses.			
• Students to find out about regional aid, etc.				(d) Memos, notices and telex:	B, C		
• Students to make a list of the advantages and disadvantages of being in the county.				• Format and uses.			
• Legal implications of buying/renting property.				(e) Presentation and interpretation of financial and other business information e.g. graphs, tables, charts – identification of trends.	B, E		
3. Deciding what to buy	J			**Oral communications**			
Make a list of the items of expenditure that the business will need to make.				(a) Personal exchanges.	B, E, F		
				(b) Telephone and telephone techniques.			
				(c) Public speaking (with the use of visual aids).			
				(d) Interviewing and counselling skills.			

Content/learning activities: Organisation in its Environment I	General objective	Content/learning activities: Finance	General objective	Content/learning activities: People in Organisations I	General objective	Relevant chapters in book	Intramodual assignments (IMAs)
Work of an accountant Accountancy firms: (a) Their objectives. (b) Their sources of finance. (c) Their legal status (how many are there in your local area? How many sole traders, partnerships, and limited companies?).	A	*Work of an accountant* Activities of a financial/management accountant in industry and commerce and in private practice.	A, C	*Work of an accountant* (a) How an accountancy practice is organised. (b) How accountants communicate with each other – communications skills required.	A, B	5	
4. Partnerships *Situation:* Sole trader is short of cash and so goes into partnership with another person. *Activities:* (a) Draw up its Partnership Agreement. (b) Find out advantages and disadvantages of partnerships. (c) Decide whether or not the partnership is to be limited or ordinary. (d) Registration of name.	A, B, C	**2. Partnership accounts** • 1890 Partnership Act. • Profit and loss account. • Balance sheet. • Accruals and prepayments.	E	**Giving and exchanging of information (contd)**	E	8	
Raising money 1. Sources of finance for sole traders, and partnerships (compare these with limited companies). Government help for small businesses. 2. Factors to consider when applying for a bank loan (in collaboration with Banking I).	A, J	*Raising money* 1. Sources of finance for organisations other than sole traders, partnerships and limited companies. 2. How to prepare a cash flow forecast for a bank manager.	B	*Raising money* 1. Interviewing skills when raising money, e.g. with bank manager. 2. Presentation of material for potential providers of finance.	E F	11, 14	4. Bank loan (p. 149)
5. Private limited company *Situation:* The partnership has now been converted into a private limited company. *Activities:* (a) Draw up Memorandum and Articles of Association. (b) Registration of name. (c) Find out the reasons for setting up limited company.	A, B, C	**3. Company accounts** • Requirements of Companies Acts. • Limited company's profit and loss account, balance sheet, sources and application of funds statement, and value added statement.	E	**Giving and exchanging of information (contd)**		9	

Setting up a business (contd)

Content/learning activities: Organisation in its Environment I	General objective	Content/learning activities: Finance	General objective	Content/learning activities: People in Organisations I	General objective	Relevant chapters in book	Intramodular assignments (IMAs)
Taking on new staff 1. Methods of recruiting and selecting employees. 2. Legal implications (outline of individual employee rights). 3. Reasons for taking on new staff. 4. Industrial and human relations.	L L L L	*Taking on new staff* Financial implications of taking on new staff: (a) Payroll (calculation of tax, National Insurance, etc.). (b) Increased costs (without higher sales could reduce profits and increase prices).	 A F	*Taking on new staff* 1. Interviewing. 2. Completion of application forms and their format.	F C	1, 14	5. Finding a job (p. 149)
6. **Public limited company** *Situation:* Business has 'gone public': (a) How a company 'goes public'. (b) Differences between private and public limited companies. (c) Advantages of public limited companies (e.g. economies of scale) and disadvantages (e.g. managerial problems). (d) Public limited companies as multinationals – their costs and benefits (as an introduction to O. and E. II).	A, B, C, I	3. **Company accounts (contd)**	E	**Giving and exchanging of information (contd)**		9	
7. **Comparison of business with other types of organisation** (a) Local authorities (an introduction for O. and E. II). (b) Clubs. (c) Co-operatives. (d) Nationalised industries. (e) Your college.	A, B, C	4. **Accounts of other organisations** • Clubs. • Nationalised industries. • Local authorities. • Your college. 5. **Valuation of assets** • Including the effects of rising prices.	E C, D			10 12	
Dealing with customers (a) Introduction to importance of marketing. (b) Outline of consumer laws (an introduction to O. and E. II).	O	*Dealing with customers* (a) Financial documents sent to customers – invoices, etc. (b) Use of sales ledger software packages. (c) Credit control and its importance.	C G	*Dealing with customers* 1. Interviewing. 2. Effective presentation of ideas, e.g. customer/client contrast.	F	6, 13, 16	6. Dealing with customers (p. 149)

Content/learning activities: Organisation in its Environment I	General objective	Content/learning activities: Finance	General objective	Content/learning activities: People in Organisations I	General objective	Relevant chapters in book	Intramodular assignments (IMAs)
1. What does success and failure mean for organisations?		**1. What does success and failure mean for organisations from a financial point of view?**		**1. Indicators of success**		13, 14, 15	
(a) Their objectives – what are they? Have they been achieved? (Re-emphasise that different organisations may have different objectives, e.g. private v. public sector).	B	(a) Importance of financial objectives:	F	(a) The appropriateness of the organisational structure.	A		
		• An introduction to the need for financial planning and control.		(b) How effectively employees work as individuals and as groups.	F		
(b) Non-financial indicators of success and failure, e.g.		(b) Financial indicators of success and failure:	G				
• Price/quality of the organisation's product and how well it satisfies customers' wants.	O	• Profitability.					
		• Liquidity.					
• How much competition does the organisation have? (Discuss market types, competition and monopoly.)	O	• Capital structure.					
		(c) Financial consequences of success:	G				
• Morale and motivation of the work-force.	L	• More money for shareholders (owners), the government, and reinvested profits.					
• Public relations and relationship with local community.	O						
• Technical and economic efficiency.	M						
• Ability to adapt to change.							
(c) Consequences of failure:	N						
• Bankruptcy, liquidation, termination of employment (and its impact upon the local economy), disposal of property.							

Policy-making (contd)

Organisation in its Environment I

Content/learning activities: Organisation in its Environment I	General objective
2. Introduction to policy-making within organisations • Types and levels of decision-making.	B
• Choosing the scale of operations – getting the resource 'mix' right.	I
3. Requirements for successful policy-making (a) Effective decision-making processes and co-operation between employees (discuss types of conflict and procedures for resolving them).	H
(b) Effective personnel policies (including manpower planning, recruitment, selection, training and industrial relations).	L
(c) Effective use of existing production technology (look at the nature and functions of technological processes used in local organisations).	F
(d) Effective marketing, i.e. the satisfaction of customers' needs and wants. (Discuss marketing mix, factors affecting demand, demand and supply in price determination.)	O
(e) Adaptability to change (see point 4 below).	
Small businesses (a) Reasons why there are so many. (b) Problems facing them (except financial ones).	C, D, E, H

Finance

Content/learning activities: Finance	General objective
2. Requirements for successful financial policy-making (a) Raising enough capital (discussed earlier in the course)	B
(b) Investment appraisal techniques.	F
(c) Effective interpretation of accounts: • Using ratios. • Profitability and liquidity.	G
(d) Financial planning and control (including budgets, break-even analysis, costing, pricing).	F
3. Role of finance in organisational decision-making • Including areas where financial considerations may be secondary in decision-making, e.g. marketing and personnel policies.	H
Small businesses 1. Financial problems: (a) Liquidity problems (ineffective credit control, etc.). (b) Lack of finance. 2. Government support for small businesses.	B, G

People in Organisations I

Content/learning activities: People in Organisations I	General objective	Relevant chapters in book	Intramodular assignments (IMAs)
2. Requirements for successful policy-making (a) An effective and appropriate organisational structure.	A	11	
(b) Factors that lead to effective action by groups and by individual employees	F	12	
(c) Effective communication and documentation systems	B, E	13	
(d) Effective presentation of ideas – verbal and non-verbal	F	14	
(e) Social skills at work.	F	15	
Small businesses Impact of IT on small businesses.	D	11, 16	7. Small businesses (p. 150)

Content/learning activities: Organisation in its Environment I	General objective	Content/learning activities: Finance	General objective	Content/learning activities: People in Organisations I	General objective	Relevant chapters in book	Intramodular assignments (IMAs)
4. **Change for organisations: its causes and consequences** *Causes:* (a) *Social and demographic change.* (b) *Technological change.* (c) *Economic change* (including changes in the degree of competition). (d) *Political and legal change.* *Consequences:* (a) Marketing: changes in markets and in customers' needs and wants. Also changes in competitors' products. (b) Production: possible de-skilling of work (see People in Organisations), and need to invest in new technology. (c) Personnel: retraining, recruitment of new employees and/or redundancies. (d) Organisational (see People in Organisations). (e) Financial (see Finance). (f) Effects of local economy and environment.	D E O F, G K, L G	4. **Change in accounting and finance: summary** (a) Legal changes (e.g. new Companies Acts). (b) Voluntary changes in accounting practice (e.g. SSAPs). (c) Economic change, e.g. rising costs. (d) Technological change (the use of information technology in accounting). (e) Financial consequences of change, e.g. the need to raise more money.	C–H	3. **Consequences of change** (a) Need for organisational reorganisation (changes in factory/office layout, departmental structure, etc.): • Organisational factors which facilitate or inhibit change. (b) Need for improvements in communication systems (particularly because of the need to consult employees about change). (c) Changes in group and individual behaviour at work (e.g. through de-skilling of work). (d) Need to invest in information technology: • Commercial applications of computers. • Methods of data storage and retrieval. • Economic and personal problems associated with the introduction of IT. • Impact of computers on the nature and method of information storage and retrieval.	A B F D	5–10 16 11	8. Bulmer's and BL (p. 150)

Intramodular assignments

Assignment 1. Your college

In groups of three, you are asked to find out the following about your college:

(a) Its objectives (what you think they might be).
(b) Its sources of finance.
(c) Its organisational structure (including the different departments, illustrated by a simple organisation chart) and a simple map of the college.
(d) Its courses.
(e) The effect of external organisations upon it, e.g. local authorities, MSC, BTEC, NATFHE.
(f) The number of its students (full-time and part-time).
(g) Its extra-curricular activities (Students' Union, social events, canteen, sports facilities, etc.).
(h) How to get to the college from three major towns in your local area.

Each person should then prepare a publicity leaflet for the college, outlining the above points (maximum 1,000 words). Part-time students should prepare it for their employers.

Sources of information:
- College prospectus.
- Interviews with staff (if possible) and students.
- Tour of the college.

Skills tested:
- Learning and studying.
- Design and visual discrimination.
- Information gathering.
- Communication.
- Working with others.

Assignment 2. Newspaper

You have just joined your local free newspaper to work for the sales manager. However, advertising revenue is low, and so the sales manager has asked you to gather some information about the organisations in your nearest town, some of which might be future possible advertisers.

She has asked you to present the information in the form of a table which illustrates the following:

(a) Names of firms.
(b) What types of organisation they are.
(c) Whether they provide a service or manufacture something.
(d) How they raise finance.
(e) Their activities.

She has also asked you to illustrate the location of the business with an appropriate map.

You should then give a brief talk in pairs about what you found out. Information also to be gathered in pairs.

Note: You can file the names of the firms on a microcomputer, if you wish.

Skills tested:
- Organising and learning.
- Working with others.
- Communicating.
- Information gathering.
- Identifying and tackling problems.
- Design and visual discrimination.
- Information processing.

Assignment 3. Buying a new home

You are working in the personnel department of a large organisation in your local area. Alan Shah is to join you soon as the head of the marketing department, and he will have to buy a house in your local area. He will receive a salary of £20,000 p.a. and at present owns a house worth £40,000 near Leeds, West Yorkshire.

You have been asked by your superior to prepare the following:

1. *Details of suitable houses for Mr Shah* (he requires a four-bedroomed detached house with a large garden and, preferably, a double garage).
2. *A statement of his moving expenses* (solicitor's fees, including VAT, stamp duty, estate agents' fees, survey for the building society/bank, structural survey and removal expenses).
3. *General information on mortgages*, including the maximum amount Mr Shah would be allowed to borrow.
4. *General information about your local area* – its schools (Mr Shah has two children, one at primary school and one at secondary school), its social amenities (both Mr and Mrs Shah are very keen on the theatre and the cinema), its hospitals, and a suitable map.
5. *A suitable letter to Mr Shah* (address: 3 The Meadows, Leeds, West Yorkshire) to accompany all the information gathered. This should make clear that any moving expenses can be claimed off the company.

Note for students: Students must visit their nearest local town, and its building societies and estate agents to obtain information about:

Mortgages.
Appropriate properties.
Local amenities.
Survey fees and removal expenses.

This work can be done in pairs.

Skills tested:
Learning and studying.
Information gathering.
Communicating.
Working with others.

Assignment 4. Bank loan

You need a loan from your local bank for your group's sole trader's business. The flat rate of interest on loans is 10 per cent p.a. You are required to carry out the following tasks:

Write a suitable letter to your local bank, requesting the loan.
The bank in its reply suggests that you should come for an interview to discuss the loan. It has asked you to bring the following:

(a) *A short description of the business* – its activities, objectives, sources of finance and organisation structure.
(b) *Market research information* – this must answer the question why you think the business will be a success.
(c) *A forecast balance sheet and profit and loss account for the next year* (year ended 30 September 1988).
(d) *A cash flow forecast* for the next year based upon expected cash incomes and expenditures for the business (expenditures should include the interest on the loan and loan repayments).

Attend the bank interview to present your case (this will be filmed).

Skills tested:
Numeracy.
Identifying and tackling problems.
Learning and studying.
Communicating.
Working with others.

Assignment 5. Finding a job

Part-time students. Imagine that a job which you want has become vacant in your firm. You are one of the leading internal candidates, but you will have to compete with people outside as well.
You are required to:

1. Design an appropriate application form and complete the form.
2. Write a suitable covering letter to accompany the form and prepare your curriculum vitae (use a word processor for this, if possible).
3. Attend an interview for the post (the interviewer will be either a member of staff, or ideally a personnel manager from a local employer). The interview can be recorded on video and played back at a later date.

Full-time students. Your present course has just finished and you are looking for a job. You are required to:

1. Visit your local Jobcentre and Careers Office and look at the local and national press to find out vacancies for jobs which might suit you. Choose *one* of these jobs which you will apply for.
2. Design an appropriate application form and complete the form.
3. Write a suitable letter to accompany the form and prepare your curriculum vitae (use a word processor for this, if possible).
4. Attend an interview for the post (as for part-time students).

Skills tested:
• Design and visual discrimination.
• Information gathering.
• Communicating.
• Information processing.
• Working with others.

Assignment 6. Dealing with customers

You are working for your imaginary business. You have been asked by your local college to prepare an oral presentation (maximum thirty minutes) about why your business has been a success.
This talk should include:

1. A brief description of the business.
2. The importance of 'putting the customer first' and how you do this (including how you deal with troublesome customers).
3. How important market research and advertising are in your success.

The talk must be given in groups of three, and each group member must contribute to it.
A written report should be handed in after the talk, which each group member must prepare individually (if possible, typed using a word processor).

Skills tested:
- Learning and studying.
- Design and visual discrimination.
- Information gathering.
- Communicating.
- Information processing.
- Working with others.

Assignment 7. Small businesses

Reggae Records Ltd is a small record company specialising in the production of reggae music. Up until now it has financed its activities through reinvested profits and shares and has not yet borrowed any money.

Its sales and profits have risen steadily since the company was formed in 1975. However, a young managing director has recently joined the business, and he is concerned that in recent years the percentage growth in its profits and sales have been decreasing. This has been due to the declining popularity of reggae music.

He is keen to increase the company's profitability much faster by expanding the company and diversifying into other areas of activity. He has been particularly interested in how Richard Branson's company, Virgin Group plc, has developed over recent years (see Chapter 11).

He has asked you, as his personal assistant, to prepare a report on how this could be done and how the expansion would be financed.

Note: Before you do this, groups of four students should discuss the possible areas that the company could diversify into.

Skills tested:
- Numeracy.
- Identifying and tackling problems.
- Information gathering.
- Communicating.
- Working with others.

Assignment 8. Bulmer's and BL

You are required to read through the case studies on both companies in Chapters 9 and 15 and BL's financial results in the table below. You are then required to prepare a report for the managing directors of both organisations which comments upon:

1. How each organisation has responded to changes in its external environment (e.g. social, demographic, technological, economic, political and legal).

2. How successful each organisation has been marketing its products, and improvements ea could make in this area.
3. The strengths and weaknesses of their compe tors' products. (For this prepare a survey que tionnaire for fellow students and others outsi the college.)
4. The liquidity, profitability, and capital structu of each organisation.

If possible, use a word processor to type your r port.

Other sources of information:
- Newspapers and periodicals (including 'C Buying Guide' in *Which?*, June 1986).
- Books from your library.
- Visits to shops to assess Bulmer's and its con petitors' products (perhaps you could arrange tasting session amongst your group as a mark research exercise!).

PS: You could also do a similar assignment o other organisations mentioned in the book, e. British Rail, Virgin and Marks & Spencer.

Skills tested:
- Numeracy.
- Identifying and tackling problems.
- Information gathering.
- Communicating.
- Working with others.

BL's financial results 1983 and 1984

	1983 £ million	1984 £ million
Fixed assets	1,014.6	908.5
Current assets	1,490.2	1,320.2
(Stocks	813.8	760.1)
Creditors falling due within one year	1,032.6	922.5
Creditors falling due after one year	651.6	458.2
(Borrowings	663.5	449.7)
Provisions for liabilities and charges	102.3	76.7
Share capital (ordinary shares 50p each)	2,139.5	2,139.5
Reserves	(1,463.2)	(1,389.3)
Other capital	42.0	21.1
Turnover	3,420.7	3,401.6
Gross profit	272.0	270.6
Net loss before tax	67.1	73.3
Interest payable	101.1	100.0

Source: Annual Report and Accounts, 1984.

Note: Reserves from the profit and loss account were in deficit – £1,695.2 million in 1983 and £1,621.3 million in 1984. These figures, therefore, had to be *deducted* from BL's total reserves. Other reserves totalled £232 million in both years, and so BL's total reserves were in deficit by £1,463.2 million in 1983 and £1,389.3 million in 1984.

Index

accountants
in industry and commerce, 33–4
in private practice, 32
accounting
financial accounting, 34, Chapters 6–10
management, 34, Chapters 12–15
accruals (accrued expenses), 59, 67
accrued income, 67
accumulated fund, 74
acid test ratio (quick ratio), 101–2
added value, *see* value added
advice note, 50
Agricultural Mortgage Corporation, 86
annual percentage rate of charge (APR), 21
annuities, 18
appropriation account (sole trader), 46–7
Articles of Association, 61, 66, 68, 83
assets
current assets, 5, 27, 47, 99
fixed assets, 4, 5, 26, 47, 66–7, 82, 99
valuation and purchase of assets, Chapter 12
authorised share capital, 68

bad debts, 57, 64
balance sheet
clubs, 74–5
limited companies, 65–8
local authorities, 79–80
nationalised industries, 76–7
partnerships, 58–9
personal, 26–7, 29
sole traders, 47–8
bank reconciliation statement, 51–2
banks, *see* commercial banks
base rate, 83, 86
bills of exchange, 88
BL, 130–32
Bolton Committee on Small Firms (1971), 84
bonus share issue, 86
book-keeping, Chapters 6 and 7
'balancing off' accounts, 42–3
computers and book-keeping, 43–4, 135–6
debit and credit entries, 36–7, 38–41
trial balance, 43

borrowing, 5, Chapter 3, 106–7
brand loyalty, 125
break-even analysis, 117–19
British Rail, 75–8
British Technology Group, 86
budgetary control, 116
budgets
for businesses, 112–15
personal budgets, 10, 26
building societies
investment accounts, 15
mortgages, 23–4
sources of finance, 87
Building Societies Act 1986, 15
Building Societies Association (BSA), 15
Bulmer's, H. P., Holdings plc, 70–72
Business Expansion Scheme, 84

called-up share capital, 68, 72
capital expenditure, *see* expenditure
carriage inwards, 57
cash book, 50–51
cash flow, 26
cash flow forecast (cash budget), 100, 115
cash flow management, 100–3
cash flow statement, *see* sources and application of funds statement
central processing unit (CPU), 134
certificate of tax deposit, 72
charge cards, 22
clearing banks, *see* commercial banks
clubs
balance sheet, 74–5
income and expenditure statement, 74
sources of finance, 87
collateral (security), 20, 83
commercial banks
investment accounts, 16
loans and overdrafts, 22, 67, 86, 87
sources of finance, 87
Companies Act 1948–85, 32, 61–3, 65
compulsory deductions, 7–8
computers
and accounting, Chapter 16
and book-keeping, 43–4
Consumer Credit Act 1974, 24–5

consumer protection, 126–7
contribution, 118
corporation tax, 67, 70, 83
cost of sales, 45–6, 56–7, 64
cost-plus pricing, 119
costing, 116–17
see also historical cost
costs
fixed, 116
semi-variable, 119
variable, 116
credit cards, 22
credit control, 100, 116
credit note, 50
credit reference agencies, 20
credit sales, 22–3, 87
creditor control, 101, 116
cumulative preference shares, 85
current assets, *see* assets
current cost accounting (CCA), 93
current liabilities, 27, 47, 67, 99
current purchasing power accounting (CPP), 93
current ratio, 101–2

database, 135
debentures, 67, 86
debit note, 50
debt collection period, 102
debt factoring, 87–8, 100
debtor control (credit control), 100, 116
debtors, 5, 47, 59, 67
delivery note, 50
depreciation, 48–9
digital PABX, 136
direct expenses, 57, 64
direct labour, 64
direct materials, 64
discounted cash flow (DCF), 95–6
dividend, *see* shares
dividend yield, 105
double-entry book-keeping, *see* book-keeping

earnings per (ordinary) share, 71, 105
Edwardes, Michael, 130–31
elasticity of demand, 104, 119
electronic mail, 136
employee relations, 127–8
employers' liability insurance, 57
employment legislation, 128

equity, 124
expenditure
  personal, Chapter 1
  fixed and variable, 3–4
  revenue and capital, 4
extraordinary items, 66

factoring (debt factoring), 87–8, 100
Fayol, Henri, 111
FIFO, 90–91
finance, Chapter 11
  long-term sources, 85–7
  medium-term sources, 87
  short-term sources, 87–8
finance houses, 16
financial accounting, *see* accounting
financial planning and control,
    Chapter 14
financial ratios, *see* ratio analysis
fixed assets, *see* assets
fixed costs, 116
fixed debentures, 86
floppy disk, 134
funds flow statement, *see* sources
    and application of funds
    statement

gearing ratio, 106–7
'going rate' pricing, 119–20
goodwill, 66
gross pay, 6–7
gross profit, 45–6

hard disk, 134
hire-purchase, 22–3, 87
historical cost, 4, 90
  problems with historical costing
    in inflation, 91–3, 107

income and expenditure (personal),
    Chapter 1
income and expenditure statement
  clubs, 74
  local authorities (revenue
    account), 78–9
  personal, 10, 26, 28
income tax,
  partnerships, 56
  personal, 7–8, 11
  sole traders, 46
Industrial and Commercial Finance
    Corporation (ICFC), 86
inflation accounting, 93
information technology, 133
insolvency, 100
insurance, 17–18
insurance companies
  sources of finance, 87
intangible assets, 66
interest cover, 107
inter-firm comparison, 98, 107

internal rate of return, 96
investment appraisal, 93–7
investment trusts, 16–17
Investors in Industry Group, 86
invoice, 50
issued share capital, 68, 72

job evaluation, 127
jobbers, 16

Laker Airways, 109–10
law of diminishing returns, 119
leasing, 87
liabilities, 27
life assurance, 18
LIFO, 90–91
limited companies (private and
    public), Chapter 9
  balance sheet, 65–8
  profit and loss account, 63–6
  sources and application of funds
    statement, 69–70
  value added statement, 68
limited liability, 61
limited partnership, 54
liquidity, 98–103
local authorities, 78–80
  balance sheet, 79–80
  revenue account, 78–9

mainframe computer, 133
management
  functions of, 111
management accounting, *see*
    accounting
manpower planning, 127
margin, 91
marginal cost, 117
mark-up, 91
marketing, 125–7
Marks and Spencer plc, 129
medical insurance, 18
Memorandum and Articles of
    Association, 61, 66, 68, 83
micro chip, 133
microcomputer, 134
microprocessor, 133
minicomputer, 133
MIRAS (Mortgage Interest Relief
    At Source), 24
money
  functions of, 3
monetary policy, 83
mortgage protection insurance, 17
mortgages, *see* building societies
motivation, 127
motor insurance, 17–18

naked debentures, 86
National Enterprise Board, 86
National Insurance, 8

National Research Development
    Corporation, 86
nationalised industries
  balance sheet, 76–7
  profit and loss account, 75–6
  sources of finance, 87
net current assets (working capital)
    29, 47
net pay, 7
net present value (NPV), 95–6
net profit, 46

objectives, 33, 124–5
operating profit, 64
opportunity cost, 4–5, 45, 94, 103
order forms, 50
ordinary shares, 85–6
organisational objectives, 33, 124–5
overdraft, *see* commercial banks

partnerships, Chapter 8
  balance sheet, 58–9
  limited partnership, 54
  ordinary (general) partners, 54
  Partnership Act 1890, 54–5
  Partnership Agreement, 54–5
  profit and loss account, 55–7
  sources of finance, 87
patents, 66
pay
  gross pay, 6–7
  net pay, 7
pay slip, 6–8
payback method, 95
pensions, 17
performance appraisal, 127
personal expenditure, 5–7
personal income, 9
personnel management, 127–8
petty cash book, 52
Post Office
  investment accounts, 13–14
preference shares, 85
prepayments, 59, 67
prestige pricing, 120
price earnings ratio, 105
pricing, 119–20
pricing by tender, 120
private limited companies, *see*
    limited companies
profit/sales ratios, 104
profit and loss account
  limited companies, 63–6
  nationalised industries, 75–6
  partnerships, 55–8
  sole traders, 45–7
product line pricing, 120
product managers, 123
project teams, 123
psychological pricing, 120

Index

lic limited companies, *see* limited
  companies
lic relations, 126
chases book, 52–3

ck ratio (acid test ratio), 101–2

e of return method, 95
es, 79
io analysis
  capital structure, 106–7
  imitations of, 107
  iquidity, 101–3
  profitability, 104–6
eipts and payments statement,
  10, 26, 28
lucing balance method (of
  depreciation), 48, 49
ated companies, 64, 69
ail co-operative societies, sources
  of finance, 87
turn on capital employed
  (ROCE), 104
turns inwards, 56
turns inwards book, 53
turns outwards, 57
turns outwards book, 53
valuation reserve, 68
venue account (local authorities),
  78–9
venue expenditure, *see*
  expenditure
ghts share issue, 86

le and lease-back, 87, 100
les, *see* turnover

sales book, 52
Sandilands Committee (1975), 93
saving, Chapter 2
sealed bid pricing, 120
security (collateral), 20, 83
semi-variable costs, 119
shares
  dividend, 66, 85
  nominal value, 66
  ordinary and preference shares, 85
social audits, 125
social responsibilities, 125–9
software, 135–7
sole trader
  balance sheet, 47–8
  profit and loss account, 45–7
  sources of finance, 87
sources and application of funds
  statement
  limited companies, 69–70
  personal, 26, 28
spreadsheet, 135
stakeholders, 125
state-backed loan guarantee scheme,
  84
statement of account, 50
Statements of Standard Accounting
  Practice (SSAPs), 63
stock, 46–7, 57, 67
  valuation of, 90–91
stock control, 101, 116
Stock Exchange, 16
stock turnover (rate of), 103
stockbrokers, 16
straight line method (of
  depreciation), 48–9

tax
  corporation tax, 67, 70, 83
  income tax, 7–8, 11
  VAT, 53
teletext, 137
trade credit, 87
trade marks, 66
trade unions, 87, 127
trading account (sole trader), 45–6
transfer pricing, 120
travel insurance, 18
turnover (sales), 45–6, 56, 64

ultra vires, 83
unit trusts, 16–17
unlimited liability, 59

value added, 68
value added statement, 68
variable costs, 116
variable expenditure, *see*
  expenditure
variable pricing, 120
VAT return, 53
viewdata, 137
Virgin Group plc, 88–9
visual display unit (VDU), 134
voluntary deductions, 8

West Sussex County Council, 78–80
word processing, 137
working capital, 29, 47, 92
working capital cycle, 99
working capital ratio (current ratio),
  101–2
workers' co-operatives
  sources of finance, 87